H. Thomas

*Teaching* ART
*in the Elementary School*

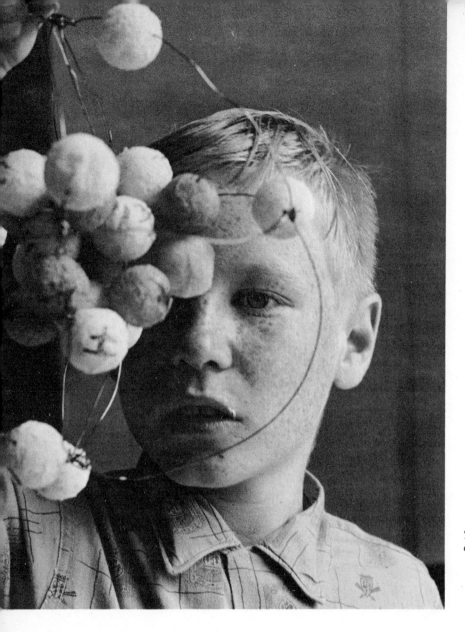

"CHILDREN . . . LIVE ON THE
FRINGES OF OUR CULTURE."

Holt, Rinehart and Winston, Inc.

NEW YORK

**Margaret Hamilton Erdt**

*Formerly Supervisor of Art Education*

*San Diego City Schools*

*San Diego, California*

# *Teaching* ART

# *in the Elementary School*

CHILD GROWTH THROUGH
ART EXPERIENCES

## Revised Edition

# *Preface*

This revised edition of *Teaching Art in the Elementary School* extends and further develops the fundamental principles of art education presented in the first edition. The revised edition provides additional contemporary art experiences that are outcomes of experimentation with new art materials, of changes and growth in children's interests, and of new techniques for developing activities.

Motivation, release, accomplishment, satisfaction—these constitute the cycle of an art experience and are recurrent in the kindergarten and elementary school life of the child. The experiences recorded in this book attempt to show the role of the teacher in helping the child to realize his potential creative and aesthetic strengths. Motivation may come from many sources: a moment of insight, an excursion, a story. Release is possible when circumstances are compatible, a comfortable and stimulating environment prevails, and good materials and tools are provided. Accomplishment requires time for work and teacher guidance that builds self-confidence and security. Satisfaction is the inner glow that comes when a child does his best and is strengthened by the approval of his classmates, and by the warm, mature appreciation of his family and teacher.

The discussion of kindergarten procedures is separate from that of the elementary because the child's experiences are differently organized in the school curriculum. Nevertheless, the kindergarten teacher provides the same effective leadership for the fulfillment of the cycle of motivation, release, accomplishment, and satisfaction that the elementary school teacher provides.

M. H. E.

*San Diego, California*
*January, 1962*

v

# *Acknowledgments*

In the preparation of both the first and the revised editions of *Teaching Art in the Elementary School,* many friends have given generously of their time and experience.

In San Diego it has been my privilege to have been associated with two outstanding school superintendents, the late Dr. Will C. Crawford and the present superintendent, Dr. Ralph Dailard, both of whom gave me inspiration and guidance in my writing. A special word of gratitude is expressed to Dr. Dailard for granting me the privilege of doing research in the instructional aids department of the San Diego City Schools after I had left the school system.

Appreciation is expressed for the help given by Robert H. Burgert, Director of the Department of Visual Education in the San Diego City Schools, and to members of his staff: Mary C. Churchman, chief librarian, and Bethel L. Merrill, research librarian, for their valued counsel; Raymond J. Blake and Ben L. Gumm, assistant supervisors of visual education, for their guidance in selecting materials; Eugene A. Souligny, photographer, Donald J. Donnelly, staff artist, and L. DeGraff Stanley, teacher-coordinator of television, for their competent assistance.

Through the interest of the Director of Music, Dr. Alex H. Zimmerman, and the assistant supervisors, Stanlie McC. Pugh, and the late Myron B. Green, musical compositions were evaluated and selected. Lillian Yardley Brewer of Guadalajara, Mexico, kindly transcribed the flute calls which I had heard when traveling in Mexico. Special help was given by Winifred Y. Robinson, assistant supervisor of physical education, in locating the records and sheet music for the Mexican marionettes.

vi

A special word of gratitude goes to William B. Steinberg, Supervisor of Industrial Arts, for his help with carpentry problems, and to the assistant art supervisors, Elinor S. Meadows, Virginia B. Phillips, and Katherine C. Melka, who participated in stimulating discussions of art education. My thanks is given to Henry F. Wiegand, art teacher, for his generosity in giving time to take many of the photographs, and to Paul Oxley for his special interest and creative insight in taking certain of the photographs of children's work for the revised edition.

The superintendent of the San Diego County Schools, Dr. Cecil D. Hardesty, accorded me the privilege of using the facilities of the curriculum library and the film laboratory of the San Diego County Education Department in the preparation of this edition. Of special assistance were Lillian Spitzer, chief librarian, Mary Lou Love of the audio-visual aids department, and Agnes Hallam, art supervisor in the county schools.

My appreciation can never be adequately expressed for the inspiration I have received from working with the teachers of three city school districts in California—Los Angeles, San Bernardino, and San Diego—and from the students in university and college courses that I taught both on and off campus.

Many illustrations of art activities for the revised edition were secured through the kind offices of personal friends: Mrs. Hook Sutherland, Mrs. Loren Campbell, and Mrs. Herbert Berlier. Special recognition goes to James T. Gibbs, a teacher in the San Diego City Schools and a long-time friend, who graciously read and evaluated parts of the revised manuscript, and to another friend, Mrs. William Wiechers, for her effective literary criticism of specific portions of the revised text.

I am indebted to Dr. Aulus W. Saunders, Chairman of the Department of Art at Teachers College (Oswego), State University of New York, and to Dr. Robert Drummond, formerly of the University of Illinois, department of art, for their careful reading of the manuscript for the first edition.

Appreciation is respectfully given to the Honorable Kyoshi Nakarai, mayor of Yokohama, who sent me pictures of Japanese school children engaged in art activities in the Yokohama schools, and to Mr. Saburo Muraoka of Chula Vista, California, who gave assistance in approaching the Mayor. Thanks is also due Mr. William DeMyer, Director of the American Cultural Center, for sending me the set of booklets, *Zuga-Kosaku,* published in Japan, which provided an overview of the total art program in the public schools of Japan.

It was my good fortune to have had the superior secretarial aid of Evelyn Adamson and Agnes Schassen in the preparation of the first edition. In preparing the revised edition, I was equally fortunate in that Mrs. Malcolm Mercer was not only an expert secretary, but also most competent and experienced in editorial work.

The illustrations that give vitality to written words about art were acquired through the gracious response of (1) school districts, (2) publications, (3) organizations, (4) art museums, and (5) community enterprises. These interesting photographs add greatly to the pleasure of the reader. I regret that space did not permit using all the pictures received for both the first and the revised editions.

1. Photographs from the following school districts are used through the courtesy of the administrative staffs:

ARLINGTON, VIRGINIA
Willie Mae Ivey, *Supervisor of Art*

ATHENS, GEORGIA
Lamar Dodd, *Head of Art Department, University of Georgia*
Charles M. Williamson, *Art Instructor*

ATLANTA, GEORGIA
Eloise Keebler, *Fulton County Department of Education*

BALTIMORE, MARYLAND
W. H. Lemmel, *Superintendent*
Leon Winslow, *Former Director of Art*

BART, PENNSYLVANIA
John Burkins, *Principal, Bart-Coler-*

*ain School, Solanco Area School District*
Kenneth M. Hoak, *Elementary Art Supervisor*
Stanley Lipman, *Teacher-Director of Mosaic Project*

BEVERLY HILLS, CALIFORNIA
R. G. Mitchell, *Superintendent*
Katharine Page Porter, *Supervisor of Art*

BOSTON, MASSACHUSETTS
Dennis C. Haley, *Superintendent*
Casimir F. Shea, *Director of Art*

BURBANK, CALIFORNIA
J. Russell Croad, *Superintendent*
Marjorie Simpson, *Supervisor of Art*

CHICAGO, ILLINOIS
Herold C. Hunt, *Former General Superintendent of Schools*
Ann M. Lally, *Director of Art*

CINCINNATI, OHIO
Claude Courter, *Superintendent*
Vera Freid, *Editorial Assistant*

CLEVELAND, OHIO
William B. Levenson, *Assistant Superintendent*
Alfred Howell, *Directing Supervisor of Art*

DETROIT, MICHIGAN
Arthur Dondeneau, *Superintendent*
Helen Copley, *Director of Art*

FORT WORTH, TEXAS
Joe P. Moore, *Superintendent*
Flossie G. Kysar, *Consultant in Art*

FULTON COUNTY, GEORGIA
Emery Rose Wood, *Director of Art Education*

GALVESTON, TEXAS
Susan Crutchfield, *Director of Elementary Education*

HONOLULU, HAWAII
Walter M. Gordon, *Superintendent*
Lurene H. Van Piera, *Director of Art Education*

INDIANAPOLIS, INDIANA
H. L. Shibler, *General Superintendent of Schools*
T. Van Vorhees, *Supervisor of Art*

KANSAS CITY, MISSOURI
Roscoe V. Shores, *Deputy Superintendent*
Rosemary Beymer, *Director of Art*

LONG BEACH, CALIFORNIA
Douglas Newcomb, *Superintendent*
Shirley Poore, *Former Supervisor of Art*

LOS ANGELES, CALIFORNIA
Raymond E. Pollich, *Associate Superintendent*
Ida May Anderson, *Former Supervisor of Art*

LOUISVILLE, KENTUCKY
Omer Carmichael, *Superintendent*
Martha Christensen, *Supervisor of Art*

MINNEAPOLIS, MINNESOTA
Rufus A. Putnam, *Superintendent*
Harold J. Gregory, *Consultant in Radio-Television Department*

MONTCLAIR, NEW JERSEY
Ralph Vernacchia, *Associate Professor, Montclair State College*

NASHVILLE, TENNESSEE
Harold D. Drummond, *Associate Professor, George Peabody College*

PHILADELPHIA, PENNSYLVANIA
Leslie Cushman, *Assistant Superintendent*
Marguerite Walter, *Special Assistant*
Martha Gable, *School-Community Relations*

PITTSBURGH, PENNSYLVANIA
Earl A. Dimmick, *Superintendent*
Mary A. McKibbin, *Director of Art*

ROCHESTER, NEW YORK
James M. Spinning, *Superintendent*
Marjorie A. Lush, *Director of Art Education*

ix

SAN ANTONIO, TEXAS
Thomas B. Portwood, *Superintendent*
Inez Foster, *Assistant Superintendent, Elementary Division*

SAN BERNARDINO, CALIFORNIA
E. J. Mueller, *Superintendent*
Fred Holland, *Supervisor of Art*

SAN BERNARDINO COUNTY, CALIFORNIA
Beulah Wolfe, *Director of Education*
Carol Poppet, *Consultant in Art*

SAN DIEGO, CALIFORNIA
Ralph Dailard, *Superintendent, San Diego City Schools*
Margaret H. Erdt, *Former Supervisor of Art*

SAN DIEGO COUNTY SCHOOLS
Cecil D. Hardesty, *Superintendent*
Agnes Hallam, *Supervisor of Art*
Florence Hord, *Art Supervisor, La Mesa-Spring Valley*
Dorothy H. Clark, *District Superintendent, Solano Beach*

SAN DIEGO STATE COLLEGE
Ruby Niebauer, *Former Assistant Professor of Education*

SAN FRANCISCO, CALIFORNIA
Herbert C. Clish, *Superintendent*
Archie Wedemeyer, *Director of Art Education*

SAN JUAN, PUERTO RICO
Commonwealth of Puerto Rico
Carmen Tuya, *Director of Art Education*

SANTA BARBARA, CALIFORNIA
Catherine C. Campbell, *Associate Professor, University of California at Santa Barbara*
Harriette Judd, *Teacher in Elementary City Schools*

SEATTLE, WASHINGTON
Samuel E. Fleming, *Superintendent*
Dale Goss, *Director of Art Education*

Color plates from the following school districts are used through the courtesy of the administrative staffs:

ATHENS, GEORGIA
Lamar Dodd, *Head of Art Department, University of Georgia*
Charles M. Williamson, *Art Instructor*

MINNEAPOLIS, MINNESOTA
Rufus A. Putnam, *Superintendent*
Ethel Christensen, *Former Helping Teacher in Art*

NEWARK, NEW JERSEY
John Herron, *Superintendent*
Leila Payton, *Supervisor*

PHILADELPHIA, PENNSYLVANIA
Leslie Cushman, *Assistant Superintendent*
Marguerite Walter, *Special Assistant*

x

SAN DIEGO, CALIFORNIA
  Ralph Dailard, *Superintendent, San Diego City Schools*
  Margaret H. Erdt, *Former Supervisor of Art*

SANTA ANA, CALIFORNIA
  Lynn H. Crawford, *Superintendent*
  Katherine C. Melka, *Former Supervisor of Art*

2. One musical score and photographs from newspapers, periodicals, and publications are used through the courtesy of the editorial staffs:

Silver Burdett Company, Morristown, N. J.: *New Music Horizons, First Book*
  Charles E. Griffith, *First Vice-President*

Standard Oil Company of California: *Bulletin*, C. R. Lyman, *Editor*

*The Louisville Courier-Journal* and *Louisville Times*, Louisville, Kentucky

*The Seattle Times*, Seattle, Washington

3. Photographs from organizations are used through the courtesy of the directors:

AMERICAN RED CROSS
  Jacqueline Wadsworth, *Director of Junior Red Cross, San Diego Chapter*

BOYS' CLUB OF SAN DIEGO
  C. A. Van Dusen, *Executive Director*

BOY SCOUTS OF AMERICA
  Marlin S. Sieg, *Assistant National Director, Cub Scouting Service*

CAMP FIRE GIRLS, INC.
  Elizabeth M. McStea, *National Public Relations Director*
  Rosemary Waters, *Executive Director, San Diego Council*

GIRL SCOUTS OF THE UNITED STATES OF AMERICA
  Dorothy C. Stratton, *Former National Director, New York City*
  Gene McFall, *Executive Director of San Diego Council*

4. Photographs from art museums are used through the courtesy of the directors:

THE BROOKLYN MUSEUM
  Hanna T. Rose, *Curator of Education*

CLEVELAND MUSEUM OF ART
  William M. Illiken, *Director*

THE DENVER ART MUSEUM
  Carl Otto Bach, *Director*

ACKNOWLEDGMENTS

PORTLAND ART MUSEUM
Rachel Griffin, *Supervisor, Children's Classes*

SAN DIEGO FINE ARTS GALLERY
Thomas B. Robertson, *Former Director*
Warren Beach, *Director*

5. Photographs were received from the following community enterprises:

*Camp Cuyamaca,* California
Denver Fox, *Director, San Diego City and County Elementary School Camp*

*Department of Recreation,* Washington, D.C.
Milo F. Christiansen, *Director*

In conclusion, a special word of thanks is expressed to Mrs. Lloyd Lounsbury, Mrs. Wesley Cooke, Mrs. George Worthington, and Mrs. James Gibbs for their courtesy in allowing me to use examples of their children's work.

M. H. E.

# Contents

*Teaching* **ART**
*in the Elementary School*

# A Portfolio of Children's Paintings

In this portfolio of children's paintings it will be noticed that only one art medium has been selected. The reason for this limitation is that if several mediums were used—drawing, finger painting, cut paper—the relationships would be less obvious. The paintings are identified by grades, and the ages of the child artists are close to the median age levels of their groups.

1. *Tempera Painting*
   *Preschool Child Care Center*
   *San Diego City Schools*

2. Harbor Scene
   *Tempera Painting*
   *Kindergarten*
   *San Diego City Schools*

1.

2.

3.

4.

5.

3. People. *Tempera Painting*
   *Kindergarten, The University of Georgia*
   *Demonstration School*

4. Going to Bed on the Train. *Tempera Painting*
   *First Grade, San Diego City Schools*

5. Boxing Match. *Tempera Painting*
   *First Grade, San Diego City Schools*

6.

6. Houses. *Tempera Painting*
   *First Grade, San Diego City Schools*

7. Roadside Market, *Tempera Painting*
   *First Grade, San Diego City Schools*

8. My Family. *Tempera Painting*
   *First Grade, School District of Philadelphia*

7.

8.

9.

10.

11.

9. Girl's Head. *Tempera Painting*
   *Second Grade, Minneapolis Public Schools*

10. Fire Engine. *Tempera Painting*
    *Second Grade, Santa Ana Public Schools*

11. Halloween. *Tempera Painting*
    *Second Grade, San Diego City Schools*

12.

12. The Farmer. *Tempera Painting*
    *Third Grade, San Diego City Schools*

13. The Bulldozer. *Tempera Painting*
    *Third Grade, San Diego City Schools*

14. Elevated Train. *Water color*
    *Fourth Grade, School District of Philadelphia*

13.

14.

15.

15. Midsummer Night's Dream. *Water color*
    *Fifth Grade, San Diego City Schools*

16. My Home in Hawaii. *Water Color*
    *Fifth Grade, San Diego City Schools*

17. Shapes and Colors. *Water color*
    *Fifth Grade, San Diego City Schools*

16.

17.

18.

18. Landscape. *Water color*
    *Sixth Grade, Board of Education, Newark, New Jersey*

19. Archery. *Water color*
    *Sixth Grade, San Diego City Schools*

19.

# Invitation to Art from a Child

It is through the child that a teacher receives her invitation to art. His enthusiasm and interest are contagious. His point of view may open a vista and a new appreciation of children's work.

Now you take art, it goes this way: when you take out your box of colored chalk and start working, lots of things can happen. One day I started drawing lines with dark brown chalk. Just any kind of lines, long lines, short lines, broken lines, curved lines; some looked rough; some looked smooth. I didn't think much about it, but you know on Saturday I went hiking in the hills, and then the funniest thing happened. I could see all those lines of my drawing in an old dirt bank that we were climbing up. The water had run down there, and there were lots of crevices and ridges, just like I had drawn them with my brown chalk. Last fall we studied about erosion, so I knew what it was, but I never expected it might make a pattern that was nice to see. The teacher had talked to us the other day about rhythm in line, but I didn't quite know what she meant, and there it was. The other kids didn't see it, and I didn't say a word.

My piece of clay looked big. The more I looked at it, the more it got to look like the big old hippopotamus at the zoo. We went there last week, all of us, in the bus, and I got awfully tired walking around all those cages. Well, about my big hippo, it just sort of grew. The other children were making bears or giraffes or other animals, but my clay still seemed to look like a hippo, so I worked on it some more. I had just about started to roll it up

1

in a ball and stick it back in the clay jar when the teacher came along. She saw right away it was a hippo, but she said it really wasn't quite finished yet and maybe I had better work some more. Now it is drying on the window sill and tomorrow I can paint it a real dark black, just like the hippo at the zoo.

My, didn't the kids in kindergarten look funny today! They were all covered up in what looked like dad's old shirt with the sleeves cut out, or an oil-cloth apron, or just flour sacks, but I guess it was a good idea, because they were messing around with finger paint. The pictures looked pretty good, snow mostly. It snowed yesterday, so they were making sleds and tobog-gans and hills for them to slide down. There were lots of snow men, too. One kid made the snow coming down with just the tip of his little finger, and you couldn't see what was going on in back of the snow. He said his house was back there, and I guess you couldn't see it because it was snow-ing so awfully hard yesterday.

Our paint boxes have just a few colors in them, seven, that's all. Just such a few colors didn't interest me; I wanted a lot of colors. That is, not a lot of different colors, but lots of kinds of one color. It is sort of hard to explain, but you can see it in a zinnia. There were some growing in our garden, and in those little petals, starting at the middle, you can see lots of shades of one color before you get to the edge of the flower. In the little tiny part that makes the center, well, it was greenish, but light, not dark; that was the middle, like a bull's-eye. And then the petals start growing and start changing color. First they are lemony, and in the next band more yellowish, then the petals turn a real yellow, but soft, and they seem to change a little speck, all the way to the edge of the flower, where they got to be a rosy orange. But with just my seven color box what could I do? I thought I'd try just the same, and the first thing I knew I had lots of samples all over my paper, and I had lots of those zinnia colors by just mixing around with my paint brush. I'd invented them myself. It was a spectrum, the teacher said, and if I'd stay in a minute after the recess bell she'd explain what that was.

2

# 2

# *Thinking through the Art Experience*

As a teacher approaches her work for the year, she evaluates the many different experiences which will further growth in children. Her earnest hope is to fulfill their needs each day for intellectual, emotional, and aesthetic experiences by providing a broad and effective program that will nurture their natural response and sensitivity to art structure. Her reward is the privilege of watching the emerging creative powers and appreciations of children as they mature through satisfying art experiences.

## THE PURPOSE OF ART EDUCATION

The purpose of art education is to awaken in children a lively and enduring interest in art. This can be done through a balanced classroom program which will sharpen children's enjoyment of art and challenge their potential creativity. Therefore, an art program must be flexible and be prepared to meet the needs of children according to their degree of maturation and natural interests. An art program should not be, and never need be, repetitious for the child. There are many avenues to art appreciation and many activities for personal and group experience.

Children are observant. They miss little in their surroundings, whether at home, in school, or on a trip. It is therefore important to display attractive examples of art that can spur vital visual experiences. Exposure to fine design is as important an experience as children can have. Many children come from homes lacking in taste, drab in color, and with nothing lovely to look at. Under such circumstances, a child's sensitivity to beauty is rarely stimulated by his immediate source of observation. For him, and for all children, the teacher can fulfill an aesthetic need. She is a missionary who brings them a priceless gift: the ability to see and enjoy the beauties of nature and of man's creative work.

Hand in hand with the aesthetics of art the teacher must consider the realities of working with her pupils. Children are active, full of vim and vigor, always eager for something to do. Children are not all creative in the same field or in the same way, but through art activities they may all spend energy fruitfully and experience fulfillment. At the end of an art period, a piece of work is either finished or on its way to completion. And how very much it means to a child to experience a feeling of accomplishment. In a good art program, every painting, every drawing, every craft activity, every newly learned process contributes to growth. What appears to be mere handwork to an unthinking person may be of great importance to the child. Mind, spirit and manual activity form a unified experience emotionally, physically and aesthetically. An art experience is, therefore, vital to every day's work in school.


WHAT AN ART EXPERIENCE MAY MEAN

An art experience for children is a natural experience. Children do not think of art as requiring years of study and training in particular and difficult skills, but feel confident that they can do the things they want to do in their own way; and so is born a child's honest attitude toward his art.

Art is a common experience because it belongs to all people wherever they may live, whatever their culture may be; by the same token, art is a common experience to all children. This is natural and normal, for history shows that art experiences and enjoyments have been the daily concern of man since he first drew with a lump of colored earth upon the wall of his cave. The cave paintings of Lascaux and Alta Mira are fascinating to children. A film and two books are available on the subject of cave paintings, both of which an upper grade class would enjoy.[1, 2*]

---

* Superior figures are keyed to the numbered references at the conclusion of each chapter.

Art is a language, a visual language, that can be read and understood by children. It is a language which children sincerely believe will tell what they have to say and will be rightly interpreted by others. Children's art expression conveys messages in the idioms of childhood; and children turn with confidence to painting, modeling, drawing to express their thoughts and ideas, emotions and feelings.

Children have a great keenness to do things; and art activities bring them wholesome experience—social relationships, companionship, fun, and investigation. A healthful companionship develops in a classroom when boys and girls are deeply engrossed in an art enterprise that calls forth all their creative effort to achieve. Art activity brings a sense of well-being to children when they take part, and participation will set the stage for rapport and harmony in a classroom. Art materials stimulate imagination; in turn, this leads to investigation by children. Who can

*Louisville Public Schools*

5

guess what fine color patterns will come when a child dips his brush into a color, or how far-reaching may be an initial experience with clay?

All of the experiences associated with any creative work in art—inspiration, production, enjoyment—become a total experience for the child as simply and as easily as do the separate pieces of a puzzle once the key is found.

## WHAT AN ART PROGRAM MAY SIGNIFY

A program of art experiences for children belongs to the children; and if a program should be planned otherwise in the mistaken belief that adult standards of achievement are right for children, then the program is of no value in the elementary school. Since art is an experience, a good program will draw upon the life experience of children and on an understanding of their interests and enthusiasms. A good program will be directed to meet expected changes in normal growth. A teacher cannot always know in advance what specific direction a program should take or how fast the children will move ahead. A program that may have seemed suitable in September may not be so in January. However, an ineffectual program can be righted because art by nature of its content is flexible and adaptable to change and revision. Children change very fast and have their spurts forward when creativity is high and their passive periods when creative expression lags and grows stale. Many times a teacher is able to stimulate creativity by finding a new interest which will become a natural inspiration for creative work. Perhaps a bridge is under construction a short distance from school. A sketching trip to the site could be a novel experience and could lead to a series of drawings and paintings of other scenes in the vicinity. Or, right within the class, there may have been some discussion about having either a May Day festival or a kite tournament. This, then, would be an opportune time to come to a decision, and to start work on all the fascinating new art activities that either choice would offer. For a teacher to ignore such possible sources of inspiration would be to put art back in the copybook era and rule creativity out of existence.

An art program is more, much more, than a list of things to do which can be checked off monthly through the year. Instead, it is a series of daily circumstances that develop out of the classroom situation and bring to children experiences of emotional, intellectual, and aesthetic

Making Costumes.
We are making our
own costumes for the
May Day dance. We
each will make a hat
_____r. We will put
__s on each hat.

*Beverly Hills Unified School District*

quality that will inspire creative work.[3] A well-planned art program will provide many opportunities for freedom of choice so that children may choose and investigate different kinds of materials. Given this freedom, it is possible for a child to experience the intangible rewards of happiness, satisfaction, honesty in doing a task, independence, challenge and response, respect for others and respect for himself—all of which contribute to art learning. The child's family life, his schoolwork, his personal interests, and his recreation are made more complete by art activities. Also, individual needs not recognized by a child, his mental hygiene, and his sense of well-being are helped by meaningful art experiences and by the subsequent satisfaction that comes from wholesome emotional release.

Degrees of maturation vary within every elementary class and are as consistently reflected in the art of children as in their other work. This diversity poses an instructional problem for the teacher; but,

7

since art is creative and not standardized by tests and national norms, children have a better chance to develop at their own rate of growth and to fulfill their own destinies than is possible in many other subjects. There are children with limited art ability, and there always will be; but they can be helped. There are children with superior art ability; but they may not always be superior unless they, too, are helped. Studies of genius groups[4] have shown that when the problems of the very superior child are not recognized, he suffers as greatly if left to grope his way as does the child with lesser endowments. Sometimes high intelligence is reflected in art production and sometimes not. Perhaps it is a wiser course for a teacher to appreciate the art qualities in children's work rather than to attempt to interpret the psychic qualities, at least until much more information is available to teachers and until classes are smaller. In large classes it is impossible for a teacher to know each child as intimately as she would like and to have the time to give the hours to analysis which the study requires. Nothing short of authentic knowledge[5] in the techniques of psychological procedures is fair to the child, for a hasty judgment by a teacher can classify a child most unjustly.[6]

As the year progresses, the children's art experiences will need evaluation from time to time in relation to goals, expected outcomes, and objectives of art education. Goals and outcomes are general and fairly constant, probably always the responsibility of the teacher, whereas objectives emerge from class needs and are defined by the teacher and children working together. The goals of art education are closely allied with the welfare of children, the purposes of elementary education,[7] and the cultural values of society. From more carefully selected art experiences for children and better teaching in the classroom, it is reasonable to expect that, as an outcome, children will have better understandings of art, and, when they are adults, will live in a richer American culture. It may be found in summing up the goals of a good art program that the art experiences have been directed toward these goals.

FIRST, fostering the growth and development of the creative, spiritual, appreciative, and aesthetic qualities, abilities, and potentialities of children.

SECOND, selecting appropriate content material in order that the art program may meet the maturation levels of children and enrich experience.

THIRD, providing favorable circumstances for art learning and competent teaching that result in desirable changes in the growth and development of children.

And LAST, giving children a deep and lasting enjoyment of art that will persist in adult life and will exert a positive influence on our own American culture.

Children understand objectives that result from classroom activities. An objective has a better chance of being achieved when it is not imposed upon children by a course of study or an authority beyond their comprehension. Objectives become valid and have meaning to children when they grow out of a specific situation which is familiar to them and can be talked over by the group. For example, a better use of color in all paintings might become an objective for a class as the result of an evaluation of a mural which had poor color. Only as objectives are thoroughly understood can there be hope for their fulfillment. Objectives are equally useful in the practical duties of classroom management, for these can be clearly stated and checked by the children. Whether every child has performed his duty in the care of art supplies is quickly ascertained. When an objective is identified and accepted, children work with a will to fulfill its purpose.

The significance of art education is its educational integrity. The laws of learning and the psychological drives of childhood are not violated in art teaching, but rather they are strengthened and supported. Learning by doing, verbal learning, and observational learning[8] are all part of an art program. Learning by doing is creative work and planning; verbal learning is discussion and evaluation; and observational learning is visual discrimination, art judgment, and response to both good and bad art structure. The psychological drives of childhood for social relationships and personality development, security, activity, success, recognition, and acceptance by other children can find fulfillment through the art experience provided that the circumstances which comprise the art program are properly directed. When this is true, it would be almost impossible for a child to fail to find in art activities some of the satisfaction which he craves.

## WHAT PRACTICE MAY PROVIDE

Many of the teaching techniques appropriate, useful, and efficient for other subjects are basic for art instruction, for art is little different from other areas of creative teaching. Art, also, has its problems of motivation, pupil response, production, and evaluation. Group tech-

9

niques, individual work, the field trip, evaluation, and integration are familiar techniques equally successful in art.

Group techniques[9] operate equally well with few and with many children, with a committee or with a class. Group work, besides building social relationships and giving opportunity for interaction, brings rewarding results. It is a pleasure to watch the cooperative planning and execution of an art project and to see the results of fine cooperation reflected in the finished work. In group activity children must get along together or there will be bedlam; moreover, fine plans for murals, dioramas, and puppet shows will fail. Children unconsciously experience the democratic process of give-and-take, of assuming leadership and responsibility, of listening to others and, equally important, of standing fast when they are right. There is always a time, too, when, no matter how good an idea may be, a child has to be unselfish and relinquish his idea in a pleasant manner. The interaction of group techniques[10] gives opportunity for unexpected character strengths to develop. Unsuspected talents often come to the fore when group work gives security to children who are afraid to go too far by themselves.

A fourth-grade class was deeply interested in a marionette project. In the group was a timid, sensitive child, with great natural feeling for rhythm and action. He enjoyed the music hour and never missed a step in folk dancing; but because he was retiring and the other children were livelier, they easily won the approval of their classmates. When the children started handling the marionettes, he quickly became dexterous with the control stick and the strings. In no time at all his little wooden character came to life and was walking and dancing and bowing up and down and about the room. It was natural that such a demonstration of skill should immediately be recognized by his classmates, and they clamored for the secrets of his clever manipulation. Through their demands he became a leader. Perhaps without the favorable circumstances of a group activity which both concealed his timidity and revealed his talents, he would not have had either a rewarding social relationship or an outstanding art experience all year.

Committee work helps a project move more quickly to completion. Committees accomplish work which under different circumstances could take weeks and even months to do. When many participate, interaction within a class acts as stimulation to all children, with the result that clever and ingenious solutions to art problems occur which might never have been discovered through individual activity alone.

Successful as the cooperative project is, children are not to be deprived of individual expression where each does his own piece of work. Many art activities are conducted this way by choice, with all the class working together during an art period. Every child has the right to work for himself and to keep what he has made. There is need for the wholesome therapy that only release and satisfaction through personal effort can bring, and for the child to have something which is entirely his own. Moreover, individual work helps the teacher to know the children better because the art production clearly shows patterns of growth. By studying these patterns, a teacher finds how she can best help children according to the needs of each one. Often a few minutes of special attention during a lesson will clear up problems for a child and he will be able to proceed with renewed confidence and vigor.

Besides providing the environment for committee and class-work, there is another art experience invaluable to children. This is the opportunity for a child to work independently at any time during the day when his other work will permit. If this is to be done most efficiently, a suitable place must be arranged in the classroom. This need is well cared for in new school buildings, where each classroom includes a workshop area, often called an art center, in an alcove or a corner of the room. A workshop has a sink, storage cabinets, and a bulletin board low enough for a small child to pin up his work. The basic workshop equipment consists of one or two easels, one or two tables, and several chairs. Art materials are set out each day on the tables. A workshop takes children away from the distractions and interruptions of class activity and gives opportunity for initiative as they fulfill a committee assignment or work out an idea of their own. A member of the art committee for a school paper might be drawing a cartoon for the next issue, while at the same time two other children could paint their kites.

Since all teachers are not assigned to new buildings, ways and means can be found to arrange workshops which function very well in an old-fashioned classroom. A pail may have to substitute for a sink and open shelves may take the place of cupboards, but it can be done. One teacher solved such a problem with very little effort. In the rear of her room was an old-fashioned and relatively commodious cloakroom with a window at one end. The cloakroom extended the full width of the class-room and was entered through an archway at either end. With a piece of

11

*Fort Worth
Public Schools*

Celotex, the teacher made a temporary low partition which divided the cloakroom into two parts. The end with the window became the workshop and the other section continued to serve its original purpose for wraps and lunch boxes. In the workshop area the hooks for the children's coats were removed and the shelf above became a convenient place to store art materials. There was ample room for an easel, a small table, two chairs, and a clay jar. A small pitcher was used to dip water from a pail as needed and an empty can was ready for its later disposal, thus keeping the water in the pail clean for the day. Two children could work here comfortably; in fact, the children liked it so well that seldom was there a vacancy in this efficient little art center.

Children should realize that the privileges of a workshop also bring responsibilities which every child has to be willing to accept. Then he will expect to clean up his materials after he has finished his work.[11] He must respect the freedom accorded to him not only by leaving the place tidy for the next child, but also by the character of his behavior. He will work independently and with little or no supervision; therefore he must be trustworthy. When every child cooperates, the art center 13 becomes a place where, absorbed in fruitful concentration, a child may follow the dictates of his own talent. The workshop has other functions as well. It may be used exclusively by a committee for several days, and often is the ideal place for setting up a construction unit. Thus the workshop is as actively engaged all the time as is the classroom.

Experiences within the classroom cannot entirely replace the values for children of direct contact with the resources and activities in a community. Field trips and excursions pay high dividends in creative expression and intellectual growth. Besides these educational values, a trip is fun for children and has untold possibilities for unexpected happenings and surprises.

Careful planning should precede every field trip and follow-up activities should be planned in the classroom. Otherwise much learning is missed by the children. Whenever possible the teacher should take the trip first. It is better for everyone if she meets beforehand the person who is to escort the class and investigates what is available for the children to see. Often a person unaccustomed to the lively ways of children is overwhelmed when the group descends upon him unless he, too, has taken time to make preparations in advance. From such experiences as visiting a farm, a bakery, or an airport will come some of the finest, most original, and varied creative work in the kindergarten and elementary grades—art which is an honest expression of the direct, personal experience of the children.

A trip to an art museum may be the high light of a school year for upper-grade children. Nothing should be allowed to stand in the way of such a trip if it is possible. Chartering a bus and packing a lunch, if the trip is a long one, is little enough to do for the rewards that await children after they arrive. A guided tour by a member of the museum staff is always to be preferred to having the teacher attempt to conduct the class herself. Museum trips may have a cultural goal—to acquaint children with great works of art—or they may be planned in order that children may see a specific exhibit related to some phase of their schoolwork.

Classroom practice would fail to fulfill its goals unless integration and evaluation were a part of the total art experience. These teaching skills are of such great importance that they are discussed in later chapters. Also, since no art program is complete without utilizing the resources in a community, a later chapter is devoted to what is available to supplement school experience.

## WHAT THE TEACHER MAY CONTRIBUTE

"And where do I come in?" the teacher may ask. The answer is, "Every step of the way." The teacher and the child are sympathetically affiliated, and one can hardly be thought of apart from the other. The teacher is the activator of an art experience for children, the link between children and art and children and materials. Her regard for art, her respect for creative work, and her own expressive experiences and enjoyment of art will aid her teaching. In regard to the materials for working, she has found that she must be persistent and indomitable in securing for children all the supplies they need, and there are many. Nevertheless, little can come of her efforts to provide supplies unless ample time is allowed in the daily schedule for creative expression. Art cannot be squeezed into another period, but must have time of its own. This the teacher must plan for efficiently. Of equal importance is the guarantee to children that they may work without interruption once they have started. It is frustrating to children to be interrupted in an art project when they

*Detroit Public Schools*

are in the spirit of creative work. Their inspiration may never again return as forcibly for that particular project. A feeling of gratification comes at the end of a school day when both children and teacher have accomplished together what they set out to do, individually and as a group. The teacher also must find ways to help the child who has special and difficult problems of his own: the child who will never show his work, but keeps it hidden away in his desk; the child who throws his work into the wastebasket, ashamed to show it to his classmates or take it home; the child who races through everything he does, spoiling his work by his hurry; the child who lacks self-reliance and asks innumerable and unnecessary questions while he is working; and the child who makes many false starts, wasting his energies, his time, and the school supplies.

The teacher is the initiator, the provider, and the encourager, the one who always stays calm when buckets of water get tipped

*The Brooklyn Museum*

*Elementary School, District of Toa Baja, Puerto Rico*

over or plaster of Paris hardens before it is used. She does not become outwardly upset if a fire drill comes in the middle of a particularly successful watercolor lesson, but sensibly says, "Hurry along, your work will be waiting for you when we return." She is the one who can make the gracious and unexpected rewards and recognitions for work well done by remembering to point out to a visitor to the room a particular painting or a piece of clay work. She may invite the principal to come to her room and choose which picture he would enjoy displaying for a brief time in his office. Her well-arranged bulletin boards in the classroom and in the hall give distinction to children's art work.

What makes good art teaching? A creative point of view makes good art teaching, with strong motivation for each new experience and with new enthusiasm for problems that must be repeated. Creative teaching implies willingness to try something new, willingness to experiment, and willingness to hunt for new materials to use. In creative teaching, fresh ideas are constantly being sought for the better use of regular school supplies, and new techniques are tried which, when successful, are pre-

17

sented to the class at the appropriate time. This open-minded approach by the teacher encourages children to be inventive, and they will respond with lively and original suggestions by the score. In creative teaching, every contribution made by a child is prized and evaluated. Perhaps it will not develop as hoped, but at least it will be given fair consideration by the teacher. To her it is very important that even the smallest talent shall not be lost, both for the sake of the child who possesses it and for the invigorating atmosphere that creativity brings to the classroom. In creative teaching, there is always some phase of a subject which eludes the teacher. This is particularly true of the fine arts. In visual art, seeing is the total experience. Seeing, in the fullest meaning of the word, is neither observing, which is too detached, nor viewing, which is even more detached, but the simple and subtle experience of seeing emotionally—for the joy it brings, for the imagination it involves, for the awe it inspires. Sensitive teachers seem to know how to evoke this awareness. It is a subtle, highly individualized experience. To see emotionally is to grow in perception, thereby reaping boundless rewards.[12]

Children are dependent upon their teacher for encouragement in their creative work. She it is who builds their self-confidence and helps them to overcome their misgivings from time to time. She is generous in her praise, but declines giving it when it is not merited. Children always respect this honesty in teachers.

Children look to their teacher for the continued motivation and understanding that keeps them at a creative task until it is finished. Her insight into behavior guides her judgment in discriminating between the child whose progress stops because of boredom and the one who is held back by lack of information. It is an easy matter to remedy the difficulties of the former; as for the child who is frustrated by something he does not know how to do, the teacher must be capable of giving him promptly the assistance he needs. Most children grow impatient if help is not forthcoming reasonably soon and will give up even when a good start has been made. Then, too, there is the child who needs a new vision, and for this child the teacher must seek inspirational material.

Helen, a sixth-grader, presented such a problem to her teacher. Helen could make many things of paper most successfully. Her Christmas tree ornaments were prettier than any other child's in the room and so were her valentines. She was so clever with paper, scissors, and paste that the teacher longed to develop her talent further. One afternoon when the teacher was at the audio-visual department she came across a film on paper sculpture.[13] Previewing the film, she found it presented a new approach to paper work. Arrangements were made to show the film at school, and after seeing it Helen could hardly wait to go to the art center and start working. Her skill in handling paper was sure and true. Not only did she experiment with the techniques demonstrated for curling, bending, and combining papers, but she also invented ways of her own with the gratifying result that she soon became expert in using three-dimensional techniques.

Probably the roots of creative teaching lie in the feelings and attitudes of the teacher[14] and her rapport with the group. Children are sensitive and must not be defeated by a negative attitude before they start; they will blossom forth when they believe that their teacher is understanding. A teacher with the feeling of freedom within herself will release the children from uncertainty, and they will work freely in their individual way. There is only one answer that a truly creative teacher could give if asked, "Have you faith in the art experience?" She has.

TURNING POINTS IN ART EDUCATION

In reviewing the roots of the present philosophy of art education, two names predominate. They are Arthur Wesley Dow of Teachers College, Columbia University, and Franz Cizek of Vienna, Austria.

The publication of *Composition*[15] by Arthur Wesley Dow in 1899 appears to be the first written expression of an emerging philosophy of art education. This book brought to attention a changing point of view in the theory and practice of art that was to influence radically the creative experiences of children. The British art educator, R. R. Tomlinson, has written of Dow: "Professor A. Wesley Dow is credited with revolutionizing Art Teaching in America; and there can be little doubt that the attention he called to the value of creative power, and the stress he placed on the teaching of composition and design, contributed enormously to the vital methods now in use in that country."[16]

Arthur Wesley Dow was professor of fine arts at Teachers College, Columbia University, and later became director of the department. His classes were a mecca for art teachers and supervisors. In his strategic position as teacher of normal courses and art training for children, he influenced grade teachers as well. His powerful and beloved personality

19

gave his students the courage to break with tradition in their teaching and to revolt against the regimentation, copying, and imitation then prevalent in the art lesson. Nor are his years of guidance forgotten. In *Art Education Today*, 1935, a number of his philosophical observations are again brought to the attention of the earnest student, who will find truth in the Dow definition of teaching: "As teaching is a process of building, there must be a foundation strong and solid, upon which to rear the structure that will be worth the effort."[17]

In the foreword to his book, *Composition*, Dow writes: "The approach to art through structure is absolutely opposed to the time-honored approach through imitation, . . . gathering knowledge of facts but acquiring little power to use them." In the conclusion of the book, Dow further strengthens his statement by writing that his "intention has been to reveal the sources of power: to show the student how to look within for the greatest help, to teach him not to depend on externals, not to lean too much on anything or anybody."[18] A summary of the Dow philosophy per se may be written in one word, "APPRECIATION," which is also the last word in his book and symbolizes the postulate of his philosophy of art education.

Following the work of Professor Dow, American education was to be profoundly influenced by an Austrian art teacher, Franz Cizek. In tribute to his philosophy of the teaching of art to children, Tomlinson writes: "No person has done more to draw attention to the charm of the unsophisticated work of children than Professor Cizek, the results of whose teaching are world famous."[19] Reports of his work with children were first brought to this country by teachers who had traveled in Europe before and after World War I. Shortly afterward, the monthly magazine of the American Junior Red Cross published articles about his art school, *Jugendkunstklasse,* in Vienna. They were illustrated with color reproductions of children's paintings; through the wide circulation of this magazine, many teachers became familiar with his work. In addition, the Junior Red Cross made available for purchase large color prints which enabled thousands of American children to enjoy "The Goose Girl," "Spring," or "Processional"—to mention but three of many titles—in the schools of many American cities and towns. The pictures had great appeal for children of all ages. By 1924, when the world-traveling exhibit from *Jugend-kunstklasse* came to this country, many elementary school teachers had an apperceptive basis for the evaluation, appreciation, and enjoyment of the child art on display. Of this opportunity Tomlinson writes: "These exhibitions were responsible for an international change in attitude toward the work of children."[20]

The opportunity to see and evaluate the Cizek exhibit caused teachers to pause and appraise the results of their own classroom practices. They were intelligent in recognizing that the work from Vienna was not the result of a philosophy built on copying or dictation. Its virility of design, variety of subject, and vividness of color were the result of magnificent teaching based on a sound educational philosophy. In homage to the memory of Professor Cizek after his death in 1947 at the age of eighty-two, Ankwicz-Kleehoven wrote that "the world of art education mourned the passing away of a pedagogue of world repute."[21]

Viola's study of Cizek, *Child Art and Franz Cizek*, was published in Vienna by the Austrian Junior Red Cross in 1936. In this study, the author often successfully captures in words the personality of Professor Cizek—as when the professor replied to a child's outburst:

> "Herr Professor, I can't draw. I can't!" Now let us pause for a moment. What would the average old-fashioned schoolmaster have replied? "You must draw. It will go all right. It only needs practice."—And Cizek? He hesitates for a moment and then has a genial thought: "How would it be if you embroidered what you want to draw?" After some time a wonderful piece of embroidery in glowing colours is produced without any previous drawing of a design.[22]

A teacher-artist now living in California who attended *Jugendkunstklasse* describes the studio as a place filled with color: paintings, drawings, and work done with paper and cloth covered the walls; craft work was displayed on tables and flowers were everywhere during the summer season. When looking back on her childhood experiences, she marvels that Professor Cizek could give his personal attention to so many eager children. He never turned a child away.

How far his work has gone!

## Reference Material

1. *Lascaux, Cradle of Man's Art*. 16mm. film, 30 min., sound, color; produced by International Film Bureau, Inc.*

* Addresses of all distributors listed are given in the Appendix.

2. Baumann, Hans. *The Caves of the Great Hunters.* New York: The Pantheon Press, 1954. (A child's book.) Janson, H. W., and Dora Jane Janson. *The Picture History of Painting.* New York: Harry N. Abrams, Inc., 1957. pp. 8–11.

3. Prescott, Daniel Alfred. *Emotion and the Educative Process.* Washington, D.C.: American Council on Education, 1938.

4. Witty, Paul (ed.). *The Gifted Child.* The American Association for Gifted Children. Boston: D. C. Heath & Co., 1951.

5. Lowenfeld, Viktor. *Creative and Mental Growth.* Rev. ed. New York: The Macmillan Company, 1952.

6. Mines, Robert. "Remember, You're Not a Psychiatrist," *Woman's Home Companion.* LXXVIII, No. 6 (June, 1950), p. 42.

   Sheehy, Emma Dickson. *The Fives and Sixes Go to School.* New York: Holt, Rinehart and Winston, Inc., 1954. "Interpretation of Children's Pictures," p. 152.

7. *Education for ALL American Children.* Educational policies Commission of the National Education Association and the American Association of School Administrators. Washington, D.C.: National Education Association, 1948.

8. Barr, A. S., William H. Burton, and Leo J. Brueckner. *Supervision,* 2d ed. New York: Appleton-Century-Crofts, Inc., 1947. (Chap. XV, p. 709.)

9. *Learning Through Cooperative Planning.* 2 reels, 16mm. film, 20 min., sound, black and white; produced by Bureau of Publications, Teachers College, Columbia University.

10. Cunningham, Ruth, *et al. Understanding Group Behavior of Boys and Girls.* New York: Bureau of Publications, Teachers College, Columbia University, 1951.

11. *Care of Art Materials.* 16mm. film, 10 min., sound, black and white; produced by McGraw-Hill Book Company, Inc.

12. *Learning to Look.* 6 filmstrips, color, 1 recording; produced by Filmscope Inc.

13. *Paper Sculpture.* 16 mm. film, 6 min., sound, color; produced by International Film Bureau, Inc.

14. Zirbes, Laura. *Spurs to Creative Learning.* New York: G. P. Putnam's Sons, 1959.

15. Dow, Arthur Wesley. *Composition.* 13th ed. New York: Doubleday & Company, Inc., 1928.

16. Tomlinson, R. R. *Picture Making by Children.* New York: The Viking Press, Inc., 1934. p. 36.

17. "Excerpts From Notes by Arthur Wesley Dow," *Art Education Today.* New York: Bureau of Publications, Teachers College, Columbia University, 1935. p. 73.

18. Dow, Arthur Wesley. *Composition.* 13th ed. New York: Doubleday & Company, Inc., 1928. (Foreword.)

19. Tomlinson, R. R. *Picture Making by Children.* New York: The Viking Press, Inc., 1934. p. 25.

20. *Ibid.,* p. 27

21. Ankwicz-Kleehoven, Hans. "Professor Franz Cizek," *Everyday Art,* 26: 34; Sept.–Oct., 1947. p. 5.

22. Viola, William. *Child Art and Franz Cizek.* Vienna, Austria: Austrian Junior Red Cross, 1936.

## READER PARTICIPATION

Discuss the wholesome contribution to child growth of sustained art experiences in the elementary school program.

Talk with children of different ages about their interests and enthusiasms. Does environment seem to affect choices? Did you find some interests common to all?

List three art experiences for children that would contribute to each of the four goals.

Name some possible out-of-school experiences that would stimulate the art program in the district where you hope to teach. Indicate the expected outcomes for child growth inherent in each experience.

Analyze the merits of both group and independent experiences for growth in creative work.

# 3

# *When Does a Child Begin?*

Art provides a means for children to find satisfaction and enjoyment through personal experience. Since the art program is flexible, the experiences may be adapted to meet the differences of personality and ability found in every classroom. A varied program makes it possible for each child to discover his own congeniality for certain art materials and techniques and to select those most appropriate for expressing his feelings and ideas. Creative work brings emotional release through a real rather than a vicarious experience.

## THE CHILD'S EXPERIENCE AND THE SCHOOL PROGRAM

A rewarding personal experience brings children strong feelings of satisfaction and security. When children grow up in a wholesome environment which provides a variety of worth-while things for them to do, their vicarious experiences fall into proper perspective and do not absorb all their interest. Today more and more children seem to be developing passive leisure-time habits of watching and listening to the adventures of others by means of television,[1] radio, and motion pictures. There is a danger when these types of entertainment become substitutes for imaginative play, for games when wits are matched against wits, and for activities that call for creative thinking. It therefore becomes doubly

24

important for the school art program to provide daily experiences for children that are creative in nature and that will fulfill many of childhood's longings for real activity.

The content of a good art program consists of many things. It is the outcome of the creative growth[2] and maturation level of children; and it is conditioned by their environment, past experiences in creative work—meager or ample—and current interests. The effective art program then becomes a flexible program that can be adapted in content and practice to meet both individual and group differences. Children neither produce spontaneous art expression nor exert their best efforts when creative work is bound by hard and fast rules and subjected to schedule and direction. Such rigidity has turned many a creatively inclined child away from art forever. Children need no crutches to lean upon or patterns and hectographed materials to depend on in art. These practices only nullify the goals of creative work. What can happen to a child is startlingly illustrated in *Teaching Art to Children*[3] by Jefferson.

SIGNIFICANCE OF PERSONALITY, ABILITY, AND MATURATION

Personality differences become more noticeable as children mature; and the scope of the art program must be broadened to provide satisfactions and meaningful experiences for all children, not only a few in the class. Children neither do, can, nor should all work in the same way; in fact, personal choices of activity, subject, and technique are what make the creative work of each child honest and vital.

There is a wide range in the native endowment of children. Some children are gifted; some children are highly sensitive; some children have manual dexterity; and some children have outstanding powers of observation. Only the rare child has everything, and no child has nothing. The ability to do good art work may appear at different times in the life cycle of a child. With some children it comes early, with others later; or it may be spasmodic, dormant for a time, then reblooming when least expected. Younger children seem to be naturally expressive and to know instinctively how to handle color, line, balance, and rhythm skillfully, particularly in painting. Older children often have an exaggerated admiration for the technical perfections of adult art and, consequently, tend to set a false goal for themselves which they cannot achieve. The teacher's guidance is most essential in helping this type of child to maintain

*Courtesy of Mrs. Loren Campbell, San Diego*

the art goals of childhood and to keep the buoyancy of his earlier expression.

Personality is expressed very early in a child's life: in the stories he tells, the pictures he draws—even in his manuscript writing. When using lined paper, Tony and Medford wrote according to the prescribed school pattern, and correctly so; but when signing his drawings, each printed his name in his own way. Personality differences were beginning to be re-expressed. Both signatures had design quality. Nor were they due to happenstance, for all art papers presented by these two children during the first quarter of their first year in school were similarly signed. Other children showed interesting hints of future development, but none seemed to express as acute a sense of design as these two children.

Maturation defines the normal progress of children toward maturity, their physical development, characteristic reactions, and special needs. Jenkins, Shacter, and Bauer have made an extensive study of the maturation levels of children and have reported it in their textbook, *These Are Your Children.*[4] The implications for creative work are most significant to art education. The elementary school teacher will find it helpful to study the charts at the front and the back of the book. The relationship of the study to art experience is so pertinent that, with reference to classroom practice and recognition of special needs in art, it has become the frame of reference for the remainder of this chapter. Art experience is a significant factor in education, for it offers opportunity for each child to progress at his own rate of growth. An overview of the implications that maturation holds for art experiences will assist teachers to plan more adequately a sound art program. Although Lowenfeld's *Your Child and His Art*[5] is addressed to parents, it has equal significance for teachers in the appraisal of the maturation levels of children.

A book to be studied carefully in conjunction with this chapter is Lindstrom's *Children's Art*.[6] The illustrations are particularly pertinent.

## IMPLICATIONS OF MATURATION FOR ART EXPERIENCES

### The Preschool Child

Under present conditions, many children spend the greater part of their day away from home. This is particularly true in urban districts where child-care centers and nursery schools are provided for the children of working mothers. At a child-care center children have many valuable experiences which they would never have at home. The

small child is active, inquisitive, trusting, and lovable in personality. While he is naturally inclined to be changeable, he also can be surprisingly intent. In all his activities he needs patient and understanding guidance from his teacher. He often tries her patience with his lively ways, continuous chatter, high spirits, and his determined and frequent excursions into disapproved behavior. Observation of his play habits[7] will give clues to his personality and guide a teacher in her relationships with him.

Soft and easily workable art materials are preferred for the preschool child: finger paint, colored chalk, tempera paint, thin, colored cutting paper, and very plastic modeling material. Better than anything that can be bought is a mixture of flour, salt, and water that a teacher can prepare herself.[8]

Only the most inconspicuous and gentle motivation is right or necessary for the preschool child, the kind of motivation that stimulates art expression by making art materials accessible, by providing a comfortable place to work, and by allowing freedom and self-direction for their use. A place to work should be provided where the child has the right to be himself, to splash with paint, to get grimy with colored chalk, to crumple, tear, cut, and scatter paper, to build with blocks and to knock them down. He needs a place where tipping over a jar of water is an accident to be expected, and where his normal activity does not disrupt the activities of other children. In short, he needs a place where he is automatically protected from destroying things not his own and where he can be a happy child[9] while preparing for the step into kindergarten. Parental understanding[10] and appreciation at this period of growth is an important factor that can influence a child's future art expression.

### The Five-year-old Child

The natural interests of the five-year-old are his home and family life, and when art activities and construction projects are related to his own life he understands what he is doing. A house built of blocks fulfills his need for noisy activity and the exercise of large muscles.

Since a five-year-old is beginning to be able to carry some responsibility and is eager to do so, a few essential work habits may be established. The child will soon remember to wash out his paintbrush when he changes from one color to another, to tidy up the easel after painting, to put away his work in some safe place, and to return to its place anything he may have borrowed. His carpentry tools should be the right size and

28

weight, and his art materials large and easy to handle. The working area should be unconfined, with large, low tables, easels, and space to work on the floor, which is often the best for his needs. Any and every type of small and delicate work puts a strain upon the muscles and eyes of a little child and, consequently, is not recommended.

When a new art material is introduced, the five-year-old needs ample time for experimentation, to feel it with his hands, to play with it, and to find out what he can do with it. This he likes to do very much. Color choices are largely accidental; often only one color is used, and he may not be able to name it. Many times a child has not developed beyond the scribbling he was doing at home or in a child-care center before he enters kindergarten, nor will he always be able to describe what he has tried to show. However, this will soon pass and he will have much to say about his work. Next, he goes through successive periods of symbolism in his work, first using forms which he can name but which are meaningless to others. Following this period, he devises symbols which can be identified because of their significant characteristics even though

*Department of Education, Baltimore, Maryland*

29

his composition is fragmentary. For some time composition will continue to be confused and have no relation to the laws of gravity, but he is satisfied. Later, depending upon his speed of maturation, his drawing and painting begin to show art structure, and even though he always enjoys making explanations they are no longer needed. His art expression speaks for itself. From now on there is a steady growth in creative power. All children seem to progress through these stages of development, but the periods are not of equal duration for every child or always as sharply marked. A teacher should not interfere with a child's pattern of growth or try to hurry his development.

The special needs of the five-year-old for activity are met in construction projects and group work, freedom in his art expression, and security in the knowledge that his teacher appreciates his every art effort.

## The Six-year-old Child

The physical characteristics of the six-year-old show slight change since he was five, and the same kinds of materials and tools that he used in the kindergarten are right for him in the first grade. If a child has had no kindergarten experience, his drawing and painting will show the same progression as that of a kindergartener, but faster progress through the successive stages may be expected. Good work habits and proper care of materials should be encouraged, and new responsibilities may be given if the child feels no added pressure.

In an art experience the six-year-old learns best by participating and using his own initiative. He may and will admire the work of the other children, but always he is waiting and wanting to go to work himself. Art activities should be of limited duration because the interest span of a child is short and he is easily fatigued. He likes to be associated with other children and to accomplish something in common with them, such as building a market and making the items to stock the shelves. All activities should be finished in a short time so that the child's patience is not taxed.

Encouragement continues to be an emotional need for the child, and he wants the warm appreciation of his teacher. He feels important when his painting is displayed or used as the illustration on a chart. He is proud to show his work and not at all self-conscious during the sharing period.

A six-year-old has many independent ways, and though he

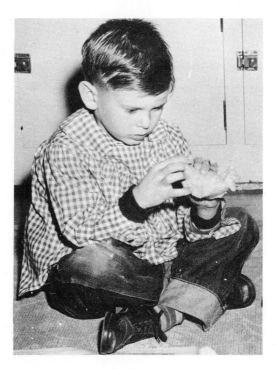

*San Diego City Schools*

may at times find it difficult to make up his mind and will turn to his teacher for help, once started he does not welcome interference.

*The Seven-year-old Child*

The most noticeable change in the maturation of the seven-year-old child is his improved eye-hand coordination and better control of the small muscles, but he still is not ready for any kind of fine, close work or an art activity that demands prolonged nervous control. Large tools and pliable materials continue to be the best to use. Since he likes to use his hands, he may have more tools and make many things for construction projects and holiday gifts. What he makes he likes to have sturdy and usable.

At this maturation level the child learns best when his experiences are concrete. He enjoys a field trip and profits from it. Like all younger children his need for activity is insatiable, and companionship with other children is necessary to his growth and security. He is highly competitive and responds to the interaction that group work gives. The individual interests of boys and girls begin to show differences which are

31

reflected in art expression and in the choices they make in art activities.

Although the seven-year-old is becoming self-critical and cautious, he still is pleased with his work and is disappointed if appreciation is withheld. Especially is he dependent upon the approval of his teacher, without which he may lose self-confidence.

### The Eight-year-old Child

The eight-year-old is an alert child. He quickly grasps the new art concepts which he is experiencing for the first time in life study units. He enjoys dramatic play and is an enthusiastic and imaginative participant. This becomes a strong motivation for related art activities in a construction unit. The eight-year-old child is interested in building appropriate settings for his dramatic activities and will work industriously to make and design costumes and accessories. His interest span is longer and he works with greater thought for detail. He has improved vision and is ready for closer work. He works with less physical fatigue because the small muscles are better developed.

*San Antonio Independent School District*

*Fort Worth
Public Schools*

The eight-year-old is careless in many things which he does, and accidents will happen which spoil his finished art work. His eagerness and enthusiasm often lead him to work too fast, but, nevertheless, there are fewer drips on his paintings and his clay work stays together. He often neglects his responsibilities and must be reminded that in art activities good work habits are essential for good results.

33

A child of this maturation level has greater capacity for self-evaluation than ever before, but at the same time he is sensitive to criticism. He is less defensive when criticism comes from his classmates because he wants their approval and, consequently, will accept their suggestions. From his teacher he needs the encouragement to keep on trying rather than to be reminded of his faults, and the constructive approach to evaluation[11] will always help him to make progress. His best incentive for diligent work comes from his classmates.

### The Nine-year-old Child

The nine-year-old is a responsible and dependable child, willing to carry responsibility, and he does it well. His interest span is longer, and he can make plans and carry them to completion upon his own initiative. These characteristics play a significant part in his art experience and contribute to the success of group projects which proceed smoothly with a minimum of teacher supervision.

*Pittsburgh*
*Public Schools*

*Long Beach
Public Schools*

The nine-year-old child's type of art expression is changing, due largely to an increasing ability to incorporate in his creative work the ideas gained through reference work. A strong interest in crafts is beginning to develop, and he enjoys working with new materials. He is eager to improve his skills and asks many questions about technique, for he tends to be both a perfectionist and a realist. He is disappointed when his performance does not match his ideal. This often leads to discouragement and loss of interest. He is grateful for guidance which is helpful but resents pressure. Unfortunately, some of the exuberance he formerly displayed in painting is lessened, and he tends to tighten up because of his new concern for technique and detail. Plenty of opportunity for quick, free, water-color work and finger painting with strong motivation for subjects which draw upon his personal experience will help him to continue to express the vigor of his earlier work. A special need of the nine-year-old is to be treated in a manner equal to his maturity.

35

*Detroit Public Schools*

Superior art ability now becomes evident in a few children, and varied experiences should be provided for them, with encouragement to carry out their own ideas.

### The Preadolescent Child of Ten and Eleven Years

In the last two years of elementary school, the ten- and eleven-year-old child goes through the emotional and physical changes of preadolescence. Within every class there is a wide range of individual differences and maturation levels, with the girls maturing more quickly than the boys. A flexible art program is the only possible way to meet so many varied art needs and to maintain interest and enjoyment in creative work. The child responds best when given every opportunity for independence in his work and thinking. A rigid, prescribed art course will crush his creative thinking and his liking for art. Interest differences between boys and girls are sharp and are seen in choices made for craft and group activities and in subjects chosen for painting and drawing. Children are

36

inventive and ingenious and will find their own materials and bring them to school to use for special purposes. Never is a diversified program of art activities more urgently needed than during the years between the beginning of the tenth year and the end of the eleventh year, when differences in maturation are marked.

Because of the preadolescent's intellectual strengths, integrated art activities that utilize reference materials and include field trips are rewarding. Murals, dioramas, maps, and illustrated notebooks provide opportunity for related art experiences. Publishing a school newspaper affords evaluation of layout and lettering. However, integration must not be emphasized to such a degree that equal opportunity for the expression of personal interests is excluded.

Problems in art techniques continue to perplex the child, and unless he is helped when he needs it, he becomes frustrated and uncooperative in finishing his work. The teaching problem is one of maintaining a balanced approach so that techniques will not dominate the child's thinking and crowd out the fine creative work which he is capable

*The Brooklyn Museum*

37

of doing. Individual patterns of performance are unstable, and drawing, painting, and craft activities alternate between good and poor work, reflecting the emotional and physical changes the child is undergoing.

Since the preadolescent child is overly critical, it is only natural that his approach to evaluation tends to be negative. When a negative attitude becomes a fixed point of view, the result is not constructive nor does it contribute to growth of creative power. Relaxed and skillful leadership by a teacher who refuses to be maneuvered into making issues of delicate situations will help the child through this difficult emotional period and increase his respect for art.

REFERENCE MATERIAL

1. Shayon, Robert Lewis. *Television and Our Children.* New York: Longmans, Green & Co., Inc., 1951.

2. Lowenfeld, Viktor. *Creative and Mental Growth.* Rev. ed. New York: The Macmillan Company, 1952.

   Mendelowitz, Daniel M. *Children Are Artists.* Stanford, Calif.: Stanford University Press, 1953. (Chaps. I–V.)

3. Jefferson, Blanche. *Teaching Art to Children.* Boston: Allyn and Bacon, Inc., 1959. pp. 256–61.

4. Jenkins, Gladys Gardner, Helen Shacter, and William G. Bauer. *These Are Your Children.* Chicago: Scott, Foresman and Company, 1949.

5. Lowenfeld, Viktor. *Your Child and His Art.* New York: The Macmillan Company, 1957. pp. 83–149.

6. Lindstrom, Miriam. *Children's Art.* Berkeley, Calif.: University of California Press, 1959. pp. 1–80.

7. Gesell, Arnold, *et al. The First Five Years of Life: A Guide to the Study of the Preschool Child.* New York: Harper & Brothers, 1940. (Chap. IX, "Personal-Social Behavior," Sec. G, "Aesthetic Development.")

   Hartley, Ruth, Lawrence Frank, and Robert Goldenson. *Understanding Children's Play.* New York: Columbia University Press, 1952. (Chaps. VI–VIII.)

8. Directions for making modeling material:

    4 cups flour     1½ cups table salt
    2 cups water    Coloring as desired
                    (food coloring is recommended)

    Mix flour with table salt. Add coloring to water and mix all ingredients together. If too spongy, add more salt. Knead thoroughly. Mixture keeps in good condition for a week and may be reused daily. Store in covered crock.

9. Gesell, Arnold, and Frances Ilg. *The Child From Five to Ten.* New York: Harper & Brothers, 1946.

10. Moore, Sallie Beth, and Phyllis Richards. *Teaching in the Nursery School.* New York: Harper & Brothers, 1959. "Creative Work on Display," pp. 340–41.

11. Strang, Ruth. *Introduction to Child Study.* 3d ed. New York: The Macmillan Company, 1951. (Chap. XV, "How Primary Children Learn," p. 379.)

## READER PARTICIPATION

Recall some of the creative experiences you enjoyed in the play-life of your childhood. Are there equally significant opportunities for children today? What are they?

Have you sought the friendship of some preschool children? Do you ever do any baby-sitting?

When did you last visit a kindergarten?

Select a small group of children of nearly the same age, a Sunday school class, a cub scout den, a summer camp group, and observe the differences in maturation within the group. How do skills and interests vary?

Describe how one or two specific art activities may be adapted effectively to children of different levels of maturation in the same class.

Discuss different kinds of experiences for art enjoyment that would stimulate an upper-grade class of children. Provide an additional enrichment experience for the small group within the class whose members have a much more mature understanding.

# 4

# *Finding and*
# *Using Source Material*

Art is related to many subjects in the elementary school program—more closely to some than to others. A careful selection of resource materials will help art relationships to develop naturally. The more opportunities children can have to experience art relationships, the higher become the possibilities for integration. Because there are many kinds of resource materials on the market, an appropriate choice may be made for every grade.

## VALUE OF RESOURCE MATERIALS

Resource materials provide one effective means of establishing an integration of art with other subjects. Integration is a mental process that brings different experiences into a natural and satisfying whole. Integration is not a made-to-order experience for children, nor can it happen at will. The teacher's responsibility is to provide the circumstances and maintain the permissive atmosphere in the classroom which will encourage its development. The ability to integrate art with other subjects is a sign of maturity and denotes an understanding of relationships that is not always accomplished by children in their elementary school life. Integration is of gradual growth, subjective and immeasurable, and may be stimulated and activated by an art program that emphasizes the meaning of art in its broadest application. Resource materials which foster integration are discussed in the following pages; integration which motivates children's creative expression is discussed in a later chapter.

## AVAILABLE RESOURCE MATERIALS

Visual aids and reference materials are varied in type and comprehensive in subject matter.[1] There are many different kinds of visual aids which are suitable for the wide range of maturation levels in every class. Now available for classroom use are art prints and study prints, charts, posters, maps, postcards, sound films, filmstrips, Kodachrome slides, dioramas, dolls, toys, and books. There are also collections of various kinds of materials packed in what, for want of a better term, are called loan boxes, because they are loaned to classes. All of this material stimulates pupil interest and increases art understandings.

It is best to choose reference material with respect for art quality as well as content so that the finest examples may always be secured for the class. Among five or six posters, one or two are likely to be better in color and design than the rest, even though each poster presents equally authentic information. Marked degrees of art quality are true for all visual aids, and the art program will be fortified if a careful evaluation is made.

## PICTORIAL MATERIALS

Pictorial resources range from large and beautiful reproductions of paintings to inexpensive postcards, and include study prints, charts, posters, and maps. Literally hundreds of colored reproductions of the work of artists are available to teachers. Commercially these are usually termed *art prints* and classified as such. In the following pages this connotation is used. Art prints beautify the classroom and satisfy children's love of pictures. They are large in size and as true in color as a printed copy of an original work ever can be. There are art prints representative of every century, every country, and nearly every artist published by a number of commercial firms and societies. Consequently, subject matter is so comprehensive that examples may be found for use in connection with social studies—historical, geographical, and cultural aspects—nature study, music, and literature. The same art prints which are selected for

41

*Indianapolis Public Schools*

curriculum work can become an excellent core for a planned program of art enjoyment and appreciation. There are a number of catalogues[2] of art prints. A school district may do three things: prepare portfolios of art prints for circulation in its schools, mount and catalogue art prints for teachers to borrow, and inexpensively frame art prints for extended loan to schools.

As a means of showing how art prints may be used for integration, a few selections will be made for units in the social studies and nature study. Since grade placement would not be the same in all school districts, the suggestions are not to be considered as final. Any arbitrary selection of this kind is always open to evaluation in terms of the art comprehension of each particular group of children and their personal preferences.

The farm is a typical primary unit and will be taken as the first example in the social studies. Any one of the snug country scenes painted by Grandma Moses[3] would be a delightful choice for children. Others could be *Spring Tryout*[4] by Thomas Hart Benton and *The Farm*[5] by Peggy Wickham. A middle-grade unit which extends children's geographical concepts is "Carrying the Mail." Since letters and packages are posted to every part of the world, art prints can be found which are typical of many postal destinations here and abroad. *Manhattan Harbor*[6] by George Grosz and *Rue Ordener, Montmartre*,[7] by Maurice Utrillo are both interesting to children. John Marin's[8] water colors of the Main Coast are redolent of the saltiness of the sea; John Steuart Curry's *The Line Storm*[9] has caught the flavor of the Midwest, and *The Waterhole*[10] by Peter Hurd can give children a view of the western plains. "Markets and Marketing" is a unit often taught in upper grades which offers children an opportunity to become acquainted with the painting of foreign artists. *Coffee Bearers*[11] by Candido Portanari of Brazil is one such example. Many ships have ports of call in the South Pacific, and there are numerous compositions by Gauguin[12] from which to choose. European markets would suggest a host of painters, Van Gogh[13] and Dufy, to name but two whose work pleases children. A final example in the social studies—in a few school districts the elementary program is culminated in the sixth grade with a unit centered on the cultural gifts of European countries. Innumerable color reproductions of the masters of the Western world, such as El Greco's *View of Toledo*,[14] Botticelli's *Madonna of the Lilies*,[15] Pieter de Hooch's *Pantry Door*,[16] and Van Gogh's *Blooming Apple Orchard*,[17] may be used for this unit and can be ordered from art catalogues.

There are human values in nature study units which can be interpreted emotionally to children through painting. What child could resist the tender feeling of Albrecht Dürer's *Study of a Young Hare*[18] or his *Squirrels?*[19] Could a child fail to respond, although in a different way, to *Red Horses*[20] by Franz Marc? Birds in flight are gone in a flash with hardly enough time for children to see, much less enjoy, the exquisite pattern and subtle color of their plumage. Audubon and Menaboni have captured both in their paintings. A list of Audubon[21] paintings available in art prints may be found in catalogues, and the illustrations in the Menaboni book, *Birds*,[22] can be shown to the class. Except for a personal experience, what better way could be found for children to see and sense nature than through the eyes and skill of the artist?

Pictures and illustrations may be taken from magazines, advertising, brochures, calendars, and other types of printed matter, and successfully used as *study prints*. Current materials become valuable teaching aids and cost no more than the price of a magazine or the effort of writing a letter. Because they are cheap or free material, study prints can be discarded without compunction when the picture becomes soiled or out of date. Study prints are used for reference work, not for copying, in connection with creative activities which necessitate more knowledge of some phase of a particular subject. There is a timeliness about current materials that cannot be duplicated elsewhere. Hence illustrations and photographs of recent developments in commerce and industry and the findings of scientific expeditions are invaluable to the teacher. A careful and persistent search will usually reward her, so that eventually she will have a bulging file of indispensable reference material for children to use. Study prints make attractive displays in the room when nicely mounted and well arranged on the bulletin board.

Handsomely designed *posters* and *charts* are an important part of the environment. Evaluation of art quality can become a natural outcome when posters are displayed. Children can appreciate design in a poster because it is a direct and simple statement. Commercial artists are producing some of the finest examples of contemporary art for posters. Since posters and charts are large in size and printed on heavy paper, they make a dramatic showing as well as presenting information. This type of advertising material is available from business concerns and government agencies either free or at a nominal cost.

Children are always fascinated by the unknown as represented by *maps*. Decorative maps have been designed by artists for classroom use. Three recently published maps of the United States are outstanding: *America—Its Folklore*[23] by William Gropper, a delineation of heroes and legends from Rip Van Winkle to Paul Bunyan; *America—Its Soil*[24] by Paul Sample, a panorama of natural resources; and *America—Its History*[25] by Aaron Bohrod, an overview of the highlights of American history. There are enough decorative maps of places all over the world to make it possible for a teacher to find the one she needs.

Carefully selected *postcards*, especially photographs of foreign countries, are a time-honored and useful aid. They are an authentic source of information about places and can help children to visualize the characteristics of another country, its landscape, dwellings, and vegetation. A typical set from Japan might include the grove of cryptomeria trees at Nikko, the sacred mountain of Fujiyama, the Inland Sea, the bamboo homes of the peasants, and the deer park at Nara. One can also make a collection of the children's favorite paintings after visiting an art museum.

AUDIO-VISUAL MATERIALS

   *Sound films* in color are probably the most popular visual aid with children. A good film successfully integrates photography, music, and art. *Geography of New England*[26] has many scenes of beauty and is an interesting presentation of the area it covers. A philosophical film that is not too mature for upper-grade children, *The Strands Grow,*[27] is helpful in developing a fuller concept of conservation. Like the film on New England, it is artistically photographed.

   Besides commercial films, a number of films are produced by industry and distributed gratis to schools upon request to the office of public relations. Films of this type are intended for educational as well as business use. Two examples which are interesting for children and very different are *American Cowboy*[28] and *Man on the Land.*[29] The first is a story of cattle grazing in Colorado. There are fine shots of the surrounding country, plenty of bronco busting, and cowboy songs. Needless to say, this film is a great favorite with boys. The second film, *Man on the Land,* is a unique production and has lots of humor. It is an animated film on the subject of oil. The production is very fine in design and color and the cartoon technique used by the artists holds the children's attention. This interesting and instructive production is probably most appropriate for fifth- and sixth-grade classes.

   The value of a *filmstrip* is its flexible continuity. A filmstrip must be described as a series of stills printed on a strip of film. The projector is operated manually, and the teacher may turn the film forward or backward as needed to emphasize a point. Usually either a tape recording or a manual accompanies the strip. A table viewer[30] for filmstrips only that an upper-grade child can operate is now available. The viewer is placed on a table and plugged into an electric outlet; the filmstrip is inserted in a slot and turned manually. It is an indispensable piece of equipment for individual study. Two filmstrips suitable for different age groups are *Farm Pets*[31] and *The Story of Corn,*[32] the first for primary grades, the second for upper grades.

   There are *Kodachrome slides* for practically every unit in the elementary school curriculum. Slides may be projected on a screen for all the class to view, or a small group may see them by using a table viewer. A new model[33] to be plugged into an electric outlet enlarges pictures on

45

a glass plate and is simple enough for a child to operate. Two sets of slides that illustrate an important period of American history are *Early American Crafts*[34] and *Early American Textiles.*[35] Manuals are provided to assist the teacher in her instruction.

If a teacher's hobby is photography, she may take pictures and make her own slides. One wildflower enthusiast who taught in a city school returned each spring vacation to her father's farm where, as a child, she had roamed the meadows and woods searching for wildflowers. It was her constant regret that children raised in the city knew so little about the wildflowers of their own state. She had found in her teaching that good pictures of wildflowers were few and difficult, if not impossible, to find. Deciding that colored slides would be a more efficient teaching aid anyway, she gave up her search for pictures and concentrated on taking colored photographs with her thirty-five-millimeter camera. It took her three years to complete her collection, which finally included all she had hoped to find: jack-in-the-pulpit, anemone, shooting star, Dutchmen's-breeches, dogtooth violet, lady's-slipper, buttercup, columbine, and crocus. The slides were an inspiration to her teaching and she was able to impart to children some of the loveliness of spring days seventy miles away from school.

Previews of films, filmstrips, and slides are a wise precaution before taking class time to show them. There are many productions of equal merit but not of equal art quality, so why not choose the best?

DISPLAY MATERIALS

Display materials are in constant demand in the classroom. There are dioramas, loan boxes, dolls, and toys—all most attractive to children.

*Dioramas* are small-scale models executed with the greatest of artistic skill. The parts of a diorama are put together in a portable case which has a cellophane·front. An endless variety of subjects may be developed in a diorama—for social studies there could be a lumber camp, a placer mine, prehistoric animals, the landing of Cabrillo at San Diego, and many others. Dioramas are realistic; nevertheless art principles are demonstrated in their construction, for good design and fine color are essential for a satisfying portrayal of factual material. Compact, unique, interesting, and portable, a diorama is one of the most important visual aids that a teacher can have for use with children. Teachers will find it helpful to refer to a film prepared by Syracuse University entitled *How to Make and Use a Diorama.*[36]

What is a *loan box?* A loan box is a collection of materials that becomes a treasure chest for children and an instructional aid for the teacher. Loan boxes are frequently prepared by the audio-visual department in a school system. Usually the contents are packed in a sturdy cardboard box with a strap to secure the lid in place. On the inside of the lid is pasted a brief description of the contents of the box, where the materials came from, what they are made of, what they are used for, and any other information of interest to children. Loan boxes may be borrowed by teachers for a period of time. When displayed in the classroom, the contents of a loan box makes an attractive exhibit.

Teachers who have imagination and are good shoppers can find many unusual things to put in boxes. The materials may be more modest than those an audio-visual department is able to procure, but the results will still be gratifying. Loan boxes serve immeasurably to advance art appreciation as well as to make a learning unit more understandable by bringing examples of art work to the class. At one school, market baskets

*San Diego City Schools*

were substituted for boxes. Each basket was painted a different color and the articles were wrapped in colored tissue paper. The baskets were easy to store on a closet shelf and convenient to carry from room to room. The contents of each basket could be identified quickly by a chart on the closet door; the green basket held things from Brazil, the yellow basket was filled with toys from Europe, and the others contained articles selected with equal thought for children's interests.

A loan box that was interesting to a fifth-grade class came while it was studying pioneer life. Said one girl, "It is like rubbing Aladdin's lamp to get so many treasures out of one small box." First to be taken out was a piece of hand-woven fabric. This, the teacher explained, had been woven on a four-harness loom, similar in operation, only smaller, to the loom used by pioneer women. Next came three utensils: a big wooden bowl, a ladle, and a dipper made from a gourd. By reading the information card pasted on the inside of the lid, the children learned that gourds grew on vines along the trails and in the fields of the Midwest.

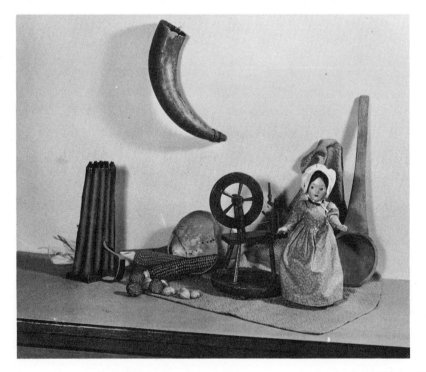

*San Diego City Schools*

Then came a pair of wool carders and a set of candle molds. Again the children learned how essential were certain things to pioneer life, for by pouring the tallow quickly the housewife could make six candles at one time. Following these came several ears of corn, the dark Indian corn and the golden corn that could be popped by pioneer children in the open fireplace on winter evenings. The next article was well wrapped, and when it was opened it revealed a miniature spinning wheel, the type that was used for spinning flax. The boys examined it carefully and figured out its working principle of treadle and wheel. Now was found a doll dressed in a bright calico dress and a white sunbonnet. Lastly, there was a paper sack containing butternuts and wild walnuts native to the woods of the Midwest.

How to display advantageously all this fascinating material from a loan box became an art experience in arrangement for the children as they assisted their teacher in setting up the contents in their classroom. By discussing the arrangement with children, the teacher felt that each article became more significant, and an opportunity was presented for the children to talk naturally about the art values of each piece. First, a proper place in the room for the display was chosen. Next followed the selection of colored papers for mat and background. Then the children experimented with placing the different things so that each would be seen to its best advantage. The first evaluation led to discarding the big bowl and the carders because they were clumsy and out of proportion to the other articles. Continuing experiences in evaluation became an outgrowth of the development of the children's sensitivity to shape and awareness of the appropriate position of each article in relation to the whole. The result was not perfect, but it was their own. There is real art learning for children when they see and handle the handcraft of a culture other than their own.

Dolls and toys are a part of child life. A *doll* exhibit may be a way to demonstrate design in clothing. The beautiful peasant costumes of European and Oriental dolls are lessons in color, pattern, texture, and culture for a class. Children may participate in the exhibit by bringing their own dolls to school and so have a share in the display. A teacher with average sewing skill can dress a doll in any period style that strikes her fancy, or she can dress it for a specific use like the doll in the loan box previously described. The doll collections in many art museums can be the incentive for planning a delightful afternoon excursion to see them.

*The Denver Art Museum*

A color film, *Dolls of Many Lands*,[37] would provide an enjoyable ten minutes for the girls of the class while the boys play baseball.

*Toys,* like dolls, have a place in the classroom, particularly in the primary grades. Toys lend themselves to charming arrangements, and if some of them are from foreign lands, they will surely lead to animated discussion about the life and culture of the country from which each toy came. Also, they provide an opportunity to talk about color and design and to find out why some of the toys are more pleasing than others.

BOOKS

There are many beautifully illustrated books for primary children, notably those which win the Caldecott award. Children's books are displayed and catalogued in public and school libraries; to list them would be superfluous.

Upper-grade classes like to have good, readable art books

50

on the library table. An excellent book for a teacher to get for her class is *Famous Paintings: An Introduction to Art for Young People.*[38] A historical report on the life of Paul Revere, for example, would be made much more interesting for the class if the illustration of Copley's portrait of Revere holding one of his silver teapots were included in the presentation.

There are not nearly enough reference books on art for elementary school children, but the title mentioned in the preceding paragraph may serve as a criterion in the selection of art books for children.

### DISCRIMINATION IN CHOICES

No teacher would ever want, or expect, to set up a classroom environment using all the resource materials given here. To do so would violate good teaching practice and overstimulate children to such a degree that they would find it difficult, if not impossible, to settle down to serious work. The teacher's task is to select the materials appropriate to the current needs of the class and to postpone the use of other material until a later and more propitious time.

### PUPIL OUTCOMES

A vital classroom environment can help children to build lasting values in art and will demonstrate the relation of art to life experiences. It is believed that respect for art comes with learning more about its importance in everything that people do, see, feel, and enjoy.

## REFERENCE MATERIAL

1. McKibben, Mary Adeline. "Resources of the Art Teacher," *Art Education Today.* New York: Bureau of Publications, Teachers College, Columbia University, 1949–50. pp. 47–55.

2. *Catalogues and Supplemental Listings.* Dr. Konrad Prothmann.

   *101 Fine Color Reproductions, Impressionists and Modern Painters.* Erich S. Herrmann, Inc.

   Catalogues of Artex Prints, Inc.

   Catalogues of Raymond and Raymond, Inc.

51

*UNESCO Catalogue of Colour Reproductions Prior to 1860.* New York: United Nations, UNESCO Publishing Center, 1950.

*UNESCO Catalogue of Colour Reproductions 1860 to 1952.* New York: United Nations, UNESCO Publishing Center, 1954.

3–21. See sources listed under No. 2.

22. Menaboni, Athos, and Sara A. Menaboni. *Birds.* New York: Holt, Rinehart and Winston, Inc., 1950.

23. Gropper, William. *America—Its Folklore. Fine Art Reproductions, Old and New Masters, 1956 Supplement.* New York Graphic Society.

24. Sample, Paul. *America—Its Soil. Fine Art Reproductions, Old and New Masters, 1956 Supplement.* New York Graphic Society.

25. Bohrod, Aaron. *America—Its History. Fine Art Reproductions, Old and New Masters, 1956 Supplement.* New York Graphic Society.

26. *Geography of New England.* 16mm. film, 10 min., sound, color; produced by Coronet Instructional Films.

27. *The Strands Grow.* 16mm. film, 17 min., sound, color; produced by Encyclopaedia Britannica Films, Inc.

28. *American Cowboy.* 16mm. film, 28 min., sound, color; produced by the Ford Motor Company. (Free film.)

29. *Man on the Land.* 16mm. film, 16 min., sound, color; produced by the American Petroleum Institute. (Purchase or loan.)

30. Standard Viewer Model 200. Standard Project and Equipment Company, Inc. Contact local or district supply company for audio-visual equipment. (For filmstrips only.)

31. *Farm Pets.* Filmstrip, 28 frames, color; produced by Eye Gate House, Inc.

32. *The Story of Corn.* Filmstrip, 31 frames, color; produced by Eye Gate House, Inc.

33. Model C.O.C. Standard C.O.C. Executive Table Viewer. Optics Manufacturing Corporation. Contact local or district supply company for audio-visual equipment. (For slides only.)

34. *Early American Crafts.* 111 Kodachrome slides, 2″ x 2″. Dr. Konrad Prothmann.

35. *Early American Textiles.* 58 Kodachrome slides, 2″ x 2″. Dr. Konrad Prothmann.

36. *How to Make and Use a Diorama.* 16mm. film, 20 min., sound, color; produced by Syracuse University.

37. *Dolls of Many Lands.* 16mm. film, 10 min., color; produced by Encyclopaedia Britannica Films, Inc.

38. Chase, Alice Elizabeth. *Famous Paintings: An Introduction to Art for Young People.* New York: The Platt & Munk Company, Inc., 1951.

## READER PARTICIPATION

Study the curriculum of any grade level to determine which subjects would provide most productive materials for the enrichment of the environment.

What other criteria, besides subject matter, would influence your choices for classroom display?

Visit your nearest museum of art in the near future.

Learn to operate a table viewer and all three types of projectors—motion picture, still film, and slide.

Collect material for a loan box and be imaginative regarding wrapping and boxing.

# 5

# *TV, a Tool*
# *for Art Education*

Educational television has proved its worth in practically all subjects in the elementary curriculum throughout the country. Since television is a visual as well as an auditory medium, televised art programs are particularly effective in strengthening art education. Children understand television and are responsive to its message.

## TV: EDUCATION'S CHALLENGE

Because art is visual expression, television holds great promise for the enrichment of the art program, and broadcasting possibilities are being extensively explored by many school systems. Particularly in inaccessible and remote school districts, educational television[1] is a necessity, and is recognized as an integral part of teaching procedures.

Throughout the nation, televised programs on elementary school subjects have been in operation since approximately 1953. At present there is an acceleration in the growth of television education. Its costs have been partially absorbed through grants made available by such sources as the Ford Foundation and The Fund For The Advancement of Education.[2] Local school districts with local broadcasting stations have found that broadcasts have not been prohibitive in cost. Television has proved an effective tool in the implementation of art education, and when the techniques of color television are perfected, the scope of television art education will be tremendously enlarged.

## TV AND THE TEACHER-PUPIL RELATIONSHIP

Teachers are finding that classroom viewing of art demonstrations is helpful in stimulating children to want to try a new technique, and that it is encouraging to teachers who may want more information on a technique. It is recognized that the more impersonal presentation of a television program can never replace the close classroom teacher-pupil relationship so basic to good teaching. But, because television has so much to offer children, and because they are predisposed toward the medium by their home experience, the effectiveness of televised art programs should not be overlooked. Children have already learned that they must watch and listen attentively if they are to follow a broadcast.

## WAYS OF TELEVISING

Art instruction for educational purposes is televised in two ways: the programs may be conducted on a closed circuit for school viewing, or they may be sponsored by a broadcasting station during the time the station is required to devote to educational programs. In either event, there must be a close liaison between the channel and the school district. An advantage of the open circuit is that school programs can be viewed by parents and others in the community, thus broadening the understanding of art experience in the community.

## METHODS OF PRESENTATION AND SPONSORING

Three general types of presentation are most frequently used. A program may be presented as an informal discussion by a teacher or a museum curator and show fine examples of creative work of every kind, including examples of children's work done in school. Or it may be a demonstration by a skillful teacher to show children how to use materials and tools. The program may also take the form of a simulated classroom situation with both children and teacher participating in the broadcast.

A program or a series of programs can be sponsored by an organization such as the Girl Scouts of the United States of America,

55

which produced a nationally televised series of programs on crafts, or by a community enterprise such as the local newspaper.

## BEFORE THE CAMERA: PERSONALITY ATTRIBUTES FOR EFFECTIVE TELEVISING

The person making the presentation should understand children—that is, understand children's powers of understanding. Whether he be a teacher or a representative from a gallery, he should be articulate, knowledgeable in the subject presented, and at ease before the television camera. The museum expert must be able to express himself in language that children can understand. For this reason, the curator of the children's department of a museum or gallery or a teacher of special classes for children would be the best representative a museum could select for television presentations.

## MINNEAPOLIS: A NOTEWORTHY PROJECT

In Minneapolis, a well-organized and well-planned program for educational television has been sponsored by the Minneapolis public schools. It is a comprehensive program dealing with every subject in the curriculum. The art programs broadcast are worthy of study and may serve as guides for other school districts that contemplate using television for the improvement of classroom instruction in art education.

In the Minneapolis program, school personnel from four instructional areas are responsible for preparing the art programs televised for the public schools. This group is comprised of two teachers, an art consultant (the city schools director of art education), a production and evaluation team, and the producer, who is also a member of the evaluating group.

Kinescopes are made of each broadcast, to be reused as needed, thus making for economical and flexible programming of art activities.

Comprehensive grade level curriculum publications for television education are distributed to the schools for teacher guidance. They include information such as broadcasting dates and program summaries. In these publications, the goals are the same for all grade levels.

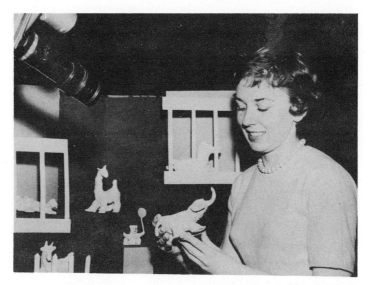

*Minneapolis Public Schools*

As presented in *Teacher's Manual, 1960–61,*[3] the three general goals for television education are:

To provide children with an opportunity for independent and creative thinking and doing.

To help children appreciate and understand art in the home, school, and community through an open and inquiring mind.

To give children opportunities for experiences in a variety of two- and three-dimensional art media.

The art section in the manuals for grades one and five scheduled the following programs for the school year. Areas covered in the first grade were: cloth materials, clay, and stick puppets; in the fifth grade: block printing, music, painting, stage design, and papier-mâché masks.

Included in the teacher's manual are questionnaires for the teacher to complete after each broadcast. Besides supplying class statistics

57

such as school and grade level, the teacher is asked to evaluate nine specific features of a broadcast. In addition, space is provided at the end of the form for the teacher's personal comments regarding the effectiveness of a broadcast in her class. When completed, the questionnaire is returned to the school radio-television department. The filing of such reports is general practice because of the assistance they give the steering committee in planning subsequent art programs.

### SAN DIEGO: A TELEVISED CLASSROOM ACTIVITY

In San Diego the city schools personnel prepared and televised four programs showing art activities. The programming was done by a steering committee, of which the art supervisor was a member. The production problems were supervised by a coordinator, a member of the audio-visual department. The commercial art department of the city schools painted a classroom set to use as a background in the television studio. A clock and a blackboard were installed. The children were taken to the broadcasting studio in cars and were escorted by their teacher and by cooperative parents.

Each program was a cooperative enterprise in which the classroom teacher selected, the children who would participate, the coordinator, and the art supervisor worked together.

Preparing a television show can be fun. Since parts are not learned, it is a freer form of expression than a play and demands more imagination by the children. Because children have something to do with their hands, they must concentrate on what they are doing and have less time to think about themselves. Absorbed in an interesting manual task, they soon become at ease and natural in both action and speech. The cue sheet of a telecast given by third-grade children might be helpful in clarifying one procedure, the step-by-step method, that has proved effective on the air. The success of the method lies in the fact that the children are always the center of interest and there were no long speeches by a nervous teacher. A program in San Diego showing how to make an Indian bowl by the coil method is used as an example of this type of demonstration. The continuity for this program is given on subsequent pages.

The group chosen for the demonstration of making Indian bowls were six third-graders, three girls and three boys. In addition, a fourth girl was asked to take care of properties, and she proved most helpful. The script, if such it might be called, and the action were worked out cooperatively in the classroom. After the second rehearsal a cue sheet was prepared for teacher and cameraman. It took three rehearsals in all to give the children the confidence they needed and time enough to develop the details of each child's separate part. There were no individual rehearsals for a single child; all the children worked together each time. In this way any change that was made was known by all. The children were seated behind three classroom tables which were placed at slight angles to each other to form a semicircle. This is good camera and mike technique because fewer adjustments for focus and none for sound need be made during the telecast. In this way the camera and the projecting mike are always in the same relative position to all the children seated at the tables on the set at the TV station.

A teacher planning to give this classroom type of broadcast for the first time might be helped by considering some further suggestions not found on the cue sheet:

1. Have the children work in back of a table. They may stand or sit as they prefer, but the table is important since in the event that a tool should drop it can easily be picked up again.
2. Have very little on the wall in back of the children, for too much material will distract the attention of the viewers as they watch the show.
3. Request the children to wear plain clothing. Loud shirts and print dresses are distracting to the viewing audience. White and colors of medium value are best because a "halo" often appears around black or other dark colors. Let the girls put on a little lipstick.
4. Use a background that reflects light, such as a painted flat, rather than a heavy dark curtain that absorbs light. As much light as possible should be reflected on the children's faces in order to convey an attractive image.

With these few cautions in mind, there is but one more suggestion to give the children before going before the camera. Tell them to look at the camera when they are talking, and the rest of the business can be safely left to the experienced cameraman. He will know when to take close-ups, how to pick up interesting sound patterns made by the tools as the children are working, and when to use all the professional methods of his craft to make a varied and interesting program.

*San Diego City Schools*

## KFMB-TV CONTINUITY

Show or Spot: *Art*

Date: *4-28-53*   Time: *1:00 to 1:30*   Anncr: *Stanley*   Sponsor: *KFMB-TV and San Diego City Schools*

Setting: The studio classroom stage set. Outline on blackboard, two Indian paintings by children on bulletin board.

| VIDEO | AUDIO |
|---|---|
| 1. Standard Opening. | 1. |
| 2. Announcer shows bowl of type completed on last week's program. Compares it with coil type of clay bowl. | 2. On last week's program, boys and girls, you saw a clay bowl such as this which was made over a clay mold. Today our art lesson will show us how to make a coil type of bowl such as the American Indians used to make. |
| 3. Announcer shakes hands with teacher. | 3. Greets teacher and asks her to introduce children. |
| 4. Teacher with children behind desk. | 4. Introduces Chris, who in turn, introduces Carol at his left, etc. |

60

| VIDEO | AUDIO |
|---|---|
| 5. Camera is on teacher, who shows curriculum guide on clay activities. | 5. Teacher states that she and the boys and girls are studying the Indian unit and have used the city schools' handbook on clay activities for directions for making bowls by the coil method. |
| 6. Teacher walks to blackboard and points to steps involved in making Indian bowl. | 6. Coil bowl:<br> 1. Base<br> 2. Coils<br> 3. Walls<br> 4. Leveling<br> 5. Polishing<br> 6. Decorating<br> 7. Firing |
| 7. Teacher and Chris at table. | 7. Chris rolls out clay into flat form, cuts out and scores base and explains processes in his own words. |
| 8. Teacher and Carol at table. | 8. Carol scores base and makes coil, talks about the purpose of slip and applies it to base. |
| 9. Teacher and Morris at table. | 9. Morris puts second coil in place on first coil already made and describes how coils should be welded together to make smooth, strong walls. |
| 10. Teacher and Marie at table. | 10. Marie states she has almost finished her bowl and shows it. She is now ready to put the last coils in place to close the mouth of the bowl. |
| 11. Teacher. | 11. Suggests to Marie that she draw her design on the blackboard. |
| 12. Marie goes to blackboard. | 12. Draws design of her bowl. |
| 13. Marie returns to her seat. | 13. Discusses welding, shows hand positions needed to support both inside and outside surfaces of the bowl and adds final coils to give the inward curve to bowl. |
| 14. Teacher to James at table. | 14. James goes to blackboard and draws his design for an Indian water jug. |

| VIDEO | AUDIO |
|---|---|
| 15. Teacher to James. | 15. Discusses James's drawing and James goes to work making this type of neck on his bowl. |
| 16. Teacher goes to blackboard. | 16. Shows that children are now ready for steps No. 4, 5, 6. |
| 17. Virginia at table. | 17. Levels base of bowl and uses stone to polish the clay. "See my stone is very smooth," etc. Polishes her bowl and states that she has polished a good deal of the bowl previous to beginning of the program. |
| 18. Teacher to Virginia. | 18. "Virginia, have you decided what kind of design you are going to paint on your bowl?" Virginia replies: "I am going to paint a snake design." |
| 19. James to Virginia. | 19. "What color are you going to use?" Virginia and James discuss what colors to use in painting on the design. |
| 20. Virginia goes to blackboard. | 20. Draws a snake design for her decoration. |
| 21. Virginia returns to seat. | 21. Begins to paint on design. |
| 22. James. | 22. Shows completed work and discusses what he has done while camera was on Virginia. |
| 23. Panorama of whole group. | 23. Children work and talk to each other. "Your bowl came out fine," etc. |
| 24. Résumé by all children at blackboard led by teacher. One child at a time steps out and points to outline. | 24. Chris says, "I did the base." Carol, "I did the coils," etc. Teacher explains about firing. |
| 25. Announcer enters. | 25. Thanks teacher and class for their art demonstration. |
| 26. Announcer closes. | 26. Concludes show and announces next week's program. |

## GIRL SCOUTS: SPONSORS OF A CRAFT PROGRAM

The Girl Scouts of the United States of America gave a series of televised programs on craft activities several years ago.[4] Kinescopes made of the broadcasts can be rented from the Girl Scouts National Headquarters at a nominal fee. This series of broadcasts won a citation in 1959 from the Institute of Education by Radio-Television, Ohio State University. A leader's supplement[5] is available for assistance in preparing the children to view the programs.

The programs are unique because the Girls Scouts participating were not limited to one age level. Brownies, Girls Scouts, and Senior Scouts worked on different levels of the same craft activity, showing the development of a skill from a simple to a complex technique in one program. Specialists in each of the crafts presented were invited to participate in the program on the air. Their comments greatly enriched the program. To unify the series, there was a running commentary by a young professional actress who utilized a puppet to catch the viewer's interest. The crafts televised in the series were: pottery, weaving, basketry, the making of masks, dolls and puppets, wood carving, leathercraft, and the making of both modern and "primitive" jewelry. The original broadcasts were given on Sunday afternoons, making it possible for parents to gain a greater understanding of the purpose and meaning of the Girl Scout program in craft activities, and enabling all interested children to view the series.

## BUFFALO: AN ENRICHMENT EXPERIENCE

Besides presenting programs by the school district, many TV channels offer art demonstrations for children on Saturday mornings and weekdays in the late afternoon. These go under such inviting program titles as that used by the *Buffalo Daily News,* "Fun to Learn about Art,"[6] a program based upon good educational practices. An eight-page pamphlet describing the program not only lists the titles of the demonstrations in the series, but also presents reasons in a chatty way for children to "Be Creative! Think Up Your Own Ideas," "Do Your Own Work, Don't Copy," "Make a Collection of Your Best Work," "Be a Neat and Orderly Worker." Included also are suggestions directed to the children's parents,

63

lists of materials needed for carrying out projects at home, and other helpful information. Art programs of this type carefully planned and educationally directed extend the scope of art and bring creative work into the home circle where it may be enjoyed and appreciated by parents with their children.

### WHAT TO LOOK FOR IN A GOOD PROGRAM

Each of the four basic types of programs is interesting to and worthwhile for children as well as stimulating to the teacher. A teacher's first thought may be, "What are the criteria for a good children's program?" The criteria are twofold. First, to maintain as natural and spontaneous responses from the children as is possible despite the unnaturalness of the situation; and, second, to present an art technique that calls for activity in

*School District of Philadelphia*

the handling of art materials so that children will have plenty to do during the televising. Added to these goals is the important part played by the teacher who keeps the action going by her unobtrusive leadership. A teacher who has a warm smile and a friendly voice and who can ad-lib with ease is able to lead the children into each new phase of the demonstration easily. By clever questioning and subtle prompting, she can give confidence to the group and carry it along with the minimum of self-consciousness. The unexpected humor and comments of children always add the human touch that makes for a successful show—and for the enjoyment of all participating in it.

ADMINISTRATIVE CONSIDERATIONS

School administrators must take care that daily schedules do not become so rigid that broadcasts are missed; there is plenty of time in the school day to permit the rescheduling of other subjects when a significant art program is to be broadcast. Furthermore, the rigid regime of a five-minute recess before or after the hour should give way to a more flexible arrangement so as not to deprive children of worthwhile experiences, otherwise unobtainable in their area, and which may never again appear on the air.

There is one problem which remains to be solved in many school districts. That is the manner in which broadcasts are watched in the school. It has often been necessary to combine several classes on one grade level in the school auditorium because there was only one television set in the school. This sometimes presents problems of control that would never occur in a classroom. Where there is a large group there is also the difficulty of having every child see the screen clearly. Distractions in auditorium situations occur which would never happen in the home classroom where the teacher is in charge of her own group.

PUBLIC RELATIONS

The teacher may find in the television program an excellent approach to public relations. By far the majority of the public never visit a classroom to see what is going on in the art program. Through television it may be possible to show some of the developmental activities provided children through different types of art experience. Adult viewers often

65

respond to these programs with surprise at the industry of children and at their desire to learn.

TEACHER AND SUPERVISOR CONTRIBUTION

Educational television programs increase the scope of the service of the supervisory department, making it possible for a classroom teacher to acquire information and see demonstrations of skill between the visits of the supervisor to her classroom and between any workshops sponsored by the office of the art supervisor. Television programs are an excellent outlet for creative teachers because they enable them to share their skills with co-workers. A program utilizes the talents of many teachers in a school district, through their contributions to its planning and evaluation, and through their suggestions for other programs needed to broaden and strengthen the general art program in the schools. Television utilizes the specific teaching skills of a superior teacher who, in recognition of her good work in the classroom, has been asked to produce a program. One very important asset of a broadcast is that it permits teachers to see a master teacher at work. In most school districts there is little or no opportunity for teachers to observe master teachers at work. It is a well-known fact that teachers appreciate the special skill of another teacher.

GAINS TO CHILDREN

Television programs bring children advantages which some local school districts cannot provide. This is particularly true of programs on the cultural aspects of creative work which call upon the resources of specialists, such as the curator of the children's program in an art gallery. In districts where opportunities for visits to art galleries and museums are rare, such visits must of necessity be dependent on parents who can take their children the necessary distance to visit an art gallery. Since all children do not come from privileged homes, and since lengthy bus trips are sometimes too expensive for many children, the televised art program initiated by a museum or art gallery fulfills their need for enrichment.

HOME-TUTORED CHILDREN'S GREATER PARTICIPATION IN ART WORK

Another contribution that a television program made at one time was one of the outcomes of the program on Indian bowl making

66

that was reported by a visiting teacher. Viewed by five different home-tutored children in her area, the program motivated them to want to make bowls themselves. When the visiting teacher returned the following week, all the children who saw the demonstration were clamoring for clay. In each of the homes the mother was eager to help and had found a suitable place where her child might work. Since these children were not bed patients, it was usually on the porch or in the kitchen. With the help of the visiting teacher, tools were found among the kitchen utensils and the school district provided the clay and fired the bowls. The children proved to have been such good observers of the demonstration that every bowl was a success and came through the firing intact. It is inspiring to think of the possibilities that may be developed through educational television for these children who must learn at home. A visiting teacher would find it difficult to give the necessary instruction for making bowls to each child in the limited time scheduled for a home visit, but she would have ample time to evaluate the results of televised instruction and suggest good follow-up activities.

READINGS FOR TEACHER RESEARCH

Two books and a magazine article are recommended to the teacher who would like to explore the broader scope of television education. The books are *Educational Television Guidebook*[7] and *Teach With Television*;[8] the article is "Classroom TV Enters a New Era"[9] in *Saturday Review*.

THE FUTURE OF EDUCATIONAL TV

Color television is the next step in television education. It, too, will bring its problems, but they will be worth solving in view of the beauty color can add to the instructional content—particularly when paintings and drawings are shown on the screen. Television will continue to be both a useful and broadening technique in art education.

Perhaps some day an artist will be discovered who can do for art education what Leonard Bernstein, Director of the New York Philharmonic Orchestra, does so superbly for music education on his programs for children.

## REFERENCE MATERIAL

1. Shayon, Robert Lewis. *Television and Our Children*. New York: Longmans, Green & Co., Inc., 1951.

2. *Teaching by Television*. The Ford Foundation and The Fund For The Advancement of Education.

3. *Teacher's Manual, School Year 1960–61*. Minneapolis Public Schools, Minneapolis, Minn.: Radio-Television Department. (Mimeographed.)

4. *Adventuring in the Hand Arts*. Girl Scouts of the United States of America Film Library.

5. *Leader's Supplement* (Cat. No. 16-03). Girl Scouts of the United States of America Film Library.

6. "Fun to Learn About Art," Station WBEN-TV. *Buffalo Evening News*, Buffalo, N.Y. circa 1953. (Booklet.)

7. Lewis, Philip L. *Educational Television Guidebook*. New York: McGraw-Hill Book Company, Inc., 1961.

8. Costello, Lawrence, and George N. Gordon. *Teach With Television*. New York: Hastings House, Publishers, Inc., 1961.

9. Scanlon, John J. "Classroom TV Enters a New Era," *Saturday Review*, XLIV, No. 20 (May 20, 1961), p. 50.

## READER PARTICIPATION

Tune in on one of the Sunday afternoon concerts given by the New York Philharmonic Orchestra for Children.

View on TV any type of an educational program available and evaluate the techniques used to present the subject. Are they based on a sound understanding of the learning process?

Outline a general plan for a series of three or four programs on art for upper, middle, or lower grades. Or, choose one art activity taught on all grade levels and adapt it to fit three different grade levels.

When reading professional magazines be alert for any announcements of programs featuring art on television.

Contact your nearest art gallery or museum and find out if any programs for children featuring art appreciation are being planned or currently presented.

# 6

# *Beginnings in*
# *the Kindergarten*

A child's art experience in school starts in kindergarten. The kindergarten program and the room environment are especially well adapted to different kinds of creative work. The flexibility of daily work and the pleasant surroundings encourage easy and relaxed responses from the child. Skillful guidance so that growth in art expression will be continuous is the responsibility of the teacher.

## CHARACTERISTICS OF KINDERGARTEN ART

Although a kindergarten child has been given crayons and pencils at home, kindergarten is still his real initiation into creative work. The first months in kindergarten are exploratory by nature, for the child is trying out many new art materials. He is beginning to become aware that he can express ideas and feelings with paint, chalk, finger paint, and clay. It is in his drawing and painting,[1] which starts with scribbling, that the kindergartener makes the greatest progress and where changes in growth are the most noticeable.[2] In time the first scribbles done for the pleasure of movement and activity become scribbling which has meaning to the child. His explanations are profuse and often fantastic and involved. Gradually, recognizable forms begin to emerge from scribbling, but their arrangement on paper is jumbled and fragmentary. Different parts of a

*San Diego City Schools*

picture are scattered over the paper—right side up, upside down, sideways. But, with time, as forms become still more meaningful their arrangement grows orderly. It is interesting to watch the development of a pattern of landscape composition which seems to be universal in kindergarten and primary grades: a strip of color across the top of the paper for the sky, another at the bottom for the ground, and the sun somewhere between.

Only the inexperienced teacher or insensitive parent would wish to interfere with the normal pattern of growth[3] or force a child to work unnaturally by giving him directions or patterns to color, copy, or trace.[4] Since children mature at different rates of speed, every child may not be as far advanced when he leaves kindergarten and will continue for a time in first grade to display some of the early characteristics.

70

Even though these characteristics of growth seem constant for the kindergarten child, they are modified for those children who attended good child-care centers, many since they were two years old. Because of a lengthy preschool experience, many five-year-olds are coming to kindergarten more capable in many ways than is to be expected for children of their age. Children that have been in child-care centers have painted at the easel and used finger paints, manipulated soft modeling materials, and learned a few work habits. They know that an apron is worn for painting and that to be overly obstreperous with any art material is not good behavior. As a result, observers are coming to believe that because of skillful guidance at a child-care center or nursery school, children have moved forward a step in every area of growth, with the happy result that

*Department of Education,*
*Baltimore, Maryland*

71

they adjust more quickly and are more ready to work with a group. Should attendance at child-care centers and nursery schools become universal, might not a new set of expectancies evolve for creative work in kindergarten? It will be interesting to see what develops.

The underdeveloped muscular control and vision of kindergarten children mean that all work must be large and free, with little detail expected. Art materials and tools must be selected accordingly.

A large quantity of the basic art materials is needed, for children work fast and are not sparing in their use of paint. No child can paint with flabby bristles; therefore, it is wise to buy good brushes that will stand hard wear. Occasionally large crayons may be used, but they do not have the same value as an art material for kindergarten children as do other materials. The following list offers suggestions as to what should be supplied:

12″ x 18″ and 18″ x 24″ newsprint, natural and colored
12″ x 18″ and 18″ x 24″ finger-paint paper (A good shelf paper may be substituted if it is not plastic-coated.)
12″ x 18″ colored paper, both poster (thin) for cutting and construction (heavy) for folding
12″ x 18″ and 18″ x 24″ Manila paper
12″ x 18″ bogus paper
Tissue paper
½″, 1″, and 1½″ bristle brushes, medium-long handle (Natural bristles are as good as bleached and are less expensive.)
1″ varnish brush
Blunt-pointed scissors for each child
One pair of 7″ scissors for teacher use
Colored chalk, large and regular sizes
Colored crayons, kindergarten size
Tempera paints: red, orange, yellow, emerald green, deep green, blue, turquoise, violet, white, black, brown, and flesh (Colors will be put out gradually.)
Finger paint (These may be made by the teacher.)
Clay, red and white (real earth clay, not an oil-base substitute)
All-purpose white glue
Wallpaper paste
Egg beater for mixing

The number of tools needed will depend upon the size of the class. The following list has proved satisfactory for kindergarten:

7 oz. claw hammer
8" or 10" half round cabinet file with handle
6" C clamps
6" screwdriver
¼" chuck hand drill
16" ten point crosscut saw
Small sawhorses, two or more
Pair of combination pliers

## CHOOSING ART ACTIVITIES

Because the sequence of art activities in kindergarten is flexible and centered on personal experience, individual differences among children are automatically cared for, and each child may develop in his

*San Francisco Unified School District*     73

own way. A child's art expression[5] is a continuous and spontaneous interpretation of what he feels, thinks, does, and sees—never a series of arranged
units with a time schedule to follow. Creative work is stimulated by walks
around the neighborhood, pets in the classroom, trips taken with his family,
the circus, stories told by the teacher, and the important holidays of the
year. A flexible art program allows time for a child to record an experience which captured his interest. If he went to the county fair on Sunday,
Monday is the day he wants to paint pictures about it.[6]

An interest may continue for several days, but in a short
time another experience will claim his attention, and again he will paint
with equal enthusiasm. Even though most children progress from one
interest to another, teachers occasionally find a child who keeps on doing
the same thing over and over. The usual reason for this is a wish for the
approval he received following a particularly successful piece of work. An
example comes to mind of a boy whose painting of a boat was the best
painting he had ever done. He was rewarded by the appreciation of his
classmates and teacher, and this gave him a delightful feeling of confidence.
In order to keep this new-found sense of security, he continued painting
boats in the hope that the rewards would be continued.

It takes skillful guidance to give a child with this problem
courage to stop painting what he knows he can do so well and to attempt
something else without loss of self-confidence. A strong new interest as well
as personal attention from the teacher during this trying time will help him.
When a tendency to repeat the same thing becomes habitual, growth in
creative power and enjoyment of art are unnecessarily delayed.

Among the materials provided for preschool and kinder-
garten children are blocks for building. Block building affords fine creative
activity; it is often amazing to see how frequently the basic elements of
contemporary design emerge as the child plays and builds with his blocks.
Blocks are now available that are beautiful in color and different in shape
from the standard blocks of previous years. However, blocks in natural
wood are also beautiful.

Blocks are an incentive to children's creative expression.
Block building results in well-proportioned structures; it affords variety in
arrangement and in the choice of sizes and shapes. It is perhaps one of the
major art activities that is carried out with little inconvenience in the
home, where the child can work independently of others.

74 When building with blocks at this age, design is purely

*Courtesy of Mrs. James*
*T. Gibbs, La Mesa*

instinctive. But it is interesting to the adult to see how the child replaces the massive block walls of his first construction with the openwork characteristic of our present building forms. Children are naturally in harmony with the changes on the fringes of our evolving culture. The interpenetration of space and matter is incorporated into the constructions of small children.

### HELPING PERSONALITY TRAITS DEVELOP

Self-confidence is a vital part of the happiness and success of the child in his art experiences. He gains it from the warm approval of his teacher and classmates—approval for every piece of earnest work he does, every little scribble, paper cutout, or clay worm. His happiness is complete when the members of his family appreciate his work and thank him for bringing it home for them to see. Self-confidence is also helped by the skillful planning of the teacher, which protects the child from undertaking art activities that are not adapted to his present level of maturity. Since there is no arbitrary art schedule, no child need be hurried into a new art activity until he is ready for it and can be expected to have a reasonable amount of success.

75

BEGINNING TO BE ORDERLY

Establishing good work habits and orderliness is as necessary in art as in everything else a child does. Kindergarten children are mature enough to learn to be careful of the art materials and to be purposeful in their use. Paint and clay should not be wasted, and tidiness helps to keep tempers down and art activities going smoothly. It is not only good training to be thrifty of materials but also of time, for many children must share the materials and tools. Children can learn to clean up their work area, to return leftover clay to the clay jar and to put on the lid so the clay will keep moist, to return tools to cupboards, and to hang up aprons in the proper place. While the major responsibility of keeping a room in order is the teacher's, children should be expected to help insofar as they are ready for responsibility.

*Louisville Public Schools*

BEGINNING TO WORK TOGETHER

Since the kindergarten child is highly individualistic in his creative work, and it is normal that he should be so, he must take the first steps in kindergarten toward working with others.[7] Group planning of the art activities for the day will give practice in this skill and will provide for free choices of daily activities. All the children cannot do the same thing at once, but by talking things over together they will realize that perhaps John did stay at the easel too long yesterday because the bell rang for lunch before Betty could paint a picture of her new puppy; that since Peggy claimed every bit of the clay left in the jar for herself, even though she did not need so much, Bobby had none for his airplane; and if they had all remembered that there was only room enough for two children at the finger-painting table, they would not have had those cross words and mean looks yesterday and everyone would have been happier and better able to do his own art work. The practical need for sharing in an art experience brings children early understandings of cooperation.

ENVIRONMENT AND ART MATERIALS

The kindergarten rooms are usually the best-equipped, largest, and airiest rooms in the school, and the teacher is careful to keep them both attractive and stimulating to the children. Pictures and flowers are as much a part of the room as are tables and chairs. The group gets real enjoyment from the frequent changes of flowers and figurines, toys, dolls, and seasonal decorations. However, to be enjoyed, the arrangements must be displayed low enough for all to see. The children's paintings and drawings are a part of the environment, and the frequent changes of work are eagerly anticipated. Clay modeling will have a place of its own for display, made attractive by the addition of colored papers for a mat and background. Throughout the year pets are brought to the kindergarten for the enjoyment of the children, and an aquarium or birds in a cage can hold the children's interest all year.

The furniture is suitable in size and design for small children, and in interest centers distributed around the room many activities are enjoyed, such as a science table, a picture book table, the playhouse corner, the toy shelf, and the art center. More than any other, perhaps,

*Burbank Unified School District*

the art center becomes a focal center for young children, for here is every encouragement for creative work. Its low cupboards store their working materials conveniently, and they can reach the drawers where colored papers are kept. The clay jar is available, and a table is ready for its use. On another table, which is covered with oilcloth or has a permanent Formica top, the materials and water for wet-chalk or finger painting are put out by the teacher from day to day. Easels are always ready for painting, and close by is a low bulletin board where paintings may be pinned up temporarily to dry. Scissors, paste, and scrap wood, along with colored chalk and extra boxes of tempera paint, are conveniently stored in low cupboards. The sink is child-high so that the children can use it when water is needed or for washing their hands. Since there are many interest centers in the room where children may go, the art center will not be over-crowded at any one time, and every child will have his fair chance to work. A well-stocked art center encourages independence and self-reliance, for there everything a child needs he can get for himself.

ENJOYING HIS ART

Evaluation is hardly the right term for the kindergarten experience of enjoying, sharing, and talking about art. At first evaluation,

78

so called, should be an individual experience between child and teacher and carried on largely when work is in progress, but gradually the wish to share with other children what he has done becomes important to a child. Since children enjoy talking about themselves and their work, it is natural for them soon to want their friends to see what they have done and to talk about it. Sharing also provides the teacher with the opportunity to give recognition for those personal traits which contribute to a child's success. She may have known that there was no paper at the easel when Paul went to paint and noticed that, instead of coming to her for more, he got the paper himself, put it on the easel, and went to work. This showed Paul's growth in self-reliance and he deserved the teacher's warm approval for it. When initiative is displayed and recognized, it is most impressive to the whole group and will bring results sooner than nagging. From group sharing may come also the selection of pictures to display for the day and the choice of clay work to show in the room for all to enjoy.

*Burbank Unified School District*

## Reference Material

1. Alschuler, Ruth H., and La Berta Weiss Hattwick. *Painting and Personality*. Vol. I. Chicago: The University of Chicago Press, 1947. (Chap. I, "The Basis of Understanding.")

2. *Beginning of Picture Making*. 16mm. film, 6 min., sound, color; produced by International Film Bureau, Inc.

3. Strang, Ruth. *An Introduction to Child Study*. 3d ed. New York: The Macmillan Company, 1951. (Chap. IX, "Development During Preschool Years" [Children's painting].)

4. Berson, Minnie Perrin. *Kindergarten: Your Child's Big Step*. New York: E. P. Dutton & Co., Inc., 1959. ("Graphic and Plastic Arts," pp. 74–76.)

5. Wills, Clarice Dechent, and William H. Stegeman. *Living in the Kindergarten*. Chicago: Follett Publishing Co., 1950. (Chap. X, "Hands Can Tell Stories, Too.")

6. Sheehy, Emma Dickson. *The Fives and Sixes Go to School*. New York: Holt, Rinehart and Winston, Inc., 1954. (Chap. VII, "The Arts.")

7. *A Day in the Life of a Five-Year-Old*. 2 reels, 16mm. film, 20 min., black and white, sound; produced by Bureau of Publications, Teachers College, Columbia University. (Metropolitan Schools Service Council.)

## Reader Participation

Make arrangements with a kindergarten teacher to visit her class three times during the year to observe the changing characteristics of the children's creative expression as they mature.

How much responsibility for care of art materials should be encouraged in kindergarten children?

Plan some experiences in color that will extend and develop children's enjoyment of color.

Explain ways of giving guidance in creative work without interfering with the child's natural pattern of growth.

Suggest ways of beginning a cooperative group activity that will not force the children beyond their maturation.

# 7

# *Children Integrate*
# *Diverse Learnings*

Careful planning in which children have a part is necessary for worth-while group experiences in art. When the teacher really believes in demo-cratic practices, guidance of group activities is a natural teaching technique for her. One premise of group planning is faith that children have much to offer when given the opportunity to use initiative; a second is belief that the greatest growth for children comes when they participate. Participa-tion develops understanding, initiative, and consideration for others, with rewards for children in satisfaction and growth. Maturity in a child is nurtured by the development of his ability to integrate a variety of learning through experience.

## TECHNIQUES OF GROUP PLANNING

There are different degrees of planning—from the simple choices in the kindergarten when the art activities of the day are decided during the morning sharing period, to the complexities in the sixth grade of producing a marionette play. Sharing of ideas does not mean that every suggestion made by children is necessarily good or possible to carry out; but rather that, as in an open forum, every idea is considered. All sug-gestions can never be used, nor do they offer equal value for child growth. Giving way unselfishly is a difficult lesson for many children, but one that

81

is often learned best through experience. Group planning with children on any grade level should be informal. By encouraging the children to talk freely, the teacher will discover the abilities and weaknesses in the group and be in a better position to give leadership.

The decision on a choice for a project will be reached after time has been given to group discussion. As always, the teacher's leadership is the strength of group planning, for, without dampening the children's enthusiasm, she can help them evaluate the details of proposed plans. She may need to remind them that certain materials will be impossible to obtain, or that time will not permit the successful accomplishment of all the plans they are making. When a teacher assumes the role of adviser, the benefits that result from group planning will follow, and children will experience the beginning practices of democratic action. A further step in group planning will be the delegation of responsibilities to volunteer committees.[1]

Care of materials and tools is one of the problems of group projects. In the early primary grades more guidance by the teacher is needed than in upper grades. A good approach with young children is to give praise when it is merited and then bring the other children into partnership. "I have noticed," a teacher might say, "that Dorothy always puts her tools away when she has finished her work. Would any of you like to help her today after you finish working on the barn?"

Upper-grade children like to be given responsibility, and a committee can volunteer to care for materials. There is an appropriate film[2] that can be shown in class which will encourage the rest of the children to cooperate with the committee.

### WORKING WITH THE SOCIAL STUDIES

An intelligent approach to an integrated art program first establishes functional and aesthetic relationships between the two subjects, then provides the classroom activities that will make possible a natural integrative experience for children. The vitality of an integrative experience for children is lost when integration does not rest upon honest relationships between art and the social studies unit. If this occurs, integration becomes superficial, devoid of opportunity for true creative expression, and no longer a means for child growth. In some units integration can be carried on effectively for only a limited time, without resorting to contrived art activities. It is far better practice to accept what it is possible to do, and then

*San Diego City Schools*

to release the class for other and more productive kinds of creative work. Perhaps this was what a sixth-grade child knew intuitively when he protested one day in class, "We have studied about dirt, we have sung about dirt, now must we draw about dirt?"

A major value of integration is that it awakens new art enjoyments in children and stimulates many a child who otherwise may have only a passive interest in art. Another fact of equal importance is that children tend to develop a feeling of kinship with another culture when they are given opportunity to work with their hands. These values are realized in the units to be described: "Shopping in a Market," for primary grades; "Mexico," for middle grades; and "Pioneer Life and the Westward Movement," for upper grades. As typical examples, each of these three units fulfills the promise of good integration.

83

*Burbank Unified School District*

## THE CONTRIBUTION OF ROOM ENVIRONMENT

The classroom environment is a delightful means of initiating a related art unit. Since the materials will be on exhibit for some time, there is ample opportunity for each child to see and to become acquainted with everything on display. The environment sets the stage, stimulates interest, and provides an art background which is in keeping with the social studies unit. Art prints may be used and, since there are a number to choose from, may be changed frequently. Smaller pictures from the teacher's file can be mounted on colored papers. Arrangements appropriate to the unit may be made by the teacher. Attractive baskets filled with freshly washed vegetables and fruits would be suitable for "Shopping in a Market," and when fruit trees are in blossom, nothing would be more lovely than branches from an apple, peach, or cherry tree. Different crafts would be the natural choice for the unit "Mexico." A serape for weaving, an olla for pottery, a batea for painted ware, and a piece of hand-blown

84

glass from Guadalajara should not be forgotten. The simplicity of design and workmanship of Mexican crafts gives children a feeling for the peasant life of the country. It might be possible for children to have a part in setting up the environment for "Pioneer Life and the Westward Movement." Many times objects which would be fitting to display can be brought from home by the children. A pieced quilt, an old pewter candlestick, a sampler, great-great-grandmother's doll, a piece of hand-woven linen would add to the art prints, pictures, and other things provided by the teacher.

Everything in the classroom which has art quality is an asset in furthering the relationship between art and cultural understanding.

CONSTRUCTION PROJECTS

Social studies units provide opportunity for construction work and building which may be developed on a large or a small scale. It is a matter of choice as to the type chosen, for both have equal value for content and learning. As an example, a construction project for a unit

on Southwest Indians would naturally be a pueblo. It may be built on a scale large enough for children to use for dramatic play, or on a scale small enough to include the whole Indian community and the mesa. For the first, children would make costumes for themselves and large pieces of pottery; for the second, Indian figures would be modeled in clay and the pottery would be proportionately small. Art is important in either type of construction and both develop craft skills. Evaluations of design, color, form, proportion, and balance are a daily occurrence during the period when construction projects are being completed.

### INTRODUCTION TO INTEGRATED ART UNITS

A well-planned social studies unit[3] meets the many individual needs that are the result of different maturation levels and art abilities within an average class.

## SHOPPING IN A MARKET

*An Integrated Art Experience for Primary Children*

### INTRODUCING A LIFE STUDY UNIT CENTERED IN THE ENVIRONMENT

"Shopping in a Market" is an appropriate unit for primary children because it is closely related to their everyday lives. Rare is the child who has not been to a market many times, helped his mother make purchases, and watched the activities of the employees. The unit provides many art activities for which children see an immediate need and which stimulate their imagination. The market is a good approach to group planning. Each child in the class has a background of understanding about markets which he is eager to share. Like all primary work, the construction must move along briskly or the children will grow impatient.

### CHOOSING A LARGE-SCALE CONSTRUCTION

Since the market is a primary-grade unit, nothing but a large market will do. Children quickly identify themselves with the vegetable man, the grocery clerk, the butcher, and the checker; consequently, any project that cannot accommodate several children will fail to satisfy

*San Diego City Schools*

them. Before starting to make plans, the group should discuss the differences between a market and a neighborhood grocery store. Some of the children who have visited both will say that a market is bigger and managed differently. Others will remember the turnstile, the checker's counter, and the wire basket on wheels. However, if more children are familiar with a small grocery store and its simpler procedures, it is an equally acceptable choice.

It is a good idea to introduce the building of a market with a short preliminary experience in block building. Through block building children will gain a better understanding of the general arrangement of a market, discover the limitations of using blocks, and find that a better market can be built with boxes and boards. The class will also realize that it is impossible to make with blocks the equipment they have seen in markets. The children will be eager to proceed and will make suggestions for the necessary equipment. All needs will not be foreseen at

87

first but will be thought of as production proceeds. As suggestions are made by the children, a list is written on the blackboard and will be referred to often as work progresses. On the list will be a counter, shelves, a refrigerator, a bakery case, a deepfreeze, and bins for vegetables and fruits; these are the major necessities for a market.

The teacher will remember, from her past experiences when using wood, that there is no better source of supply than apple boxes, orange crates, and the shallow boxes called "trays" in which perishable fruits and vegetables are packed. The wood is soft and easy for children to saw and nail. A few boxes and trays should be broken up to supply extra pieces of wood as needed. Boxes and a few boards of soft pine should provide enough wood for everything the children will need.

It will be well to start with the counter since it is the most simple to make. The teacher will ask which children wish to make it, and when two or three have volunteered she will suggest that they look over the stock of wood and take what they need. It will not take long for them to discover that two boxes with a board across makes a fine counter. This rapid demonstration gives confidence to the watching children and becomes the general procedure for making the other items in the days that follow. Before the group is dismissed, the teacher will print with black crayon the name of one of the counter makers on each box and on the board chosen by the volunteers. This will identify the wood as theirs and prevent later misunderstandings as more wood is selected by other children for their work. In addition, the names of the children making the counter will be listed on the blackboard under the caption "Counter Makers." Committee work has begun and group techniques have started. Sometime soon the counter makers will nail the board in place and be ready to paint.

Each piece of equipment is developed in a similar way. Group discussion is followed by opportunity for children to volunteer to do the work. Then comes evaluation, with choices made for the best kind of wood to use—a board, vegetable tray, apple box, or orange crate. Next, difficulties of construction, such as adding a shelf, must be identified. Labeling every piece of wood with the name of a group leader should not be forgotten, nor the listing of the names on the blackboard. Last, the carpentry work will give children opportunity for creative thinking and independent work. Teacher help is promised to every group when needed, but, for the most part, children are able to carry on with independence when careful preplanning has taken place.

TEACHER GUIDANCE FOR MAKING THE MARKET

## The Shelves

Vegetable trays make the best shelves. Pile three trays, one on top of the other, end to end. This will make two shelves, but the children will want more. By adding a shelf to each tray there will be five shelves. Knock a couple of trays apart and use the ends for the shelves. They will fit into the trays perfectly. Put an end piece into a tray in the middle and check to make sure it is straight. Put the tray on its side on the floor and nail the shelf in place. Turn the tray over and nail the other end of the shelf. Put shelves in the other two trays.

*San Diego City Schools*

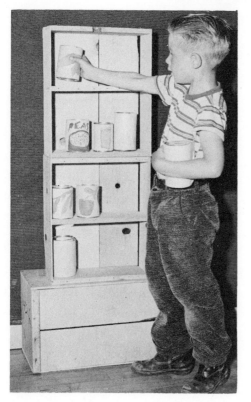 

*San Diego City Schools*

*The Refrigerator*

Use an orange crate. The center division board will make a shelf when the crate is on end. Make a door from four pieces of lath. Cut two pieces the length of the sides of the crate and two as long as the width of the crate. Nail them together like a frame. Cover the frame with a piece of cellophane. Staple in place. Make two hinges from two strips of an inner tube. Nail hinges in place. Use a spool for the knob.

*The Bakery Case*

Use an apple box. Remove the bottom of the box; this opening becomes the back of the case. Remove one side of the box; this opening becomes the top of the case. All that remains of the box are the ends and one side. Put the box on its side, since this is the way it is to be used. Nail narrow strips of wood across the middle of each end of the box. The strips are the supports for the shelf. Cut a piece of wood the correct length for a shelf and place it in the box. Put a sheet of cellophane over the

90

top and front of the box and staple in place. Cut a piece of lath the length of the case and nail it across the top of the back opening. This will protect the edge of the cellophane. Tack a piece of muslin over the back opening of the case. The muslin may be lifted as the children put in or remove bakery goods. Put two apple boxes or orange crates upright on the floor for a stand for the case.

### The Freezer

Two apple boxes are used. Put them together with the bottom of the top box resting on the bottom of the lower box. Nail the two together. Follow the directions given for the refrigerator door for making the lid, and nail the hinges to the top box. The lid will open upward so that the children can reach down inside the freezer.

### The Vegetable and Fruit Bins

Six or eight small wooden or cardboard boxes of the same size are needed. Place them in a single or double row and tack the sides together. Use an apple box or an orange crate lengthwise as a stand, or make a low counter.

### The Turnstile

A piece of soft pine twenty-four inches long is used for the post and the end of an apple box for the base. Drive a nail through the center of the base into one end of the post. Stand the post on the floor. Cut two pieces of lath twenty-four inches long for the crosspieces. Drill a hole in the middle of each piece. Place both pieces of lath on the top of the post and drive a nail through the holes part way into the post. Turn the crosspieces into position and the turnstile is finished.

### The Scales

Scales are made from two paper plates, string, and a piece of black paper. Use one plate for the dial. Turn the plate over and put numbers on the bottom with crayon, starting with zero. Cut an arrow out of black paper and fasten it to the center of the plate with a paper fastener. Punch two holes in the rim of the plate, one hole above zero and the other on the rim directly opposite. Put a short piece of string through the hole over zero and make a loop so that the scales may be hung up. Divide the rim of the remaining plate into four equal parts and mark with a pencil.

91

(The teacher may have to do this for the child.) Punch a hole in the rim at each pencil mark. Cut two pieces of string thirty inches long. Put them both through the bottom hole on the dial. Divide the strings and pull the ends even. Tie each end of one string through a pair of opposite holes. Tie the ends of the other string through the remaining holes. Pull the strings so that the plate is balanced below the dial. The scales are now finished.

## The Clock

The easiest task of all is making the clock. Use the reverse side of a paper plate for the face of the clock. Put on the numbers with crayon. Cut two hands out of black paper and fasten them to the center of the plate with a paper fastener. Decorate with tempera paint and hang the clock on the market wall.

## The Awning

Sometimes an awning is put over the market if it is not too large. Measure the distance from the back to the front of the market and add a foot. Use this measurement and cut strips of wrapping paper. Paste or glue the strips together and reinforce the seams with masking tape, if necessary. Draw a line one foot from the front edge of the awning. Make a fold on the line. If scallops are to be made along the front edge, use a tin can for a pattern and cut out the scallops with scissors. Paint the awning with stripes or a solid color. A post must be put at each front corner of the market to support the awning. Cut two pieces of soft pine five feet long. Nail to the boxes at each front corner. Lift up the awning and tack the front corners to the top of the posts. Tack the back of the awning to the wall. The scalloped edge should hang down in front. The teacher must put up the awning for the children.

## Sanding and Painting

The children probably will not be satisfied unless they paint what they have made. If the class wishes to decide upon a color scheme, well and good; if not, the market will be just as attractive, and perhaps gayer, painted according to the choices of the various committees. Besides, it is fun for each group to make its own color decisions. A little sanding may be needed so that the paint will flow over the rough spots more smoothly, but only a little sanding. Primary children should not be

92

held back from the pleasure of painting by laborious hours of sanding. Tempera paint covers well on the soft wood of the construction and dries quickly. A new, practical paint for classroom use is the now available Latex base paint, which is water soluble. It has the added advantage of being easy to clean up when spilled.

ACTIVITIES COMPLETING THE UNIT

### Murals

A worth-while outcome of the market is a mural. Interest is stimulated by the many activities of dramatic play which the children have experienced. By now they are thoroughly familiar with every aspect of a market and are ready to paint. This may even be the first mural painting the class has done. Teacher guidance in the mechanics of getting started is necessary. After planning the composition of the mural the children paint directly on the paper just as they paint at the easel. It is always best for primary children to paint the figures first and then put in the background. Because the children will have such a full background of information, they will not lack for ideas when painting.

### Modeling

While vegetables and fruits may be modeled in clay and papier-mâché, sawdust mix is better. It is a good preliminary experience for the children to hold vegetables and fruits in their hands to get the feeling of rounded forms and to feel the shape, indentations, and lumps. When modeling starts, put the vegetables and fruits away so the children will work creatively. When completed, paint the vegetables and fruits with tempera paint.

### Sawdust Mix

| | |
|---|---|
| 2 cups of sawdust | ½ cup of wallpaper paste |
| 1 cup of plaster of Paris | 2 cups of water |

Mix the ingredients together and start to model before the plaster hardens.

### Painting and Drawing

Many pictures will be painted at the easel every day and an exhibit can be arranged before the unit is over. Chalk and crayon

San Diego City Schools

drawings of market scenes will be spontaneous and original. From them illustrations can be chosen for the reading charts prepared by the teacher.

*Paper Work*

Vegetables and fruits which are bulky in shape may be made of crepe paper and stuffed with tissue paper cuttings. Children are clever in making lettuce, carrots, corn, bananas, beets, and other garden products.

*Labeling Foods*

Labels for canned foods may be made by the children. The teacher cuts paper of correct size, and children paint or draw a picture on the label and print the name with crayon. Goods labeled by children look far better on the shelves of the market than a miscellaneous assortment of trade names.

A REWARDING OUTCOME OF A GROUP EXPERIENCE

"Shopping in a Market" was a pilot experience in group activity for a certain first grade. Throughout the course of the construction activities the children showed growth in sharing and consideration for each other when working together. Because of this growth in group relationships, the class was able to come to an unselfish decision when faced with an unexpected dilemma after work was completed. During the final week of construction the children had put forth their best efforts in order to have everything completed a few days before the day on which their mothers were to come in and see the market. Everyone had cooperated with the exception of the twins. The twins had been impossibly uncooperative in the last few days and their flighty ways had exasperated the other children. It took tact on the teacher's part to smooth ruffled feelings in the group. She knew that the twins' behavior was the result of their excitement over the prospect of being flower girls at their sister's wedding on Saturday. Everyone in the class was glad on Friday when at last the work was done and it was time to go home: the lumber taken away, the saw, nails, and paints put back in the cupboard, the room neat and tidy.

The following Monday brought the dilemma. It was a big wedding cake made by the twins out of a white hatbox. The box was decorated with a profusion of painted doves, hearts, flowers, and bowknots. The cake caused consternation among the children for, although they admired it as a work of art, they did not know what to do with it. The vegetable clerks said it belonged in the bakery; the bakery clerks said it would not fit in the bakery case; and the grocery clerks refused to have it on their counter, which was the only place in the market large enough to hold it. The twins were distraught as they saw their wonderful idea and hard work so emphatically rejected. Finally one of the carpenters had an idea. He thought that a special place could be built for the cake. The teacher picked up his suggestion and discussion started as to how this could be done. A small addition to the market at one side seemed the best idea. Because the solution came from one of the group and was accepted by the children, it was not much of a hardship to get out the lumber and tools and go to work again. It was found with the guidance of the teacher that very little change in the construction of the market was needed. The work was finished the next day and all was in order once more. When the mothers came on Wednesday they admired the cake along with the vegetables, the refrigerator, the bakery case, the turnstile, and all the other work of the children. The twins shared in the general good feeling in a way that would never have been possible had not group work developed good relationships.

## THE MEXICAN UNIT

*An Integrated Art Experience for Middle-grade Children*

INTRODUCING A LIFE STUDY UNIT WITH AN
INTERCULTURAL BACKGROUND

Mexico is an example of a life study unit based on another culture. The study of Mexico is interesting to children because the life of the people is different from anything they know. There are many possibilities in the unit for craft work,[4] drawing, and painting. Closer pupil identification with a new culture is encouraged by creative work.

CHOOSING A LARGE-SCALE CONSTRUCTION UNIT

Popular choices of third- and fourth-grade children for a construction project are a native home and a market stall. Group discussion will decide which to make and committees will volunteer to do the work after a period of class planning. A house large enough for children to enter can be built of large cartons, refrigerator boxes, or wrapping paper tacked to a framework of wood. A tile roof is made from oatmeal boxes cut lengthwise and fitted together by overlapping the halves. After the boxes are painted an earth red, they look much like real tile. Or a thatch roof can be made of palm and banana leaves when these are available. An adobe color for painting the house can be mixed from inexpensive calcimine. A dado of pink, blue, or terra cotta may be painted around the lower part of the house as is often seen in Mexican villages. Tile designs may be drawn and painted around the window and door, or every child may design and paint a tile and paste it in place. Other ideas will develop as the construction progresses, and perhaps a string of peppers, a dipper made from a gourd, some pottery, and a bench will be added before the project is completed.

96

Through study of the unit,[5] the class will learn that a Mexican market is a community enterprise where the peons bring their wares to sell. In large markets there are stalls where business is carried on every day, while a small village market is set up for only one day a week. The peon brings with him a primitive shelter, which when the day is over he dismantles and takes home again.

The stall for a market can be built of vegetable trays and apple boxes following the general directions given for the market in the primary grades. The back of the stall is made of three rows of trays standing on end. Put a shelf in each tray. When all the trays are placed against the wall of the classroom, the shelves provide plenty of space in which to put children's work—bowls, figurines, ollas, jícaras, bateas, and so forth. A row of apple boxes is put around the stall with an opening left for children to enter. A covering is really not necessary, but since nearly every class wants one, an awning is the best way to solve the problem. Children of this age can make and install an awning themselves. When completed, a market stall is colorful and gay.

If preferred, children may make a primitive shelter similar to those used in village markets. The only problem is to find a way to erect the four poles in the classroom. In some rooms they can be nailed to the floor. Where this is not possible, each pole is embedded in a large can filled with dirt, rocks, sand, and a portion of quick-setting cement. Pour water into the can so that the mixture will harden. Tie the corners of a sheet or a large square of muslin to the tops of the poles, and the job is done. The poles may lean a bit and the sheet may sag, but so they do in Mexico.

## CHOOSING A SMALL-SCALE PROJECT

A village plaza and a market with many stalls are good small-scale projects which can be arranged on the floor. The classroom wall in back makes a convenient place for tacking up a mural.

Careful planning should be done by the children before starting the unit. A practical child with a lot of common sense makes a good group leader for the whole project. Planning will include deciding what to put in the plaza and identifying the construction and art problems. Volunteering for committees will follow, for unless responsibility is shared, the value of the project is lost to all but a very few children. Relative proportions of people, houses, trees, and everything else must be considered. A good approach is to decide on the height of the figures first. Do not make them too small. The floor plan becomes a design problem as the children grow aware of the pattern made by grass, paths, flower beds, and the placement of the bandstand and fountain. Figures of men, women, and children are modeled in clay and painted. Or they may be made of wire and dressed with cotton material. An old man feeding pigeons, a woman with an olla on her head, a man with a tray of tortillas for sale, acrobats and a group of watching children, and Mariochis, the strolling singers of western Mexico, are all typical. A plaza scene can epitomize village life and provide a wealth of art activities for children.

### ACTIVITIES FOR THE UNIT

#### Backgrounds

Every construction unit, large or small, is improved by the addition of a background. Backgrounds are drawn with colored chalk or painted on a piece of wrapping paper cut as long as the unit. A simple landscape makes the best background. People and details are superfluous and only distract from the interest on the construction.

#### Murals

There are many subjects for a mural on Mexico. The customs and occupation of the country and the people are colorful and unusual. The famous basket market at Toluca, the fishing village at Lake Pátzcuaro where butterfly fishing nets are still used, and the floating gardens of Xochimilco make possible subjects. Children may paint people wearing the simple clothes of everyday life or the elaborate China Poblana, ranchero, and fiesta costumes worn on special occasions. Stories about breaking the piñata and the Christmas celebration, Las Posadas, are often read in class and may be delightfully portrayed in a mural.

#### Dioramas

When selecting a theme for a diorama, any of the subjects previously mentioned for construction or murals which the children have not done would be appropriate. A native craft shop or an Aztec ceremonial would be successful. Reference reading will provide the information needed

98

*San Diego City Schools*

for the scene. All kinds of art and scrap materials are used. Children will paint, model, carve, construct, and sew.

*Clay Work*

Clay is the perfect craft medium for the Mexican unit. Children work naturally with clay, often with the same directness of technique that a Mexican potter uses. Bowls, pots, jugs, ollas, and fruit compotes are satisfying to make. Two articles unique to Mexico which children can make are the painted pig bank[6] and the bird whistle.[7] Both must be fired in order to be strong enough to use.

Tilemaking is a flourishing industry in Mexico. With a few simple pieces of equipment, tiles can be made in the classroom. Decoration is an important design problem and should be based on primitive Indian and Aztec motifs such as the Old Man of Oxaca and the featured Toltec serpent, or geometric designs equally prevalent in Mexico.

Figures of Mexican people may be modeled in clay. Five or six representative of the daily life of the people, which could include making tortillas, grinding corn, riding a burro, and taking produce to market, are attractive.

Techniques for clay work are given in Chapter 10.

*Weaving*

If wished, children may do some weaving for the unit, using looms which they make themselves (directions are given in Chap-    99 ter 10). Unfortunately, the fine, firm texture of Mexican weaving can never be approximated with the wools and yarns provided in school. A woven rug is useful in a diorama.

*Marionettes*

A class often will write a play about Mexican life which can be produced as a marionette show (see Chapter 8). Dancing can be featured in the play by using records. *Los Viejitos*,[8] the dance of the old men, can be done with marionettes. Each character wears a grotesque mask and carries a cane. The dance consists of the marionettes' stamping their feet and canes in rhythm with the music. Another choice for a dance is *El Jarabe Tapatio*,[9] or the hat dance. In this the marionettes dance around a big sombrero on the floor. Sometimes during the performance, perhaps at intermission, the recording of *Chiapanecäs*[10] should be played for the pleasure it gives children. As the music is played, children clap vigorously with their hands from time to time. It is very jolly.

*San Diego City Schools*

A unique custom still carried on in remote villages of Mexico might be included in a play. On the hour throughout the night, the guardias, or night watchmen, whistle a signal to reassure each other that all is well with them. In early days, and often in remote villages today, the signal was played on an Indian flute made of clay, called a barro. The original flutes had three notes; modern flutes have two. A boy in the class could learn the call and whistle it backstage at the appropriate time. These are the signals heard in the State of Jalisco.

The costuming of a play gives opportunity for clever use of cotton goods, silk, and velvet, and for colors typical of Mexico. The painting and making of the properties can be the work of one committee as others prepare the stage and make the marionettes.

*Using Plant Materials*

Many articles in Mexico are made from plant materials: straw, palm grasses, gourds, maguey, sisal, and hemp.[11] There are dolls and animals made of cornhusks, and mats and baskets woven of palm fibers and grasses. Bracelets are made of colored raffia wound around circlets of cardboard. Charm strings are painted gourds and seeds of different kinds and sizes tied together with colored raffia.

Cups, dippers, and small bowls are made from wild gourds. When it is thoroughly dry, cut off the top of the gourd, remove the seeds, and scrape the inside clean. Paint designs on the sides and shellac the gourd. In Mexico, these are called jícaras. Both collages and mosaics can be made from plant materials. Suggestions for procedure are given in Chapters 9 and 10.

101

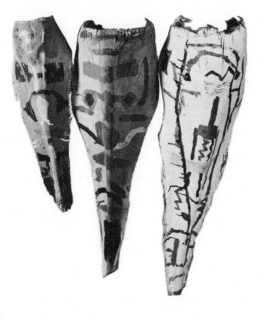

*San Diego City Schools*

### Painting and Drawing

The Mexican scene inspires children to paint deserts, mountains, volcanos, plantations, farms, jungles, and lakes. Houses have roofs of thatch and tile. Palm huts are found in torrid regions. The Mexican landscape and the native costumes of the people result in interesting composition.

### A Movie

A sequence of pictures showing native customs, such as a series illustrating a fiesta, can be developed as a movie when a story is written to accompany the pictures. The movie box, probably used many times previously, can be repainted and decorated in the Mexican manner.

Directions for making a movie are given in Chapter 8.

### Uses for Design Problems

Designs in paint and crayon, using Mexican motifs, are useful for book and portfolio covers, as patterns on paper or cloth, and on tiles.

102

*Decorative Maps*

When maps are drawn, they should be authentic and as geographically accurate as possible. The best method for map drawing is to project a map slide on a large piece of paper pinned to the bulletin board and draw the outlines in chalk or pencil. Many ideas gathered from reference reading can be used as symbols to typify different parts of Mexico —cactus for the desert regions, oil wells for the Gulf Coast, temple ruins for Yucatan, and so forth. A border design around the paper unifies the map.

*Posters*

Travel in Mexico is an incentive for poster making. Cut paper is a good method to use and gives the class an opportunity to work

with a new technique. Cut-paper letters are easy to read, to cut out, and to arrange on the poster. When a class is studying the Spanish language, brief slogans in Spanish should be used. "Vamos a México," "A México por Avion," or "México le Hermosa" give children a practical application for phrases they have learned.

### Musical Instruments

Drums and painted gourds for children to beat and shake in dance rhythms are painted with designs and decorated with ribbons and streamers of colored paper.

### Painted Ware

Uruapan is famous for its painted ware. The technique is a direct and simple style of free painting on wood that children may do. Shallow wooden bowls or plates are used, the designs being painted on the inside. Designs are bold both in style and in color—leaves, flowers, and birds in pure color. When the paint is dry, give the inside of the bowl a coat of clear lacquer. In Mexico this type of bowl is called a batea.

## PIONEER LIFE AND THE WESTWARD MOVEMENT

### An Integrated Art Experience for Upper Grades

#### INTRODUCING A LIFE CULTURE UNIT WITH A HISTORICAL BACKGROUND

The unit "Pioneer Life and the Westward Movement"[12] is a vigorous example of the historical unit enjoyed by children and provides numerous opportunities for individual and group work through art expression. The activities are simple for children to do, and many in the class will have ample time to participate in several. Often the members of a class have a rich home background of the traditions and ideals of this historic period and already have an appreciation for its arts and crafts. With such a background and the opportunity in school to work with his hands, a child will soon develop a feeling of rapport with the problems and struggles of pioneer life. In addition, the teacher will wish to develop

*Burbank Unified School District*

a deeper feeling for nature and more respect for the ingenuity of the pioneer man and wife who made a home for their family largely from what nature gave them to use. The film, *A Pioneer Home,*[13] depicts the arts and crafts of this period. It is, moreover, a sensitive and beautiful portrayal of family life and relationships and will serve as a motivational introduction for the unit.

CHOOSING A LARGE-SCALE PROJECT

The subject most often chosen by children for a construction project is the kitchen of a log cabin, but other themes, such as a cabin and a trading post, have been developed with equal success. Perhaps the kitchen is chosen more frequently because it provides a perfect setting for dramatic play and a place to put everything made in the class.

Every construction project, whether on a large or a small scale, proceeds according to the general plan outlined for other units.   105

Through teacher leadership, the class discusses the project and identifies the problems, secures certain materials, volunteers for committee work, and evaluates progress.

The first thing to do in making the kitchen is to tack up strips of wrapping paper for the wall. Make the kitchen as long as possible. On the paper paint logs, a window, and a door on the wall, and build a fireplace of cartons. To indicate the filling between the logs, make the lines as far apart as the width of the logs. Measure the width of the logs with a yardstick and put a mark where every line should be. Do this at each end of the paper. The quickest way to put on the necessary lines is to use a piece of string cut a little longer than the length of the paper. Rub the string with a piece of chalk. Have two children hold the ends of the string against the lowest mark for a log. Have another child take hold of the string in the middle, draw it toward himself, and then let it go. The string will snap back against the paper and leave a light line of chalk dust. Repeat until all the lines separating the logs are on the paper. However, it is a sensible idea to have one child lightly paint a dark line

*San Diego City Schools*

of color over the chalk because it may be accidentally rubbed off. Decide where the fireplace is to be and draw the window and door accordingly. Mix several shades of brown with tempera and paint the logs, using a little shading on the logs to make them look rounder. A view of the forest painted in the window gives color.

Use cartons to build the fireplace. Pile them up and leave an opening in the center for the hearth. Cover the cartons with wrapping paper painted to look like stones. The kitchen is now ready for everything the children will make and is an ideal setting for the culmination of the social studies unit.

### CHOOSING A SMALL-SCALE CONSTRUCTION PROJECT

Small-scale construction projects offer possibilities for this unit. Two themes, each with different values, have proved rewarding to fifth-grade classes. One is a stockade; the other is a wagon train encampment.

A stockade with its pioneer people is a worth-while project when the children can gather small dry branches to cut up and use for logs. Before work is commenced, something must be found to use for a wooden foundation which is large enough for the stockade. An old table top, a piece of plywood, or pine board laid on the floor will do. Before starting to work, the children should decide upon the scale for the construction, including, of course, the people. There are tasks for four major committees. One committee cuts branches into short lengths for the logs of the stockade, whittles a sharp point on one end of each log, and builds the stockade. Another committee cuts logs for the cabins, notches each log a half inch from both ends, and builds the cabins. A third models the people and animals in clay and paints them, and a fourth committee does all the extras which complete the stockade. This includes putting in trees, sprinkling dirt and gravel on the wood foundation, making a well and, perhaps, some benches.

The stockade is built by gluing and nailing the logs upright to the foundation board. Use all-purpose white glue and three-quarter-inch brads. Make a gate that opens. Make the cabins by piling up the logs one by one. Put a few drops of the same glue between the logs and later fill in the crevices with clay. Make a door and window by cutting some of the logs shorter, thus leaving an opening in the wall where each is to be

107

*San Diego City Schools*

located. Cigar-box wood is good for the door and the roof, but a log roof may also be used.

When the stockade is finished and all the people are inside, it looks impregnable to the bloodthirsty Indians crouched without.

The encampment project is started by having every child in the class make a pioneer man, woman, or child. The adult figures are from twelve to fourteen inches high and each is nailed to a small square of wood. The method used for making the figures, wire skeletons wrapped with strips of paper, is described in Chapter 9. The figures are dressed in calicos and cottons with black oilcloth used for the men's boots and scraps of felt for their hats. There are many characters: the captain of the wagon train, the surveyor, scouts, Indian guides, stockmen, musicians, and women and children. Making a large covered wagon and the oxen for it is undertaken as an extra responsibility by a committee of boys. The wire and paper-strip method is used to make the oxen. While this is being done, the other children paint the background or scurry around attending to all other details, such as getting wood and rocks for the campfire and finding the toy coffee pot, frying pan, and lantern. When completed, the children's work is arranged on the floor with the background behind it.

Both the stockade and the encampment are long-term projects at best. At least two months should be planned for their completion.

ACTIVITIES FOR THE UNIT

*Backgrounds*

A scenic background long enough to encompass the construction project should be made. This may be the choice of a group of children with a particular interest in landscape painting. The color of trees, mountains, and sky will add greatly to the effectiveness of the project.

*Murals*

There are many events in the lives of the pioneers on their journey west that are full of feeling and could become the incentive for painting a mural. The excitement of leave-taking from the old home, a wagon train fording a river, and an Indian attack would fire the children's imagination to do creative work.

*Dioramas*

Because a diorama is a compact composition, it is well suited for the portrayal of a historical event. In their reference reading, children will gather the significant facts of the westward movement. There are landmarks along the way, many of which would make a good diorama. The use of plant materials in outdoor scenes is always a nice accent.

*Wood Work*

Many articles made of wood are within the abilities of children of this age to construct. The experiences develop skills in carving, hammering, gluing, sawing, and whittling. Some require coarse work, others fine work. Proper tools, nails, and a generous supply of soft pine are needed. Knocked-down apple boxes and orange crates will be useful for many small articles. No patterns except those which children make themselves are necessary.

The problems of making a stool, cradle, churn, trencher, and spoon are not difficult for fifth-grade children to solve. Make the stool by cutting three pieces of wood (mop handles are good) for the legs and nailing them to a round piece of wood for the seat. Use soft pine for the seat and cut around a circle with a coping saw. If the seat can be a piece of

110

*San Bernardino City Schools*

wood sawed off a log, all the better. Make a cradle by nailing rockers on a wooden box. Draw a pattern for the rockers and trace it on a pine board, then cut out with a coping saw. A pair of wood coat hangers can be adapted for use as rockers. Get a nail keg for the churn. Turn it upside down and use the bottom for the top of the churn. Drill a three-quarter-inch hole in the top and put a piece of dowel through it for a churn stick. The end of an apple box is the right size for a trencher. Fasten the wood to a worktable with a C clamp. Gouge a shallow well out of the center with a chisel. Round the outside edges with a file. Sand the wood and stain a walnut brown. Carve a spoon from a twelve-inch piece of soft pine. Sand and stain. These articles can be made in less than a week by a committee of five children.

The boys often think that a crane and a bed warmer can be girls' work while they apply their energies to making the Kentucky rifle, powder horn, and the spinning wheel. The crane is no more than a piece of wood cut the proper size to fit in the hearth and then painted black. Punch a hole in a carton inside the fireplace and stick the end of the crane in the hole. Make a bed warmer from a long piece of thin wood for the handle and two pie tins or paper plates for the container to hold hot coals. Decorate the lid of the container with a punched design. Draw the design on the lid and punch the hole with a nail or an ice pick.

111

SEATTLE NOVEMBER 13 1851

ALKI SCHOOL

*Seattle* Times *and Seattle Public Schools*

The boys feel that nothing is as important as the Kentucky rifle and the powder horn. The horn is carried by a piece of leather lacing which serves for a shoulder strap.

Draw a pattern on paper for the rifle and cut it out. Trace around the pattern on a piece of soft pine board and roughly saw it out. Round the rifle into shape with a file. Carve a trigger with a penknife or drive a nail into the rifle at the proper place. Stain or paint the rifle a dark brown.

A real horn should be used for the powder horn and can be procured at a packing house. Discarded horns are usually well dried out and not at all unpleasant to work with in the classroom. The most time-consuming part of making a powder horn is scraping the outside clean with a knife. This probably will take about two weeks. When the horn is thoroughly scraped, saw off the tip two inches from the end. Put the tip aside; later it will be made into a powder measure. Carve a small wooden plug to fit into the natural hole in the horn where the tip was sawed off. The plug keeps the powder from spilling out of the horn. Carve a groove around this end of the horn an inch from the end. Now the other end of the horn, where it was attached to the skull, must be covered. Cut out a thin piece of wood to fit in the opening. Drill a hole in the middle.

112

*Churn*

*Stool*

*Bed warmer*

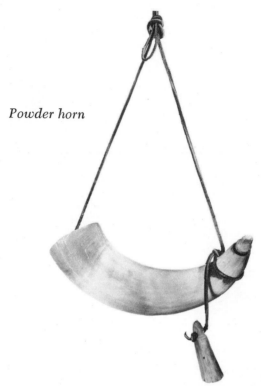

*Powder horn*

*San Diego City Schools*

Put an end of the lacing for the shoulder strap through the hole and tie a knot. Glue the wood into the opening with the knot on the inside. Tie the other end of the lacing around the groove in the horn, leaving an end about four inches long. Finish the powder measure by drilling a hole in the tip. Tie the end of the lacing through the tip of the measure. Powder horn and measure are now completed.

A simplified spinning wheel consists of four parts: a stand, wheel, staff, and spindle. The materials needed are a piece of pine board three quarters of an inch by eight inches (length to be determined by the size of the wheel), three-quarter-inch dowels, two pieces of wood three-quarter by one by four inches, a big spool, and two stove bolts. The tools needed are a crosscut saw, a hammer, a file, a brace with a three-quarter-inch bit, a hand drill with a three-sixteenth-inch bit, a C clamp, and some shingle nails. Use a wheel from a discarded bicycle or baby buggy.

Make the stand first. Cut the board the right length to hold the wheel and other parts. Round the edges of the board with a file. Drill

114

three three-quarter-inch holes in the board, one hole at the center of one end of the board (this is the front) and holes in each corner at the other end of the wheel (this is the back). Cut three legs of three-quarter-inch dowel. Put glue in the holes and insert the legs.

Make the spindle next. Drill a three-sixteenth-inch hole in one end of each of the two short pieces of wood. Put the spool between them and fasten together with a stove bolt. Turn the stand on its side. Place the spindle about a third of the length of the board from the front. Hold the spindle firmly in place and drive the nails through the board into the ends of the spindle. Put the stand back in position.

Now put on the wheel and staff. Hold the wheel in position over the back of the stand and mark where an upright on each side of the wheel should be installed. Drill a three-quarter-inch hole at each mark. Measure the height for the uprights and cut two pieces of three-quarter-inch dowel to measurement. Clamp the dowel to the worktable and drill a hole through each dowel about a half-inch from the end. Put glue in the holes and insert dowels. Put a stove bolt through the drilled holes in the upright and the hub of the wheel.

To put on the staff, drill a three-quarter-inch hole at the front of the stand. Cut a piece of three-quarter-inch dowel the same length as the uprights, put glue in the hole, and insert the dowel. Make a holder for the wood out of wire or narrow strips of wood bent into shape. Fasten on the staff.

## Clay Activities

There are a number of worth-while experiences in clay in this unit. A short, old-fashioned candlestick with handle, a water jug, and a cream pitcher and sugar bowl, if fired, can be used in the kitchen. Other clay activities are modeling figures of pioneer people and the animals encountered on the trip west—buffalo, beaver, wolf, bear, and deer. Animals are always of interest to boys.

## Needlecraft and Sewing

In this unit, more than any other in the social studies, there is need for some instruction in sewing. A pieced quilt, braided rug, sampler, and cover for a pine needle pillow, as well as the simple costumes to be made for dramatic play, can be sewed by children. Each of these activities provides experience in color and design, as well as sewing skills.

Improvement is slow, for most children have little home practice in sewing. Many must start at the beginning and be taught to thread a needle, tie a knot, and use a thimble. What if the stitches are uneven at first? What if there is a hump in the middle of the braided rug? What if the sampler is puckered where a thread has been pulled too tightly? These are only evidences of a child's sincere effort to meet a new problem. Sewing activities should be voluntary with only those children choosing to sew who want to learn. Sewing is not good for the nervous or immature type of child.

A pieced quilt will be needed for the baby's cradle. Squares of cotton prints are sewed together like a checkerboard. To plan a pleasing color harmony, the squares should be laid on a table and changed about until a well-balanced color pattern is made. If this is done, the quilt when finished will not have all the red pieces in one place and all the greens massed in another. A quilt does not have to be lined, but a careful pressing on the wrong side with an iron will help its appearance a great deal.

Soft and pliable cotton goods are the best to use for a braided rug. The material should not be too heavy for children to hold in their hands or too stiff for them to sew. Tear strips of three different colors lengthwise of the goods. Braid them, keeping the tension as even as possible. A loose braid is to be preferred to a tight one. Use a medium-coarse upholstery needle and coarse linen or carpet thread for sewing the braids together. Begin the sewing with a small circle or oval and sew the braid around and around until the braid gives out or the rug is large enough. Stretch and pull the outer edge of each row of braid as the next braid is sewed to it, so that the material in the braids will be accommodated to the curve of the rug. If the braiding has been done too tightly, the sewing will be more difficult and there may be a hump in the middle when it is finished. However, this is not too important and no rug should be ripped apart and redone just because of a hump.

A sampler can be framed in wood and hung on the kitchen wall just as was done in olden days. Simple designs are best; the child's name, the date, and a border problem will be enough for a beginner to attempt to cross-stitch. Draw the design with crayon on a piece of quarter-inch squared paper, using the same colors as have been chosen for the embroidery threads. Carbon the back of the paper with a soft pencil. Pin the pattern to the material for the sampler and trace it through with a sharp pencil. An embroidery hoop will make the cross-stitching easier for the child. When the sampler is finished, press it on the wrong side.

116

*San Diego City Schools*

Any loosely woven cotton material makes a suitable cover for a pine needle pillow. Gathering the pine needles can be a good excuse for a walk in the woods some afternoon. A design may be cross-stitched on the cover, the blanket stitch being put around the edge after the pillow is stuffed. The woodsy fragrance of the needles will be pleasant to the children.

Making simple pioneer costumes is one of the most rewarding of the sewing activities a class can have. Very little sewing is needed, and the results are gratifying. Sunbonnets, caps, shawls, and aprons for the girls look better when the children have made plain gathered skirts to wear with them or have borrowed something of mother's to bring to school. The blue jeans most boys have at home or wear to school are easily adapted for men's costumes. A vest is an addition that is easy to make. The traditional Daniel Boone costume is usually considered a necessity. Perhaps mother can help by making the jacket and trousers, but son should cut the fringe to trim them and make his cap.

*Beverly Hills Unified School District*

## Weaving

Weaving was one of the most important crafts of the pioneer woman. She felt great pride in her coverlets and guarded her designs and dyes jealously. *Irish Chain, Wheel of Fortune, Dogwood Blossom,* and many other patterns were handed down in families until they became a traditional part of the culture. There is little of the art that a child can understand unless the teacher has a coverlet to show or can procure a four-harness table loom for the purpose of demonstrating pattern weaving. Any weaving that the class can do with the ordinary looms and wools will not satisfy the children because it is little more than a repetition of the coarse weaving previously done in the Indian and Mexican units. However, many schools do have four-harness looms in table or floor models. Although children are incapable of stringing a four-harness loom, they can follow a simple weaving pattern with success.

## Painting and Drawing

The whole panorama of American scenery is open to children in painting and drawing experiences related to the unit "Pioneer Life and the Westward Movement." The children in their imagination follow the famous old trails through the passes, over the mountains, by the rivers, and across the deserts, in bad weather and good, in heat or cold, by day and night. Films and Kodachrome slides will help children to visualize the land and water forms that are unique in many regions and unfamiliar to the immediate school environment. When the time arrives for the culmination of the unit, an exhibit of water colors and chalk drawings displayed in the room and hall gives recognition for work well done.

## A Movie

Making a movie can be a three-way integration of history, story writing, and art. Children can adapt a favorite story such as *Paul Bunyan and His Great Blue Ox,*[14] which is also related in a film.[15] Or they can write a narrative of the events occurring in a day's journey, starting with the early morning call to awaken, preparing the breakfast, hitching up the wagons, forming into columns, traveling over the prairie, resting for lunch, giving the alarm of an attack by Indians, forming the wagons into a barricade, repulsing the attack, continuing the journey, making camp for the night, enjoying songs, music, and stories around the camp-

119

*San Diego City Schools*

fire, and keeping watch through the night. These events, plus others children would include, make a half-hour show for the class and other fifth-graders in the building to enjoy.

*Decorative Maps*

The fifth grade marks the beginning of significant map work for children. They have the maturity to visualize historical events and to interpret meanings with symbols. The art skills of map making offer opportunity for a group of children to plan and work together, so that when a map is completed, it is representative of a truly cooperative effort. The Appalachian Mountains in the East, the Rocky Mountains in the West, the major waterways—the Great Lakes and the Ohio, Mississippi, and Missouri rivers—will be put in first. The fun begins as the famous trails are added; the Wilderness Road through the Cumberland Gap, the Lancaster Road to Pittsburgh, and the early and scattered settlements along

120

the way to Boonesborough. Next will come the trails to the Far West; the Oregon, Santa Fe, Mormon, and California trails, each drawn in a different color and symbol. The small drawings that illustrate the hazards of the journey—the varied terrain, the wild animals, and the Indians encountered —call for information gained through reference reading and class discussion. To complete the map a border design and compass would add to its attractiveness.

## Using Plant Materials

The successful use of plant materials depends entirely upon what is available in the region where the school is located. Plants for dyeing cotton goods can be found in New England that children living in Wyoming would know nothing about. It should be remembered that, before starting to dye any material with dyes made from local plants, the advice of a chemist or pharmacist must be sought in order to find the correct mordant. Dyes may be made from butternut hulls, hickory, oak galls, and walnut hulls; from some berries such as pokeberries and sumac berries; and from the leaves of sassafras, sumac, maple, and peach trees.

Plant materials may be used in many other ways: a hearth brush from long pine needles and a broom from some stiff, wild underbrush. Cornhusk dolls were made by pioneer mothers for their little children.[16]

### SUMMARY OF THE SOCIAL STUDIES

As reported in the descriptions of the integrated art units, "Shopping in a Market," "Mexico," and "Pioneer Life and the Westward Movement," it is readily seen that a good unit provides numerous related art activities for children. The teacher wisely determines in advance those activities which she feels are best suited to the maturation of the class and which she believes can be modified to meet the needs of her class. Then final decisions will be made by the group as to which activities they want to embark on. Obviously, there will not be time for a class to engage in all. During the course of several integrated units in a year, the teacher should check the children's individual choices, and if she finds that a child is repeatedly choosing the same type of art work, she should encourage him to try something else. Otherwise, there is the chance that he will miss the broader art experience that would contribute to his greater growth and general enrichment.

We have a happy rabbit.
He is soft and fluffy
and white. See him
nibble on the carrots.
He likes to nibble on the
...er and wood...
...n to play...
...to have him...

*San Bernardino County Schools*

### WORKING WITH THE LANGUAGE ARTS

Illustration requires skillful introduction to be successful. Stories chosen must be those that children like, with the result that Superman and space ships compete with the more conservative stories on library lists. In choosing a story or poem for illustration, the best results come when the writing is strong in mood and has many word pictures and much action. Story and plot can be fantastic; nevertheless, they must have some substance of reality if they are to provide the makings for an illustration. It is this quality of reality that makes the illustrations of children's own writing so strong. Original poems, stories, and sentence stories about class and personal experiences are thoroughly understood because they really happened.

Sentence stories during the morning sharing period in primary grades are one of the most natural motivations for art expression. Children will undertake the most difficult of compositions, illustrations full of people, and activity such as a teacher might never imagine possible. A striking example comes from a first grade where one morning a boy told about going with his father to a boxing match the night before. The teacher was considerably taken aback, but the class clamored for details. The picture which he painted at the easel following the sharing period was much more vivid than his story had been (see color plate No. 5).

Often in a school district the writings by children throughout the year are evaluated by the language arts steering committee and those considered most significant are published by the district in an anthology. Illustrations by children add greatly to a book of this kind, as was done in *Creative Writing,*[17] the publication of a city school system.

*Spacemen go in a rocket.*
*Oh what fun!*
*Someday I'll go in a rocket*
*Like everyone.*

*San Diego City Schools*

123

*Arthur Denny's Dream*[18] is a reference storybook for children. It was written by a teacher in the Seattle schools, illustrated by a group of the children in her class, and published by the school district. Colored reproductions of the children's work add immeasurably to the attractiveness and interest of the story. The book is the outcome of a pressing need for reference material related to the settlement of Seattle and was undertaken as a project for the civic celebration of the Seattle Centennial in 1951 in which the schools participated. The teacher-author gathered the material from a number of different sources and rewrote it in language suitable for fourth-graders to use for independent reference reading. The atmosphere of the early times is well expressed in the crisp illustrations. An effective classroom bulletin board arrangement of Cherry Grove, Illinois, the home of the settlers, resulted in the use of cut paper for the illustrations. As work progressed, the children consciously adapted their compositions to the layout of the book. This unique project, creative for both teacher and children, met a real teaching need with results equally

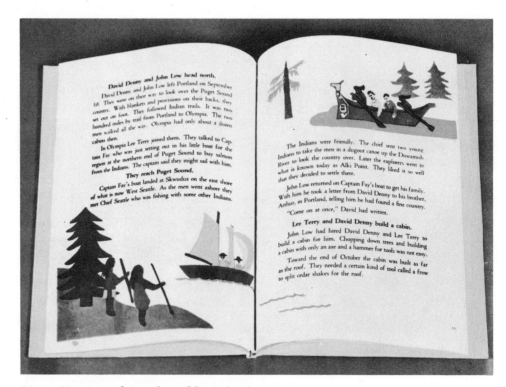

124    *Marie Hatten and Seattle Public Schools*

*San Diego City Schools*

rewarding to the children and to the school district sponsoring the project.

Hand puppets and marionettes can be a means of presenting plays written in class and are a good related language and art experience. Many times an old and loved story is rewritten by a class. When a group of sixth-graders took over the story of Puss-in-Boots, this seventeenth-century character became a doubly engaging fellow in the language of eleven-year-old writers. Successful play production means lots of work, and there are important tasks for every child in the class.

Frequently, a class will write a play or pageant for the culmination of a unit in the social studies. The construction project already made serves as an appropriate background. An understanding teacher does not let all the glory go to the actors, but gives equal recognition and appreciation to the children who carried the responsibility for the art part of the production.

A strong program in the language arts is likely to include a monthly or quarterly school paper. Often, it is the sixth grade that edits and prepares the material for duplication. School papers are popular and

125

*San Diego City Schools*

sought by the children almost before the Mimeograph ink is dry. Here is an opportunity for children to learn about good spacing and layout. Moreover, drawings will be used. This is one of the very few times in the elementary school when a pencil is the right tool to use. Cartoons, pictures of sports and school events, the designing of a masthead can all be traced on a stencil. A call upon the school secretary by the editor in chief will give him and his committee information about details.

### SUMMARY OF THE LANGUAGE ARTS

The language arts hold great promise for a fine integrative art experience for children. While the scope may not be as broad as that of the social studies, the close relationship between language expression, personal experience, and creative work is equally sound for language arts as for social studies.

### WORKING WITH MUSIC

Inspirational leadership is needed for the integration of music with art because an emotional response in children is indispensable

126

to both arts for creative work. There are several ways of providing related experiences, depending upon the character of the music.[19] Children may illustrate descriptive music as they would a story, *The Carnival of Animals*[a] for example; or they may develop designs interpreting music that has a sharply defined rhythm pattern, such as Verdi's *Grand March* from "Aïda."[b] For a gratifying integration of music and art, the children should know and like the music and hear it expertly performed. A scratchy or imperfect record, or an amateur pianist, will distort rhythm and melody, greatly confuse the children, and hinder an artistic result. A poor musical performance is particularly distressing for the child with a high degree of musical sensitivity.

When descriptive music is used, painting with water color and tempera can be a part of a full cycle that stirs children aesthetically. A cycle would include listening, dramatizing, responding rhythmically, dancing, and singing the theme. Each of these experiences helps to build

*San Bernardino County Schools*

127

a feeling for line, form, and color. Among the appropriate descriptive music for children are passages from Mendelssohn's *A Midsummer Night's Dream*[c] (see color plate No. 15), Beethoven's *Sixth Symphony* (the "Pastoral")[d] and Copland's *Appalachian Spring*.[e] *Toccata* (Little Train of Caipira)[f] by Villa-Lobos and *La Mer*[g] by Debussy are short compositions that bring different pictures to mind. A unique musical form that is appropriate for children is found in Prokofieff's *Peter and the Wolf*.[h] The voice of the narrator synchronizes story and music for the children. There are many recordings of all these compositions by the world's

greatest orchestras and musicians which can be the inspiration for creative work by children.

In descriptive music, the children are entitled to know the intent of the composer. What he did, where he went, what he saw, and what he wanted his music to tell are important for a related experience. Rossini's thunderstorm in *William Tell*[i] describes something he saw, and Tchaikovsky's music for the sugar plum fairy[j] something he imagined and wanted others to visualize.

The school music program stresses creative composition by children in all grades. Early compositions are short melodies resulting from a keen experience, but, later, the music grows in length and complexity. Accompaniments for bells or Autoharp are often written by the teacher on a chart and illustrated by a painting or drawing by a child.

Mood in music stimulates many children to creative work as effectively as does descriptive music. The emotional feelings expressed by the composer in his music are often translated into vivid abstractions of line, form, and color by children who are sensitive and responsive to quality and pattern in music. Mood in music in an auditory and transitory experience may stimulate some children to find its echo in equally expressive visual forms of line, color, and value which they will instinctively choose. In creative work of this nature, the teacher should be careful never to give the class any hints by naming the composition or telling anything about what she thinks was meant by the composer. The finale of Mozart's *Symphony in E-Flat Major*[k] is gay and classical in feeling; Gershwin's *An American in Paris*[l] is gay and modern.

Last of the music experiences to be described is the development of designs representative of the rhythm of the music. Children like to do this and become proficient during repeated playings of the music. The music must have a clearly defined and simple pattern of accented beats; 4/4, 2/4, and 3/4 time stimulate the surest response in children. In the upper grades the children will return to the basic rhythm after the music has stopped and embellish it with more color or design, yet never break the fundamental musical pattern. With all children it is helpful for them to have previously experienced the music kinesthetically in such ways as dancing, playing rhythm instruments, or marching. *Candy Shop*[20] is an example of 4/4 time that has been used in primary grades and that can develop naturally into a color pattern. *London Bridge*[21] is in 2/4 time, and *Minuet*[22] by Boccherini is in 3/4 time.

129

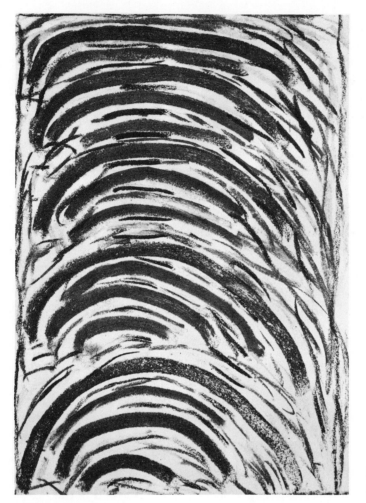

*San Diego
City Schools*

*Candy Shop*

McConathy, Osbourne, et al. *New Music Horizons, First Book.*
By permission of the publishers, Silver Burdett Company.

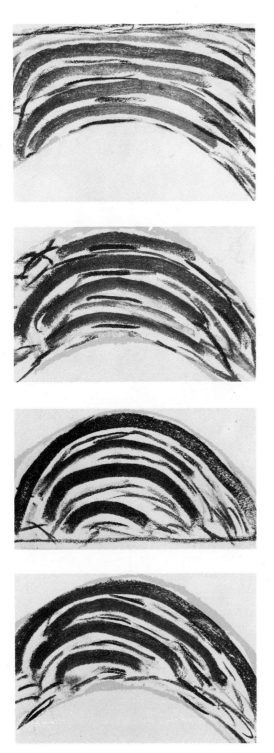

*Charles drew his rhythm in colored chalk.*

*He immediately perceived four beats to the measure*

*but, he suspected there was something wrong because all the beats he was hearing were not equally accented.*

*His first rhythm unit was better than the second, so he returned to it, but by now he had identified the major and minor accents in the measure.*

*Finally he caught the rhythm perfectly. He would have continued repeating his design many more times if only the paper had been longer. That is what he said.*

131

*Amaryllis*

*San Diego City Schools*

Any material may be used, but finger paint seems especially good for music because movements can be free and quick.

SUMMARY OF MUSIC

Correlation of art[23] and music provides a rich variation in an art program. The music selected must vary from grade to grade, its choice being determined by the maturation of the children, their previous music experience, and their enjoyment of the composition.[24] Music often relaxes children and frees their fancies to roam.

132

THE INTEGRITY OF ART: A CHAPTER SUMMARY

The integrity of the correlated art program lies within the teacher's hands. Should she allow the integrated experience to dominate the year's work, she would be depriving the children of their just right to individual art experiences and establishing a bias that is neither intelligent nor fair to children or to art.

REFERENCE MATERIAL

1. Cunningham, Ruth. *et al. Understanding Group Behavior of Boys and Girls*. New York: Bureau of Publications, Teachers College, Columbia University, 1951. (Chap. I. "The Significance of Groups," pp. 1–12; Chap. II, "Group Interaction," pp. 13–55.)

2. *Care of Art Materials*. 16mm. film, 10 min., black and white; produced by McGraw-Hill Book Company, Inc.

3. Kyte, George C. *The Elementary School Teacher at Work*. New York: Holt, Rinehart and Winston, Inc., 1957.

4. *Arts and Crafts of Mexico*. 16mm. film, 11 min., sound, black and white; produced by Encyclopaedia Britannica Films, Inc. *Native Arts of Old Mexico*. 16mm. film, 20 min., sound, black and white; produced by International Film Bureau, Inc.

5. Ross, Patricia Fent. *Made in Mexico*. New York: Alfred A. Knopf, Inc., 1952.

6. Morrow, Elizabeth. *The Painted Pig*. New York: Alfred A. Knopf, Inc., 1930.

7. Hamlin, Julia Duncan, and Victor D'Amico. *How to Make Pottery and Ceramic Sculpture*. New York: Simon and Schuster, Inc., 1947. (Project XVII—"Toys," pp. 74–75.)

8. Sedillo, Mela. *Mexican and New Mexico Folk Dances*. Albuquerque, N.M.: University of New Mexico Press, 1950. ("Los Viejitos," p. 47, piano score.)

9. *El Jarabe Tapatio*. RCA Victor record 79147; Columbia record 7011; Decca record 10325.

10. *Chiapanecás*. Album "Mexican Folk Dances," Bowmar record 1567B.

133

11. Shanklin, Margaret Eberhardt. *Use of Native Craft Materials.* Peoria, Ill.: Chas. A. Bennett Company, Inc., 1947.

12. Christensen, Erwin O. *The Index of American Design.* New York: The Macmillan Company, 1950. (Teacher background.)

13. *A Pioneer Home.* 16mm. film, 11 min., sound, color; produced by Coronet Instructional Films.

14. Wadsworth, William. *Paul Bunyan and His Great Blue Ox.* New York: Doubleday & Company, Inc., 1926.

15. *Paul Bunyan and the Blue Ox.* 16mm. film, 6 min., sound, color; produced by Coronet Instructional Films.

16. "Cornhusk Dolls," *School Arts,* LI, No. 3 (November, 1951), pp. 97–98.

17. *Creative Writing,* Vol. 16. San Diego, Calif.: San Diego City Schools, 1960.

18. Hatten, Marie. *Arthur Denny's Dream.* Seattle, Wash.: Seattle Public Schools, 1953.

19. Recordings listed for correlation of music and art may be had in the 78 rpm, 45 rpm, and 33⅓ rpm speeds. Since different schools have different types of record players, no catalogue numbers are given. The teacher can find the record for her machine in the catalogues of the major companies: RCA Victor, Columbia, Decca, Imperial, and so forth.
    a. Saint-Saëns, Charles Camille. *The Carnival of Animals.*
    b. Verdi, Giuseppe. *Aïda.*
    c. Mendelssohn, Felix. *A Midsummer Night's Dream,* Op. 61, No. 1.
    d. Beethoven, Ludwig van. *Symphony No. 6 in F,* Op. 68, No. 1.
    e. Copland, Aaron. *Appalachian Spring.*
    f. Villa-Lobos, Heitor. Toccata ("Little Train of Caipira").
    g. Debussy, Claude. *La Mer.*
    h. Prokofieff, Serge. *Peter and the Wolf,* Op. 67.
    i. Rossini, Gioacchino. *William Tell,* "The Thunderstorm."
    j. Tchaikovsky, Peter. *Nutcracker Suite,* Op. 71.
    k. Mozart, Wolfgang Amadeus. *Symphony in E-Flat Major.*
    l. Gershwin, George. *An American in Paris.*

20. McConathy, Osbourne, *et al. New Music Horizons, First*

*Book.* Morristown, N.J.: Silver Burdett Company, 1944. ("Candy Shop," pp. 30–31.)

21. McConathy, Osbourne, *et al. New Music Horizons, First Book.* Morristown, N.J.: Silver Burdett Company, 1944. ("London Bridge," pp. 4–5.)

22. Boccherini, Luigi. *Minuet.*

23. *Design to Music.* 16mm. film, sound, 6 min., color; produced by International Film Bureau, Inc.

24. Gesell, Arnold, and Frances Ilg. *Infant and Child in the Culture of Today.* New York: Harper & Brothers, 1943. (Appendix E, "Musical Records for Infants and Children," pp. 385–88.)

## READER PARTICIPATION

Under what circumstances have you participated in group activities? How effective were they?

Report upon some successful group teaching that you have observed.

Name some of the practical problems involved in initiating group activities in art.

In your opinion, which social studies units in the elementary curriculum would contribute most effectively to creative work? Explore one unit thoroughly and identify all the possible art activities that might be developed.

Review the language arts program for purposeful creative art activities.

Listen to six of your favorite records and evaluate their possibilities for art interpretation.

What are the expected outcomes for a related art program in the social studies? in language arts? in music?

Why has integration become so significant in current educational practice?

# 8

# *Art Contributes to*
# *Group and*
# *Individual Experiences*

Many art projects are equally good for small groups and individual activities. Group sharing of ideas leads to group sharing of work with the happy result that lengthy projects can be accomplished within the natural interest span of children. Each of the activities to be discussed could be undertaken in a modified form by an individual child. Every child likes to work by himself as well as with a group.

## ART ACTIVITIES FOR SMALL GROUPS

Murals, dioramas, a movie, hand puppets, and string marionettes are fun to do when children work together. Group work gives companionship which children need and enjoy, and individual work the opportunity for complete independence.

## MAKING A MURAL

Much of the success of a mural lies in the careful planning that is done before children start working. Good group discussion results in decisions in which every child has taken part. Preplanning is time well spent, and will lessen the misunderstandings and disappointments that

136

sometimes occur when one child does the work of another, not intentionally but because he failed to understand how much he was to do. Since all the children cannot do things of equal importance, the teacher is generously appreciative of whatever a child may have done, whether it was painting the figures or the sky.

Under most circumstances, all the children in a class cannot work at the same time on one mural and have a rewarding experience; there is not enough to do that is worth while. Hence, several murals should be planned for the year. A mural[1] is not difficult to organize, and once both the general plan and the details are talked over with the class a pattern of procedure can be established that all will willingly follow.

### THE COMMITTEE EMERGES

Group discussion provides opportunity for children to volunteer to work on a mural and to indicate what each would like to do. Since several murals will be made during the course of the year, committees may be kept small, to perhaps six or seven children at a time. Nevertheless, situations do occur when an entire class wants to take part in the work, no matter how small the task may be. Under such circumstances, to deprive any child would be an unnecessary and keen disappointment for him. Responsibilities for doing different parts of the work will vary. Some children will volunteer to do the figures, others to develop the background, while some child will agree to take care of the art materials in addition.

To remind committee members of their responsibilities, the tasks and duties of each may be written on the blackboard. An informal summary seems more suitable for primary children than the brief outline used in upper grades.

### *Our Mural*

Betty and Phil are going to paint the people.
Mary will paint the trees.
Tom has asked to paint the sky.
Jimmy has offered to take care of the paints
and help paint the sky.
Nancy will wash the brushes and help Mary
with the trees.

*Mural Committee*

Figures—Bill, Jerry, and Mollie
Animals—Joe and Frank
Background—Harry and Dorothy
Care of Materials—Sam

### CHOOSING THE SUBJECT

The subject for a mural may come from many sources. The decision may be made by the class or be left to the committee. Although the majority of the subjects for murals are related to the social studies, there are many other interests which are vital and important to children and which should not be overlooked. If the circus comes to town, the children will naturally find it fun to make a circus mural. If a field trip to the tide pools at the shore were a part of the science program, it would make an interesting subject for a mural. Personal interests and group experiences never fail to stimulate art expression.

### TYPES OF MURALS

Three types of mural composition seem prevalent in children's work: figure, panel, and scenic. The interest in a Halloween carnival would be centered in the large figures and their fantastic costumes. Consequently, a simple background would be sufficient and would least detract from the center of interest. The history of aviation, a series of related events, would be best presented in a panel mural to avoid the problem of unifying contrasting backgrounds. The first balloon ascension in France, Lindbergh's transatlantic flight, and Air Force tests in the Mojave Desert are effective as separate panels. A farm with its many points of interest—people, animals, buildings, machinery, fields, and orchards—quite naturally develops as a scenic mural. When murals are made several times during the year, it is good teaching to vary their compositions.

### PREPARING TO WORK

The committee must make an early decision as to which art materials to use: paint, colored chalk, or cut paper. Crayon is never

138

the best choice because children find it an everlasting chore to color large areas of paper heavily enough to produce rich, vibrant color, and because crayon is such a hard material that it demands close, fine work, restricts a free and easy technique, and results in a stiff and formal mural. After the art material has been chosen, the size of the paper is next decided. There is usually no limitation other than the suggestion that early murals in the first grade should not overpower the children by their size. Wrapping paper with a finish that will take either tempera paint or colored chalk is used. Paper with a shiny or slick surface should never be ordered. White, Manila, and brown wrapping papers all have their special uses. Twenty-four-inch, thirty-six-inch, and forty-eight-inch widths are stock sizes. Strips of paper may be pasted together with all-purpose white glue so that scarcely a pucker will show.

*San Antonio Independent School District*   139

*Indianapolis Public Schools*

The blackboard and the bulletin board are both appropriate places to put up the paper for a mural. When the paper is once in place, it should be left there until the work is completed. Paper tears and loses its crispness when handled too much. The blackboard provides the firmest and smoothest backing for painting and chalk drawing, while the bulletin board is the better place for cut paper. On a bulletin board, different parts cut out of paper may be pinned in place and changed if necessary before permanent pasting or stapling. The floor is a convenient place for primary children to work when painting or drawing with chalk.

Thought must be given to the practical problem of where 140 to put the working materials and tools. A conveniently placed table to hold paints and brushes, boxes of colored chalk, colored paper, scissors, and paste should be provided. Apple boxes on end make efficient stands for individual children. Boxes are light and easy to move as the child changes his position at the mural. If all the paraphernalia which children need is underfoot or balanced precariously on the seat of a chair, accidents are bound to happen and tensions develop.

## CHOOSING A TECHNIQUE

Shall the mural be painted with tempera, drawn with chalk, or made of cut paper? Each technique has its own charm and is appropriate for all grades and all subjects.

*Tempera* is a very versatile painting material. New and striking colors can be mixed, grayed colors can be made, and all the pastel shades are possible by mixing basic colors with white. With such a full palette, tempera is ideal for murals. Lots of accents of white add sparkle, and sharp blacks give contrasts. Since tempera is an opaque paint, spots and mistakes may be painted over and will hardly show when the mural is completed. If the paint tends to chip off the paper, a small quantity of casein glue can be added to the paint.

*Colored chalk* is the quickest technique. A wide range of colors is manufactured and ready to use. Colors may be blended and shaded; when put on heavily, they are handsome in texture and rich in tone. Sharp accents in a dark color, usually lines, strengthen a composition. A chalk mural should always be sprayed. The new plastic sprays in self-operating cans are best, but a regular fixative may be used. Unfortunately, fixatives change some colors while plastic sprays do not. Children should wear aprons, and newspaper should be spread on the floor to catch the chalk dust. Buttermilk can be used as a chalk binder for murals when the work is done on the floor. Paint the buttermilk on the paper with a wide brush as needed. Draw while the buttermilk is still moist. Buttermilk not only sharpens colors but prevents them from rubbing off. If the odor of the buttermilk seems unpleasant in the classroom, bottled laundry starch will work as well. The thing to remember is to let the paper dry completely before picking it up; paper softened by starch tends to tear easily if picked up too soon. Starch also keeps the chalk from rubbing off.

*Cut paper* is a flexible method that permits easy changes during the work. If the position of something in the mural, a barn for

141

example, throws the composition out of balance, it is a simple matter to move it elsewhere.

Cut paper is exciting when there is variety in the paper used and when the different parts are not pasted down like so many pancakes. A compact composition is best, for a scattered arrangement loses its freshness. Decorated, metal, and regular school colored papers are all used. Overlapping, fringing, bending, pleating, folding, curling, and twisting the paper makes a more unusual mural and gives a feeling of the third dimension.[2] Pinking shears can be used for fancy edges. Holes can be punched in strips of paper for dotted patterns. Odds and ends of buttons, rickrack braid, paper doilies, and shelf edgings are a few extras that add variety. Patterns and tracings should never be permitted; the children's free cutting is the only acceptable procedure. Every child in a class can have a part in a cut-paper mural.

### MAKING A MURAL: PRIMARY GRADES

Painting murals comes naturally to primary children[3] if they have had plenty of opportunity to paint at an easel; otherwise, it is

*Battle Creek Public Schools*

a tremendous change from small desk work. If painting experiences at the easel have been limited, it would be wise to encourage more easel work before undertaking the first mural. Usually a week is long enough to devote to painting a mural; after that enthusiasm begins to lag. When interest is gone, the children's spontaneity of expression is also gone.

Murals are always initiated by talking it over first and finding out who would like to work on them. When ideas seem slow in coming, dramatic play during the planning period will crystallize the children's thinking. On most occasions it is easier for primary children to put in the people, children, and animals first. Children who have had easel experience paint quickly, and probably in an hour the figures will be completed to the last hair bow and belt buckle. Color is a free choice, but if there is not some discussion about it first, all the children may choose the same color. Not that this matters too much, but after the mural is finished the children themselves are often disappointed. In the first few murals, and perhaps all year, backgrounds are very simple: no more than a little ground, sky, and the sun. By the second grade, backgrounds become more important and many details are developed. Children do not need to be told what to do; they know very well what they want to do. The role of the teacher is to keep this fine independent spirit alive. The entire process of mural work is informal, relaxed, and uninhibited. Who cares much about drips? Certainly not the children, for they have discovered long since that something can always be painted over a drip and no one will ever know it was there.

MAKING A MURAL: MIDDLE AND UPPER GRADES

Children have had many previous experiences in making murals and by now, in the upper grades,[4] they are purposeful in their approach. Keen interest in reference work and details finds creative outlet in murals which develop from the social studies.

When paint or chalk is used, murals may be planned in several ways. After group discussion, all the pupils may draw small sketches and then choose the best for the mural; or they may take parts from several sketches and combine them in a new composition. A committee of a few children may make together a larger sketch and submit it for approval. Or one or two children may draw the mural directly on the wrapping paper and then have it evaluated by the group. When either of the first

143

*Department of Education, Baltimore, Maryland*

two methods is used, the sketching paper must be cut to the same proportions as the dimensions of the wrapping paper. A drawing on nine-by-twelve-inch paper will be hopelessly distorted if transferred to a three-by-fifteen-foot mural. Six-by-thirty-inch sketching paper should be used; then the composition will be enlarged with greater accuracy. Not that precision is the aim, but when a good composition is made, children are disturbed if the basic proportions of a sketch cannot be retained. Drawing on wrapping paper is done with chalk or charcoal, not pencil. Chalk and charcoal lines are easy to erase when evaluation demands a change. Minute details should not be drawn, only the basic outline of the composition.

After the drawing for the mural is complete, color should be discussed. Children are mature enough in the upper grades to appreciate the importance of color distribution and emphasis. They are clever in mixing new and subtle shades with paint—lemon yellow, blue red, chartreuse, terra cotta, peacock blue, and others. Many beautiful extra colors are manufactured in chalk ready for children to use.

A cut-paper mural is approached in a very different way. While the class may share in the general planning, the production is better if it is left to a fairly small committee. A preliminary sketch is wasted effort since all the parts are separate and can be changed about until the most pleasing composition is made. It is stimulating to art judgment to

144

*Board of Education, Cleveland, Ohio*

try the hills high and then low, to put the trees in one place and then another, to group the figures where they add the most interest. Color distribution and emphasis develop as the children select the papers to cut. Different kinds of paper and three-dimensional forms, as suggested in a preceding section, take away the flat and static look of many cut-paper murals. Upper-grade children can develop a strong quality of design with cut paper and have a smart, crisp mural as the result. Ordinarily, cut-paper murals should be considerably smaller than other types. Their style is lost if large areas of background are left bare.

Murals are wonderful examples of cooperative work, clear thinking, and competent use of the elements of art. Children rightfully experience great pride in the achievement of a beautiful mural. Originality, imagination, and responsibility are the roots of a good mural.

A CHILD IS A CHILD

Often the most creative work occurs when the children take charge. This happened in a third-grade class during the period in world events when South African affairs were foremost in the news. Native customs and cultures were shown on TV and the children were interested and stimulated by what they had viewed at home. Their 145

*Fulton County Board of Education, Atlanta, Georgia*

enthusiasm was infectious and nothing would deter a group from making a mural depicting native life, even though the subject was remote from their classroom studies. When completed, the mural was spirited and colorful.

A few days later, one of the class inquired what a Congo mother who was holding the hand of a toddler had in her other hand. Obviously, it was not a fruit or a basket. The young painter's answer was a surprise to the teacher, but accepted as a matter of fact by the class. The painter replied: "Why her purse, of course."

## MAKING A DIORAMA

A scene from a story, a historical event, a patriotic occasion, or a holiday affords opportunity for imaginative development as a diorama. Since the work is small and detailed, a diorama is suited to the muscular coordination of the more mature child. A diorama[5] is an excellent individual problem.

146

Some children may have had the opportunity to visit a museum and see some of the large-size dioramas that have been skillfully, artistically, and scientifically prepared to depict prehistoric life, historical events, and present-day animals, birds, and reptiles in their native habitats, as well as cultural life groups of other races and times. If possible, a class trip to a museum should be arranged by the teacher. This trip would be a most meaningful, informative, and interesting introduction to the project of making a diorama. A museum visit challenges children to be inventive in the portrayal of their choice of subject and stimulates individual research, not only in the classroom, but also in the children's department of the public library.

Everything in a diorama is made separately and then arranged in a box. Children have here a compact and concise three-dimensional design to work out. The arrangement is determined by the size of the box, its length, depth, and height. Assembling the parts is a

practical experience, for whatever is made may be tried in the box before it is finished and permanently installed. Evaluation of proportions is carried on continually and, through comparisons, decisions are made. Color is evaluated in order to find the best hue and value. Children will find for themselves the colors which attract attention and can be used for emphasis. If the background is to appear far away, color values must help, not hinder, the illusion. Also, children can experiment with the arrangement of the scene, trying the parts first one way, then another, until the best is found. Since all parts of a diorama are solid shapes, houses, people, everything can be shifted in any direction. It is a mistake to use silhouettes because they will destroy the three-dimensional effect. Figures of people may be modeled in clay and painted, or made of wire covered with strips of paper and then dressed in cotton clothes. In many ways, the latter technique is more colorful and attractive.

A problem that must be solved in the construction of a diorama is how to fasten the numerous parts in place firmly so that they will not fall over if the box is jarred. For parts which do not have a base to stand on, such as trees made from small branches, there is no better method than to stick the ends in a small lump of Plasticine. Thumbtacks and cellulose tape are successful in holding wood, paper and wire in place; all-purpose white glue will hold anything not made of metal. Odds and ends come in handy for many things. A piece of glass with blue paper underneath becomes a duck pond; small dried weeds may be painted pink, yellow, or white to look like flowers; straw makes thatch; fringed paper, banana leaves; and cellophane, windowpanes.

It is the last-minute imaginative touches which children think to add that give a diorama its exceptional charm.

## Making a Movie

"Movie" is a term that children have applied to their way of making a motion picture.[6] When finished, a movie operates on the same general principle as a filmstrip, the "film" being a long strip of wrapping paper, like a scroll, on which the story and pictures appear. The strip is fastened to two rollers which are fitted into a wooden box, and as the rollers are turned the story unfolds.

The teacher should make the movie box for primary chil-

*San Diego City Schools*

dren, but older children are capable of making their own box. One method of making a movie box is to drill two three-quarter-inch holes in the middle of the two sides of a box, each hole three inches from the end. Measure the width of the box and add six inches to it. Take this measurement and use it to cut two pieces of three-quarter-inch dowel for the rollers. Turn the box on its side. Put one roller through a hole in the top of the box and fit the end into the opposite hole below. Do the same with the other roller. If the holes are too small for the rollers to turn easily, remove the rollers and file the holes a little larger. Paint the box an attractive color on the outside. Put a valance across the top of the opening and curtains on each side.

A long narrow mural can be used for the continuity of a movie in primary grades. Cut a strip of wrapping paper which fits easily in the box. Fasten the paper to the blackboard with tape. Start the painting by printing a title. The movie may be a story children love, perhaps 149

*The Three Bears,* or the happenings on a field trip, such as a visit to a farm. When the mural is finished, fasten one end of the paper to a roller with tape. Wind the mural on the roller and fasten the remaining end to the other roller. The work is done; it is time for the first show.

An upper-grade movie can be developed as a related language activity. Two small committees, one to write the story, and the other to draw the pictures, will prepare the movie while the box is being made. The story is written in paragraph form and typed on separate pieces of paper. If available, use a primary-grade typewriter. Pictures are drawn to accompany each paragraph. The pictures should be bold in color and strong in line. Crayon is the best material for achieving this. Paragraphs and pictures are pasted alternately—about four inches apart —on a long piece of wrapping paper used for the scroll. A title and ending should be nicely lettered with crayon.

*San Francisco Unified School District*

## Puppets and Marionettes

Puppetry is equally successful in primary and in upper grades. The hand puppet is more appropriate for the primary grades and string marionettes for upper grades. Nevertheless, many older children choose puppets in preference to marionettes.

### HAND PUPPETS

Puppets are slipped over the hand and are simple to make. Plays are delightful because they are spontaneous. Many times the children speak extemporaneously, with the engaging result that no two performances are ever quite alike. Only a few puppets can appear at one time, usually three at the most. The best kind of play is a series of incidents with plenty of comedy, like the traditional Punch and Judy show. Liveliness is essential if the audience is to have a good time. A color film, *How to Make a Puppet*,[7] is helpful to children and teacher alike.

### Making a Hand Puppet

First, the head of the puppet is made of papier-mâché or of either of the following materials:

3 cups of sawdust
1 cup of wallpaper paste
Enough water to mix ingredients together. Do not make it too stiff. Use before it hardens.

*or*

½ cup of table salt
¼ cup of cornstarch
¼ cup of water
Mix the ingredients thoroughly and cook over low heat, stirring constantly until mixture stiffens into a lump. Use modeling mixture when it is cool enough to handle.

Put a ball of the modeling material on top of the forefinger of the left hand and model the general form of the head. Exaggerate the size of the head and features. A big nose, popeyes, deep wrinkles, wide grin, sharp chin, and big ears all add character. Remove the head from the finger and finish the face. Smooth the surface as much as possible.

151

When We Give
Our Puppet Show

1. We will read so
   everyone can hear.
2. We will try to make
   it sound as if the
   puppet is really talking.
3. We will move the pup...

How We Made
Papier Maché

1. We tore old papers
   into tiny bits.
2. We put water with the
   paper and let it stand
   all night.
3. We squeeze... the
   water. The...
   in paste and...

*San Bernardino City Schools*

Paint the face with oil paints. Tempera can be used, but it will not reflect light as well. Use raveled burlap, the fuzzy inside of a shoe polisher, or a metal sponge for hair and glue it to the head. Make the hands out of the same material as the head or from a piece of muslin. When muslin is used, cut out two mitten shapes from a double piece of muslin. Cover the muslin with all-purpose white glue. Allow the glue to dry slightly and bend the muslin into a cupped shape. The hands are sewed to the under-shirt later.

*Making the Costume*

The costume consists of two parts, an undershirt that shields the hand and a costume to cover it. The undershirt is not indispensable, but it stiffens the costume and adds bulk. Make the undershirt with kimono sleeves to fit over the child's hand and to extend below the wrist. Cut a small hole for the neck and have the sleeves as long as the

152

middle finger. Sew the sides together and fit over the child's hand. Push the forefinger through the hole for the neck, put the thumb in one sleeve, and put the middle finger in the other sleeve. The difference in the length of the puppet's arms will never be noticed in the performance.

Make the costume to cover the undershirt by the same pattern. The costume should fit loosely. Soft pliable materials and bright colors are best. Each child should do the sewing for his own puppet.

Put the undershirt, with the hands sewed to it, over the hand, put the costume over it, and put the head on the forefinger. It is time to start practicing for the show.

*Making the Puppet Theater*

The puppet is manipulated from below the stage, the child holding his hand above his head. Use a tall three-panel screen for the theater. Cut out an opening in the center panel just above the head of a child of average size. Make the opening twenty inches high and as wide as the panel will permit. Place the side panels of the screen at an angle and nail a board across the top to keep them from closing. Tack a

*Cincinnati Public Schools*

dark curtain to the board. The children with their puppets stand between the curtain and the screen when giving the show.

Children thoroughly enjoy puppets. Role playing is quickly assumed even by the most reticent child. The very nature of a puppet show is boisterous and demands that action and words shall go together. Every bit of imagination a child has finds expression through the actions of his puppet.

### MARIONETTES

Marionettes are manipulated by strings. Like the making of puppets, making marionettes is an old folk art.

Can marionettes be made an easy way? Yes, there are

*San Diego City Schools*

simplified techniques for elementary school children. Marionettes provide step-by-step growth for children and effective correlation with literature, writing, speech, music, and art when the project is carefully planned, well organized, and production is on a level with the maturation of the group.

*An Overview of the First Steps*

If children have never seen a marionette show, and few have, the teacher should find interesting ways of introducing the project. Books may be placed on the library table, a film viewed, and a marionette brought to class. Sometime during the project, the class would enjoy being told or reading *The Adventures of Pinocchio,*[8] the most famous of all marionettes. The film, *Puppetry: String Marionettes,*[9] will be of particular interest because it demonstrates how action is accomplished by pulling strings. The same kind of a marionette that the children will be making can be brought to class for examination. Once they have handled the control stick, children will be eager to start.

Some of the value of a marionette show is lost unless the children write their own skits and plays, either adaptations of stories or original plots. Often the play is an outgrowth of a unit in the social studies, and many American heroes have trod the puppet boards in elementary schools. Likewise, children have many imaginative and fanciful ideas to develop. A variety show, *Animal Adventures in the Woods,* given by sixth-graders, was full of comical incidents and greatly enjoyed by the audience.

Children find satisfaction in a project when every child does his share of the work and when the spirit of the work gives opportunity for leadership. In such an atmosphere pupils are willing to help each other. Identifying the problems, selecting the subject for the play, writing the play, deciding where to set up the stage, and estimating the time it will take to finish the work are all discussed by the class. It is usually better practice to initiate marionettes in the second semester, for by then the children will have learned to work together.

The number of marionettes to be made depends upon the number of characters in the play. The more marionettes, the better the production and the more fun for the children. All the marionettes are never on stage at one time, so a five-foot stage in the classroom is ample. The friendly, informal atmosphere of the classroom should not be sacrificed for the efficiency of an auditorium. What if a curtain cord does get tangled, or an electric wire to a spotlight is disconnected from its outlet? These are

155

experiences children have; if there are no obstacles that are within the ability of the group to overcome there is less learning. Rather than lose the naturalness of the classroom situation, let the room be upset for the few extra days it will take to entertain the other classes in the school.

Reviewing the plans for a marionette show, the children recognize that each child cannot do everything, and that a class must divide into committees: play writers, stage carpenters, scenery painters, marionette makers, and a prop man and his helpers. There are worth-while activities for all. A marionette show is one of the superior integrated units for experience in organization. Children must accomplish the regular day's work and at the same time work out the problems of the show. This may take as long as three months; hence it becomes the responsibility of every child to cooperate in keeping the room as neat and orderly as possible.

*Specific Problems of Production*

Wood is recommended as the best material for making marionettes. Wooden marionettes are flexible to operate and the clatter of their feet on the stage floor makes a pleasant sound. Securing the wood and other materials and tools is a realistic problem that must be met before launching the project. Children grow impatient if, at the time set for starting work, there is not enough wood or if another class has borrowed the tools; nor can costumes be made without needles and pins. Lists of things needed, along with the duties of the committees, should be written on the blackboard. But whatever intervenes, when the day comes to start work the children should not be disappointed by some oversight on the part of the teacher.

Half-inch dowel and scraps of three-quarter-inch soft pine are used for the bodies of the marionettes, lath for the control sticks. A scrap box full of dress goods, materials, and discarded costume jewelry should be collected. Darning needles, No. 7 needles, and thread should be available. A pair of pinking shears saves time otherwise spent in hemming skirts, and scissors for every child who is sewing are a necessity.

Other necessary tools are a hand drill that operates like an egg beater, with an eighth-of-an-inch bit, a back saw (not to be confused with a hack saw), two C clamps, and a hammer. A staple gun is a timesaver when putting up scenery and fastening many things together. For gluing there is nothing that can excell all-purpose white glue. Sandpaper, spools of carpet thread, wallpaper paste, a half yard of muslin, tacks

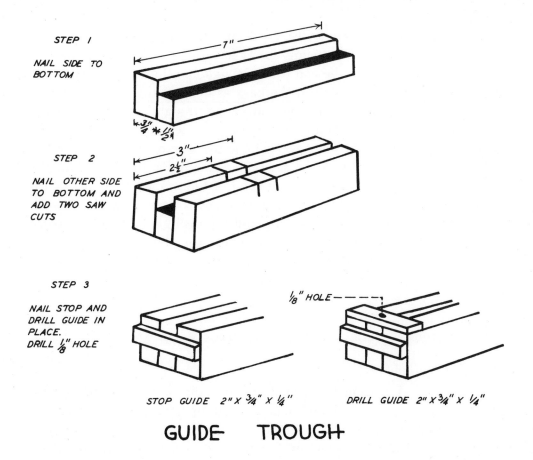

STEP 1

NAIL SIDE TO BOTTOM

7"

3/4" * 1 1/2"

STEP 2

NAIL OTHER SIDE TO BOTTOM AND ADD TWO SAW CUTS

3"

2 1/2"

STEP 3

NAIL STOP AND DRILL GUIDE IN PLACE.
DRILL 1/8" HOLE

1/8" HOLE

STOP GUIDE 2" X 3/4" X 1/4"

DRILL GUIDE 2" X 3/4" X 1/4"

## GUIDE TROUGH

*San Diego City Schools*

and nails will be needed. Other incidentals can be obtained when necessary. Most important of all to the efficiency of the project is a small piece of equipment called a guide trough which the teacher will have to make.

### Making a Guide Trough

A guide trough is a carpentry device which assures accuracy when making the arms and legs for a marionette.

The trough is made of three pieces of soft pine. Cut two pieces for the sides, seven by three-quarters by one-and-one-half inches. Cut one piece for the bottom, seven by three-quarters by one-half-inch. Nail the sides to the bottom so that there will be a trough between them

157

one-half-inch wide and one-half-inch deep. Make two slots in the sides of the trough to use when sawing dowel for arms and legs. Measure two and one-half inches from the end of the trough and draw a line across the top of the trough. Saw a slot on the lines as deep as the trough. Draw a second line three inches from the end of the trough and saw a second slot. Finally, make a stop and a drill guide. Cut two pieces of thin wood, each three-quarters by two inches. Nail one piece across the middle of the end of the trough closest to the saw cuts. This is for the stop. Nail the other piece across the top of the same end of the trough. Drill an eighth-of-an-inch hole in the middle of this piece. This is the drill guide. A small opening will be left between the stop and the drill guide. Should a piece of dowel get stuck in the trough, the dowel can then be released by poking a nail through the opening. Always clamp the trough to a table when using it.

TEACHER GUIDANCE FOR MAKING A MARIONETTE

*Making a Marionette*

A marionette is made of movable parts of wood tied together with carpet thread and manipulated by strings. When a guide trough is used and directions are followed step by step, production moves along briskly. The dimensions used will make men marionettes fourteen inches high. The size may be reduced proportionately for women and children.

*Making the Head*

Make the head large as compared to the size of the body. It is made of two parts and sewed together. The face is a mask made from strips of paper pasted together; the back is a square of muslin stuffed with cotton.

Make a model for the mask in Plasticine. It should be about two and one-half inches long and proportionately wide. Exaggerate the features to accentuate the character of the marionette. When the modeling is completed, lay it aside and start cutting strips of paper for the mask. Cut enough newspaper strips for the first three layers and paper-towel strips for the last layer. Make the strips about five inches long and a little more than one-quarter of an inch wide. Mix a bowlful of thin wallpaper paste, using an egg beater. Dip a newspaper strip into the bowl of paste. Smooth the paste on the strip by drawing it through the thumb and forefinger of the other hand. Lay the strip across the middle of the Plasticine model. Press it down firmly to squeeze out extra paste. Repeat until the whole face is covered, being sure that the strips overlap a little. Put on a second layer of strips lengthwise. Put on a third layer crosswise. Change to paper-towel strips for the last layer and put them on crosswise, but in the direction opposite to that of the newspaper strips beneath. Let the mask dry thoroughly and remove from the Plasticine. Trim around the edge of the mask with scissors and bind with strips of paper towels. Gently sand the face with No. 0 sandpaper.

Now make the back of the head. Cut a piece of muslin eight inches square. Lay a wad of cotton in the middle. Gather the four corners of the muslin together and stuff them into the back of the mask. Sew the muslin to the mask, using an over-and-over stitch. The stitches

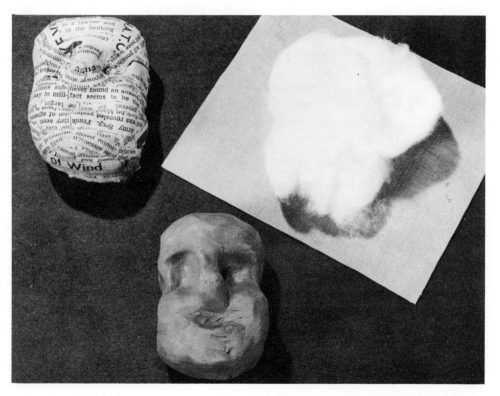

will not show when the hair is put on later. The face can be painted now, but it is better to wait until later.

*Making the Torso*

Make the torso of three-quarter-inch pine. Use a C clamp when sawing. Cut a piece of wood five inches by two and a half inches. Draw a waistline across the piece of wood three inches from one end; the larger part is for the chest, the smaller for the hips. Measure one-half inch from each end of the waistline and put a pencil mark. Draw a line from the pencil mark on one side to each corner on that side. Do the same on the other side. Saw across the waistline, cutting the torso into two parts. Saw off the side edges on chest and hips. Join the chest and hips together with a hinge made of a piece of muslin tacked to the chest and the hips. The hinge permits the marionette to bend when the strings are pulled. Clamp the chest to the table and drill holes in each shoulder corner and one in the middle for the neck. Clamp the hips to a table and drill a hole in each hip corner. When assembling the marionette remember that the hinge is on the front.

*Making the Arms*

The arms are made of half-inch dowel. Each arm has two parts, upper and lower. Clamp the guide trough to a table. Insert a piece of dowel and saw four pieces, using the two-and-a-half inch slot. Drill a hole in both ends of the two pieces of dowel for the upper arms. Drill a hole in one end of the pieces for the lower arms. Tie the arms together loosely with carpet thread. Tie the arms to the torso.

*Making the Legs*

Each leg has two parts. The lower leg is longer than the upper. Cut two pieces of dowel at the two-and-a-half inch slot for the upper legs. Drill a hole in each end. Cut two pieces for the lower legs at the three-inch slot. Drill a hole in one end. Tie the legs loosely together with carpet thread. Tie the upper legs to the hip holes.

*Making the Hands*

Hands should be big in order to be seen when the marionette gesticulates. Hands may be carved of balsa wood or made of muslin as described for hand puppets. Muslin hands are attached to the arms by

160

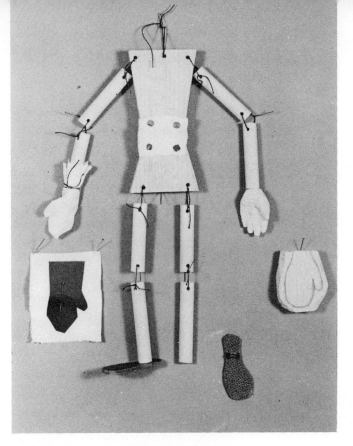

gluing the cuffs of the mittens (hands) to the ends of the arms. In addition, tie a piece of carpet thread around the cuffs. Paint the hands later.

### Making the Feet

Make the feet of cigar-box wood or Masonite. Use a coping saw for wood; a power saw for Masonite. Draw a pattern for a foot and make it large. Trace the pattern on the material to be used and cut out two feet. Drive a nail through the bottom of each foot into the end of the dowel for the lower leg. Paint the feet.

### Costuming the Marionettes

Costumes should be made very simply. Long full skirts, full sleeves, and trousers cover skinny arms and legs. Blouses and jackets are made with kimono sleeves.

A good selection of materials and colors adds to the dramatic effect of the show. Prints, bits of lace and velvet, soft cottons, and rayons all work up well. Stiff or heavy materials interfere with the action of the strings. All clothing should be loosely fitted to the marionette. Since marionettes are made in only three sizes, a pattern committee can make a set of patterns for all the children to share.

### Putting on the Head

First tie a loop of carpet thread through the neck hole on the torso and then proceed to attach the head as follows: Thread a needle with carpet thread. Double and make a knot in the end. Insert the needle in the mask about where the ears should be and push the needle through the head, leaving an end four inches long. Cut off the thread four inches from the head and make a knot. Put the ends of the thread through the neck loop in opposite directions and tie together firmly. Do not cut off the ends. Thread the needle again in the same way and put it through the mask under the chin. Leave ends about three inches long and knot the loose end. Put the ends through the neck loop in opposite directions and tie firmly. Do not cut off ends, but poke them all under the blouse. The ends of the threads are not cut off because carpet thread stretches and the knots will have to be undone and tied tighter at intervals.

### Finishing the Head and Hands

Carpet warp, cotton roving, raveled burlap, and yarn are

*San Diego City Schools*

all good for hair. A generous amount should be used, about a hundred strands for carpet warp. Lay the strands across a piece of narrow tape and sew down the middle by hand or on a sewing machine. Glue the hair to the head. Girls are clever at arranging hair for women and giving men a neat haircut.

Now is the time to paint the face. Protect the costume with a piece of paper. Use oil paints because they reflect light on the stage. Stress the character of the marionette when painting. Paint the hands to match the skin color of the face.

Costumed and painted, the marionette is now ready to have the strings attached.

163

*Attaching the Strings*

   Elementary school children can handle seven strings with practice. Tan or black carpet thread is used. Cut seven strings six feet long. This may be too long when the strings are attached to the control stick, but the thread can always be cut shorter. Sew a string to each side of the head on a level with the eyes. Put the needle through both the mask and

164

*Denver Museum of Art*

the muslin. Tie the arm strings around the wrist. Put knee strings on men, girls, and boys. Women in long skirts do not need them. Put the knee strings through the long trousers with a needle. Put a thumbtack in the middle of the back of the hips. Tie a string around the thumbtack and put the string through the clothing with a needle.

### Making the Control Stick

Ordinarily two controls are used for a marionette, but since this is a simplified project, one is sufficient. The strings are fastened to the control stick with thumbtacks. The control stick is held in one hand, the other hand thus being free to pull the strings.

Use three pieces of lath for the control stick, which is made like a cross with two transverse bars. Cut a piece of lath ten inches long for the centerpiece of the cross. Cut two pieces of lath eight inches long for the bars. Put the centerpiece on the table and place one bar crosswise on top one inch from an end. Nail it in place. Put the second bar two inches from the first and nail in place. Put thumbtacks a half inch from the ends of the centerpiece and on both bars. This is the top of the control stick, and the bars are at the front.

Tie the strings around the thumbtacks as follows, being sure that when finished the marionette will face the front. Tie both knee strings to the tack at the front of the control stick. Tie each arm string to a tack on the first bar. Tie each head string to the tack on the second bar. Tie the hip string to the tack at the back of the control stick. Hold up the control stick and readjust the strings so that no string is too short or too long. The full weight of the puppet is carried by the head strings. The strings should be long enough for the feet of the puppet to touch the floor when the child holds the control stick chest-high. It is possible that the strings may have to be changed again when the child stands on the bridge and lowers his marionette to the stage.

### Further Experience for Mature Children

Children who through practice have become skillful in using the control stick which has been described may wish to try handling two sticks. Cut a piece of lath or other light wood twelve inches long. Remove the knee strings from the control stick and fasten them to the new stick with thumbtacks. The first control stick is held, as formerly, in the right hand; the second stick in the left hand. Marionettes can be made to walk much more realistically when the knee strings are manipulated separately from the other strings.

## Making the Storage Bags

Although storage bags are not essential, they are most convenient to have for a bag keeps the marionette fresh and clean. Each bag should have an identification tag.

### TEACHER GUIDANCE FOR BUILDING A CLASSROOM STAGE

Constructing the stage is as rewarding an experience for the carpentry committee as is making marionettes and painting scenery for other groups. The stage, if it is to be the work of the children, must be of simple construction. It will not have the refinements associated with a marionette theater, but it will serve the classroom purpose very well. The building of a permanent marionette stage is difficult even for adults and beyond the carpentry skills of children. A temporary stage, however, can be constructed from materials of little or no cost—apple boxes, kindergarten tables, two long pieces of wood, plywood or Celotex, heavy cardboard, and a sundry assortment of nails, screws, eyes, wire, curtain rings, and string.

The teacher meets with the carpentry committee to identify the problems of construction. She will explain that a marionette stage consists of three parts: the stage proper where the marionettes perform; a higher platform in back, called a bridge, where the puppeteers stand to manipulate the marionettes; and a framework in front of the stage for the curtains.

## Making the Bridge

Use two old kindergarten tables placed end to end for the bridge. Three or four puppeteers will be able to stand on them at one time. If two more tables are available, put them in back of the first tables. A larger bridge is always more comfortable and safer to stand on.

## Making the Stage

Use eight apple boxes. Put them bottom side up on the floor in front of the bridge; four in back against the legs of the tables, and four in front.

166

*San Diego City Schools*

*Making the Stage Wall*

A wall at the rear of the stage serves two purposes: to conceal the legs of the puppeteers standing on the bridge, and to provide a place for putting up the scenery for the play. Use panels of plywood or Celotex for the wall. Each panel should extend from the stage to the waist of a puppeteer standing on the bridge, very probably twenty-four inches. Place a panel at one end of the stage and push it back against the edge of the table top. Hold the panel upright and drive nails through it into the edge of the table. Drive a couple of nails into the stage floor to brace the bottom of the panel. Put up as many panels as necessary to go across the back of the stage.

*Making the Framework*

The framework is built in front of the stage. Two wires are stretched across it for hanging up the curtains. The framework is com- 167 posed of two six-foot uprights supported by four apple boxes. Use a piece of surfaced soft pine six feet by four by two inches for each upright. Put one upright at the front corner of the stage against the apple box. Nail it to the apple box. Put an apple box on end next to the upright and nail them together. Put a couple of bricks in the apple box to keep it steady. Put a second apple box on top of the first. Nail the ends together. Nail side to the upright. Put up the other upright in the same way. Put a screw eye on the stage side of each upright near the top and stretch a wire between the two screws. Put a screw eye in each upright twenty inches above the stage and stretch a wire between them. The framework is finished.

Large pieces of plywood or cardboard may be put over the floor of the stage to cover the bottom of the boxes. However, the better choice is plywood, because cardboard deadens the clatter of the marionettes' feet.

### Decorating the Framework

The framework may be decorated in either of two ways. It may be painted an attractive color, including, of course, the sides of the boxes used for the stage; or the uprights may be painted and the remainder covered with corrugated paper. Place a screen on each side of the stage for wings to conceal the puppeteers and workers backstage.

### Making the Curtains

Curtains should be made of soft material which hangs in folds when gathered. Make a pair of curtains for the stage. Sew a diagonal row of small curtain rings on the inside of each curtain so that when the curtains are closed the rings form a V. Put the curtains on the wire and thumbtack the sides to the uprights. Put a screw eye on the back of each upright on a level with the wire. Run a long piece of soft cotton string through the screw eye and the rings on each curtain. Tie the string to the last ring. Sew a weight to the front corner of each curtain. Make a curtain to hang on the top wire. It should hang over the stage curtain about two inches.

### Lighting the Show

A baby spotlight may be put on the top box supporting the uprights of the framework. Bridge lamps may also be used backstage.

*Painting the Background Scenes*

Every marionette play needs an attractive background. A change of scenes between acts adds interest for the audience and color to the performance. A small committee can volunteer to paint the scenes with tempera. Measure the size of the back wall to be sure that the paper will fit the space.

Backgrounds are simple to install on the stage wall, and a change for every act presents no problem. To install more than one background, the last scene is first thumbtacked or fastened with cellulose tape to the back wall. The other scenes are put over it in reverse order of the play, with a separate fastening used for each one. By this method the scenes can be removed one by one and it is a matter of only a few minutes to replace them for the next performance.

*Stage Props*

A few props will probably be necessary for the play. When placed on the stage they must be either backstage or at the front, leaving the center and sides clear. Props placed at the side interfere with the entrance and exit of the marionettes. Branches should not be used for trees because the strings of the marionettes often become tangled in them.

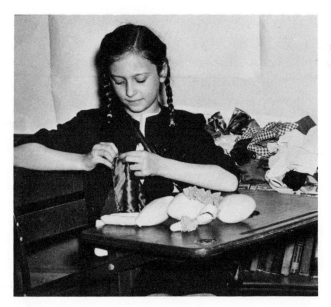

*Department of Education,*
*Baltimore, Maryland*

## The Last Act

After the final show is over the stage can be dismantled, the wire rolled up, and the marionettes taken home. All that is left as a reminder of the rewarding and happy experience is a small pile of lumber in the storeroom waiting for next year's class of eager children.

## Cloth Marionettes

While wooden marionettes are successful, a teacher may wish at some time to try another method for making them. Cloth marionettes are not difficult to make and are made in the same way that a rag doll is made. Children have great fun stuffing the different parts of the body and making the costumes.

### SUMMARY OF PUPPETRY

A delightful sequence of making puppets and marionettes can be developed by teachers of an elementary school if class projects are planned together. By doing this, it is possible for children to make different kinds of puppets and marionettes in different grades and so have a broad experience.

# REFERENCE MATERIAL

1. *Making a Mural.* Filmstrip, 37 frames, color; produced by McGraw-Hill Book Company, Inc.

   *Mural Making.* 16mm. film, 6 min., sound, color; produced by International Film Bureau, Inc.

2. Becker, Edith C. *Adventures With Scissors and Paper.* Scranton, Pa.: International Textbook Company, 1959.

3. D'Amico, Victor. *Creative Teaching in Art.* Scranton, Pa.: International Textbook Company, 1942. (Chap. III, "The Child as Painter.")

4. See preceding reference.

5. *How to Make and Use Dioramas.* 16mm. film, 20 min., sound, color; produced by Syracuse University. (Teacher background.)

6. D'Amico, Victor, Frances Wilson, and Moreen Maser. *Art for the Family*. New York: The Museum of Modern Art, 1954. pp. 94–95.

7. *How to Make a Puppet.* 16mm. film, 12 min., sound, color; produced by International Film Bureau, Inc.

8. Lorenzini, Carlo (pseudonym: Collodi). *The Adventures of Pinocchio*. New York: The Macmillan Company (The New Children's Classics), 1951.

9. *Puppetry: String Marionettes.* 16mm. film, 11 min., black and white; produced by Encyclopaedia Britannica Films, Inc.

Jagendorf, Moritz. *The First Book of Puppets.* New York: Franklin Watts, Inc., 1952.

Lewis, Roger. *Puppets and Marionettes.* New York: Alfred A. Knopf, Inc., 1952.

## READER PARTICIPATION

Organize a small group of fellow students or teaching associates and make a mural.

Make and learn to operate a puppet or a marionette.

Plan how you could construct from salvaged materials a stage in a classroom for a marionette or a puppet show.

Try to attend in the near future a marionette show given by children.

# 9

# *Each Child*
## *Will Find His Way*

What makes an art program? Actually the materials and activities are the same for all grades, but interests and motivations vary. Children work with paint, paper, clay, and chalk on every level. Designs, landscapes, figures, and crafts are done in every grade. Personal interests, life experiences, and practical needs are incentives for creative work year after year. The teacher is the judge of the best program for her class, for only she knows the children intimately and can intelligently select those art experiences which will contribute the most to growth.

There is opportunity for each child to find his own way of expressing experiences through creative work, and since he is not held to adult standards of performance, each child's art will be representative of his own capacity. The value and enjoyment of the creative experience will be greater for all children when they have been helped to build strong inner feelings of security in art.

### DESIGN

In all activities that comprise every program of art experiences for children, the goal of creative work is good design. Whenever evaluation takes place, the quality of the design is of first importance. Children make designs for two reasons: drawing and painting for enjoyment, and for the decoration of craft work.

Children draw and paint designs with a vigor that is refreshing. Design is chiefly self-motivated—a natural way of expressing space and color relationships. (See color plate No. 17.) Teachers have found that if design is presented theoretically children respond with a stereotyped piece of work; when it is spontaneous, children's work shows an instinctive use of the principle of design—unity with variety—to an astonishing degree for their maturation. It is also characteristic that many of their designs have a strong feeling of mood.

Children, we are told, live on the fringes of our culture. They have a ready acceptance of prophecy and nothing is too incredible to be believed. It is not to be wondered, then, that creative work in design has many of the attributes of the work of forward-thinking artists. Teachers see this over and over again in the work of children who, it may be reasonably believed, have had little or no visual stimulation that is suggestive of non-objective or abstract art. Children seem to have a natural sophistication which, while disarmingly childlike and primitive in render-

*Pittsburgh Public Schools*

ing, is also surprisingly mature, and they will often accomplish what adults strive in vain to do. Children are sensitive to contemporary design, and also have a natural flair for primitive design, probably because it is so direct and forceful.

Children are continually making designs for the decoration of craft work. In this the teacher needs to keep the right approach to related design, guiding children to realize that the material of the craft determines choice of motif, color, line, dark and light, and texture. This is strikingly demonstrated in primitive art where design is natural and untutored. A teacher can do two things to clarify the concept of related design. She can provide visual experiences which illustrate related design by showing children fine examples of pottery, textiles, and other crafts, and she can guide children through evaluation to a better understanding of the concept of related design.

Recognizing that design is fundamental to every activity in the art program, a choice among many possible activities must nevertheless be made for this discussion. Such art activities as making mobiles, stabiles, masks, collages and posters, as well as wire sculpture, contemporary stitchery, three-dimensional arrangements on a picture plane, and designs of line, angles, and space have been selected. These are problems in which design is obviously a factor.

MAKING A MOBILE

Mobiles are a design form particularly representative of contemporary culture. A pioneer artist in this type of design is Alexander Calder. He has been working in this field for many years. One of his early masterpieces was among the first mobiles purchased by the Museum of Modern Art in New York City.

A mobile is a three-dimensional, suspended design that changes with every shift of the air current. Its movements may be gentle and languid one minute, abrupt and swift the next, thus presenting a fascinating and constantly changing study in line and color. A mobile may carry out a realistic theme, such as a study of birds or fish; it is equally, or perhaps more successful, when abstract shapes are used.

Making a mobile is a thought-provoking art experience. Because of the subtle design and good craftsmanship it entails, why not save this rich experience for upper-grade children? Of course, should a

*San Diego City Schools*

teacher find that a mature class of primary children would profit from this kind of art activity, there is no reason why a simplified approach cannot be used. During a holiday season, making a mobile might prove a welcome change; the results of such an endeavor can be very attractive for such occasions as Christmas, St. Valentine's Day, and Easter. But do not turn a coat hanger into a so-called mobile. If pieces of wire are needed to make a mobile, the teacher can cut them with wire cutters from a wire hanger; retaining the original shape of an object that is used as a base for a mobile is most unfortunate. Nothing can disguise the fact that it is, and will continue to be, a coat hanger.

      Mobiles may be introduced to sixth-graders by showing the color film *Make a Mobile*.[1] The framework of a mobile can be made of wire or thin strips of balsa wood. Doweling can be used with equal effectiveness.

      Bend baling wire or 14- to 18-gauge copper wire into a free-flowing line for the basic structure of the mobile. This may or may not form a completed contour. Line is the most important art factor in a mobile, and children should experiment until they are satisfied with the shape of the structure. When the wire is ready, hang the mobile on the picture wire. The children are thereby able to work on all sides of the mobile and to evaluate their progress from all angles. Since each pendant is a design in itself, its position on the mobile must be carefully selected. As the pendants are suspended on the wire, one by one, they act to balance the mobile. Balance is essential to the rhythmic movement of a mobile.

Mobiles of wood are equally handsome. Cut several pieces of one-eighth-inch balsa wood or doweling of different lengths for the framework. Choose a piece for the major crosspiece at the top of the mobile and suspend the other pieces below it. Use threads of different lengths. The suspending thread does not have to be tied in the middle of the piece of wood, but can be tied at any place and balanced later by the pendants hung on it. Experiment until a pleasing arrangement of horizontal lines has been achieved. The wood may be painted one color or different colors, or not painted at all. Hang the mobile on a picture wire and suspend the pendants with thread so that the mobile is balanced and will move and change in the breeze.

Pendants, the suspended objects on a mobile, are made from a wide assortment of materials which children can collect and bring to school. Clever pendants have been made from such ordinary things as Ping-Pong balls, metal rings, bottle tops, pine cones, scraps of plastic, pieces of tin, beads, and every kind of paper that can be found. Paper can be folded into unusual shapes. Cutouts of paper, thin wood, or tin give a feeling of airiness in keeping with the spirit of a mobile. Color gives accent to shapes and helps to develop the theme and mood. Quiet little patterns of lines, dots, crosses, and other symbols can be painted on pendants. Each pendant is suspended by a piece of black silk or thread; hence a spool of one or the other must be provided. In addition to this spool, wire and wood, the following materials and tools are also needed: all-purpose white glue, a pair of tin snips, a pair of wire cutters, and scissors. A long piece of picture wire should be put up somewhere in the room to hang the mobiles on while children are working on them. Later, when completed, the mobiles may be displayed in various places in the room, a few at a time so that each may be separately appreciated.

Evaluation of mobiles stimulates discussion as to how successfully the principle of design—unity with variety—has been accomplished. Making a mobile is a new and exciting design experience for children.

Wire and wood mobiles are very different in character. Both are interesting to make.

MAKING A STABILE

Stabiles[2] reflect the tenor of the times towards space and abstract thinking in design. An artist of note working in this field is Richard Lippold. His work is on display in many art galleries.

A stabile is a three-dimensional structural form projected into space. Whereas the mobile is representative of movement in space, the stabile is static in design, but expresses movement through the arrangement of its linear parts. Stabiles can be made of wire or wood, or a combination of both.

In making a wire stabile, the wire must be pliable enough

*Courtesy of Mrs. Hook Sutherland, Los Angeles*     177

for children to handle and bend with ease. One long wire or several short lengths of wire can be used. Some children find that a long piece of wire gets in the way and hampers their movements. The gauges of aluminum wire suggested for mobiles are also suitable for stabiles.

Stabiles made by children should be mounted on a base. The best possible type of base is a block of balsa wood. Balsa wood is soft enough to permit the insertion of the ends of any piece of wire in the wood, and thus provides an anchor for the stabile from the time the child starts to work with the wire.

The tools required are very simple: a small nail saw or a coping saw for cutting balsa wood, blunt-nosed pliers, a wire cutter, a gun stapler loaded with quarter-inch or half-inch staples, and plenty of dressmaker pins. Children will find that they can hold the wire in place with pins and then secure the wire permanently with a gun stapler.

Areas within the stabile can become a decorative feature of the finished work, provided the interpenetration of space is not lost. If, for example, a crossing wire forms a loop, twine and yarn can be strung across the opening to give an interlacing effect. Enclosed areas made by the crossing of three or four wires can be filled in with colored tissue paper or cellophane. Another ingenious method of filling an area is to use a piece of colored paper perforated by a paper punch. This carries further the feeling of openness, characteristic of a stabile. Accents of paper must be carefully glued in place.

When fine wire is used for interlacing, wrap the ends tightly around the heavier stabile wire and cut them off neatly so that no ends will show. When string is used as a means of adding decorative interest, a drop of transparent, fast-setting glue on the wire of the stabile will hold the string in place, provided a clothespin is clamped on the wire while the glue sets. When satisfied with the wire structure, remove the pins and fasten the stabile to the balsa wood with the gun stapler. If no gun stapler is available, use a tack hammer and ordinary staples.

Sensitivity to line direction is required when making a stabile of wire. The criteria of a good stabile are: the right amount of decorative accent; a basic form that is not overloaded.

A stabile of balsa wood is considerably easier for a child to construct than one of wire. All that is needed for a stabile of balsa wood is a nail saw or coping saw (the former is better because it has no blade which can break), plenty of dressmaker pins, an awl or nail, scissors, and

*Courtesy of Mrs. Hook Sutherland, Los Angeles*

possibly some all-purpose white glue. It is not necessary for a stabile to be straight and angular in design. Curves can be made if one-eighth-inch balsa doweling is used. To make curves, wrap the doweling in a moist, hot towel for an hour or two, then bend it into a curve. Balsa wood lends itself to preliminary experimentation because it permits the child to build up structural pieces with pins. When a satisfying design is achieved, press the pins firmly in place; if any ends protrude through thin pieces of wood, remove them with a wire cutter. All-purpose white glue can be used to secure two parts wherever needed. Since balsa wood doweling comes only in very small diameters, half-rounds can be glued together with all-purpose white glue and secured with a few rubber bands while the glue is setting.

One quality of design to be sought in a wood stabile is the feeling of thrust: thrust in every direction—forward, backward, upward, downward, and obliquely. Like a piece of sculpture, a stabile, whether of wire or of balsa wood, should be pleasing from every angle. This art        179

*Courtesy of Mrs. Hook Sutherland, Los Angeles*

principle is often difficult for a child to follow as he is preconditioned by previous art experiences to working on a picture plane, and, except for clay work, has had fewer experiences in three-dimensional forms.

A delightful and quick art experience is making a miniature stabile of ordinary toothpicks. This activity can only be satisfactorily completed if transparent, fast-setting glue is used. This kind of glue is usually available in small-size tubes. Only a very small amount of glue is needed for a toothpick stabile.

To make the foundation pattern for the miniature stabile, the child inserts into a balsa wood base a number of toothpicks at varying angles to form the uprights on which the stabile will be built. To anchor these upright toothpicks firmly in the balsa wood, make tiny holes in the wood base with a small awl or nail. Put a drop of glue on the end of the toothpicks before inserting them in the tiny holes.

180

Build up the miniature stabile by gluing toothpicks in place, one after another, at varying distances apart and at varying angles, using a drop of fast-drying glue. A pair of tweezers greatly facilitates the handling of the toothpicks.

The miniature stabile is a further expression of interpenetration of space for the child.

WIRE SCULPTURE

Wire sculpture is an outcome of present cultural patterns in art, patterns which are departing from old conventions and moving into new frontiers of design. Wire sculpture is a linear expression of imaginative and natural forms and is a new experience for children. It is most successfully undertaken in the upper grades. Action is achieved much more easily in wire sculpture than in painting or drawing because the child is not perplexed by the problem of foreshortening. When bending wire, a

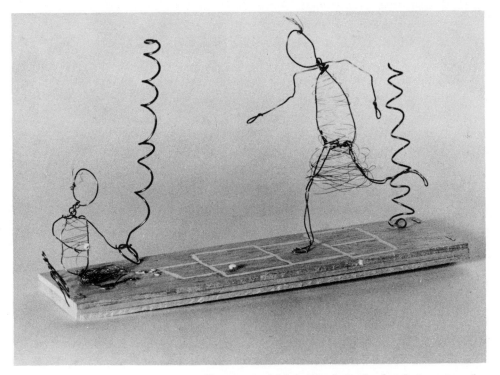

*Courtesy of Mrs. Hook Sutherland, Los Angeles*     181

child must usually catch the action in his first attempt or he is not likely to catch the spirit of the action at all. If the first attempt fails, he had better start again with a new piece of wire. Wire sculpture requires balance, an important art principle which children are not often called upon to employ, except in a mobile. In rendering subjects such as a running football player or a ballet dancer, balance is essential.

Because wire sculpture is a linear expression of imaginative and natural forms, dragons, witches, witch doctors, men from Mars, creatures of the sea, and prehistoric animals are effective subjects. Animals with distinctive characteristics with which children are familiar, such as the giraffe and antelope, are also good subjects for wire sculpture.

For wire sculpture, any available wire that is easy for children's hands to bend is practical. It must be very pliable, but hold its shape after bending. Sixteen-gauge aluminum wire is good for sculpture in wire.

The tools required are: a wire cutter, a gun stapler loaded with quarter-inch staples, which will probably be used only when the finished sculpture is fastened to the base, and blunt-nosed pliers, should the wire be too resistant for the children to bend with their fingers.

Prepare a piece of balsa wood for the base, to which the wire sculpture will later be attached. Lighter wires can be wrapped around the original wire shape to achieve greater contour in the animal or figure the child has made. Because one should be able to see through this type of sculpture, nothing should impede the vision of the viewer.

Not much guidance can be given children in making a wire sculpture; they just have to experiment and find out for themselves. There is one factor, however, that does influence their understanding of this type of sculpture. For many children, a wire-sculptured form, such as that of a person in an active position, has little reality. "It is not even a skeleton," as one child said. But if the action of a figure is given support by providing some indication of its environment, the children immediately seem to see the personality or characteristics of what they have made. Imagination quickly fills in the details not shown.

A fine wire, such as the kind that comes on spools, can be wrapped around a wire sculpture to add to the depth. Or the heavier wire of the figure itself can be used again. Spirals can be made by wrapping a piece of heavier wire around a pencil, as was done to represent trees in the illustration.

182

CONTEMPORARY STITCHERY

Stitchery, like all forms of creative expression, has a historical background. But, unlike the other arts, its possibilities for expression by children have only recently been fully explored. Perhaps the word "recently" should be qualified. Referring back to Cizek's words quoted in Chapter 2, we recall that he answered the child who felt so inadequate in drawing by suggesting that she "embroider" her art idea instead of trying to draw it. From what we are told by Cizek's biographer, the result was satisfying to the child.

Today, stitchery offers children a novel experience and a new technique to learn. Young children enjoy stitchery just as much as their older brothers and sisters. Most boys of elementary school age are not yet inhibited in practicing this art when it is properly presented. The results of contemporary stitchery are new and different.

Easily acquired materials and tools are used in stitchery: a piece of fabric, thread and yarn, a needle and scissors. Wood or cardboard frames to which the fabric is stapled or tacked are helpful in keeping the fabric taut when large size work is undertaken and detail introduced by children in the upper grades. Young children usually find a frame more bothersome than helpful. Thimbles are not necessary and certainly would be obnoxious to the boys. Any fabric which a needle can pass through easily and that is comfortable to hold can be used. For sewing, there are D.M.C. embroidery threads and different kinds of yarn available. Bumpy yarn and pliable twine can be couched on the fabric with a sewing thread.

Beginners need to know the following basic stitches: the running stitch for outlining and a filler called the satin stitch for solid areas. Equally simple are the cross-stitch, the lazy daisy and chain stitch, which are practically the same, and the back stitch. Another stitch for older children is a plain couching stitch. Many children are inventive once they get started on stitchery and will develop their own stitches for making pigtails, curls, crew haircuts, the center of a flower, or the stripes on a tiger.

Each child draws his own picture or design on paper. It can then either be drawn freehand or traced on the fabric to be used. For added color, texture, interest and accent, older children can apply as appliqué pieces of different fabrics to the basic background. Pinned to

183

*Department of Public Instruction, Hawaii*

the background fabric, the appliqué is sewn in place with a running stitch or with a new stitchery technique called the buttonhole stitch, which is easy to do.

An excellent source of information for teachers undertaking stitchery for the first time is the book *Adventures in Stitches.*[3]

The background color of the fabric can be of importance in unifying the composition. When the background is allowed to show, it will add to the attractiveness of the finished work.

Contemporary stitchery is an entirely different art concept from embroidery per se. It makes an excellent classroom project; when a large piece of fabric is used on a frame, several children can work on it at the same time. For a large project of this kind, a frame of wood is obviously essential.

In evaluating contemporary stitchery, the same art principles apply as in evaluating painting and drawing. The composition should repeat lines and colors, provide contrast, and modify shapes in order to

184

achieve a feeling of repetition with differentiations in contour and size. The children make a picture, abstract or realistic, with needle and thread.

COLLAGES

Collage is a French word meaning the gluing together of a composition on a picture plane. It may have a subject or be an abstract arrangement of shapes and colors. This is called a surface pattern. A collage is distinctive in quality, and is generally considered to be a collection of heterogeneous pieces or scraps of paper and pictures combined into a unified, meaningful whole. Max Ernst is a contemporary artist who uses collages as a serious art form.

*Courtesy of Mrs. Loren Campbell, San Diego*    185

A collage[4] is made from collected materials—and therein lies the fun for children. They like to look through magazines and clip pictures and swatches of color. Discarded greeting cards and scraps of gift wrapping paper also find many uses. Often newspapers will have just what a child is seeking. Another source of clippings is the discarded drawings and paintings done in class. Often a child does not need to rely solely on his own work, but may draw upon a common collection saved by the teacher. Many times a drawing or painting that is disappointing as a whole will contain one or two excellent parts which can be cut out and trimmed to fit a particular space. When the pieces are assembled, the result is charming and naive.

A collage subject was once chosen by a sixth-grade boy who was an ardent baseball fan. He found more material than he could use in the sports sections of daily newspapers. The gray-white of printed news articles and the strong blacks and grays of photographs were dramatically set off by a color accent: two yellow stubs from a pair of tickets for a ball game.

The composition of a paper collage is more attractive when its arrangement is compact and tight, with few or no areas of the background paper showing through the pattern. Adding details by painting or drawing on the collage detracts from the purpose of the art experience. Everything that is used should be found by the children themselves. If something necessary cannot be found, the child is challenged to make another arrangement before gluing, rather than resort to drawing in details.

When a collage is completed it is, indeed, a synthesis of feeling, visual perceptions, ingenuity, and individuality.

## THREE-DIMENSIONAL ARRANGEMENTS ON A PICTURE PLANE

The concept of design is furthered by arranging on a flat surface in a pleasing and expressive composition objects that are emphatically three-dimensional in form.

Since children are inveterate collectors, they will have fun searching for what they need for three-dimensional arrangements. Nature will, for example, provide dried grasses, grains, and leaves, bulky seeds and seed pods, dried beans and peas, nuts, pine cones, sea shells, pebbles and small bits of colorful rocks, and pieces of bark. Cereals, such as different kinds of rice and processed breakfast foods, are also suitable. A long list of

186

*Courtesy of Mrs. Loren Campbell, San Diego*

manufactured articles, such as snaps, buttons, the working parts of an old clock, pieces of doweling cut into thick and thin disks, bottle stoppers, keys, tube caps, and parts of discarded toys can also be put to use. Surplus material can be sorted and stored in boxes to be shared by all the children.

Chipboard or thin plywood makes a good background for a three-dimensional composition of this kind. Many trial arrangements should be placed on the background before the parts are glued in place. The child is continuously evaluating and subconsciously arriving at aesthetic decisions while he works. As the design arrangement nears completion, the elements of design seem to emerge spontaneously; the principle of unity with variety is evident in the imaginative combination of the varied materials.

When a child is truly satisfied with his work—and he may have to think about it for a day or two—he is ready to glue the objects into place. All-purpose white glue is best to use, particularly if metal pieces      187 are to be attached. If the child applies the glue with a toothpick, sticky fingers, which are a hindrance to efficient gluing, can be avoided.

To repeat, a child must find by himself everything that he uses. Otherwise, half of the learning in the experience is lost. If he cannot find something that he feels is essential to his arrangement, he is challenged to attempt a new arrangement.

Making three-dimensional arrangements is one of several art experiences which are peculiarly well fitted to help each child to "see."

### MASKS

Masks of witch doctors, savages, idols and pagan gods are challenging design problems. A dramatic introduction to mask making in the upper grades is the color film *The Loon's Necklace.*[5]

To make a mask, model the face from scrap clay, using a board covered with oilcloth as a base. Exaggerate the features so that they will be well-defined when the work is completed. Cover the model with Vaseline. Cut newspaper into one-inch strips, dip one strip at a time into a bowl of fairly thin wallpaper paste, and cover the clay with a layer of overlapping strips. Press the strips firmly into the indentations in the clay. When the paper is dry, repeat the same procedure two or three times, pasting each new layer of strips in the opposite direction from the layer below. Leave the mask on the clay and put the whole thing on stilts to dry. When dry, remove the mask and scrape it clean on the inside. Bind the edges with paper strips dipped in wallpaper paste. Paint the mask with tempera and decorate. Buttons and beads can be used for eyes; excelsior, frayed rope, yarn, wood shavings, and packing straw are some of the materials which can be used for hair. Rings in the nose and ears add to the awesome look of the mask.

When completed, a mask is an example of good workmanship and highly imaginative design.

### MAKING POSTERS

Making posters, the last of the selected design experiences, is totally different from the other three, both in approach and in meaning. Posters are to advertise something—a school picnic, a parent-teacher meeting, a new safety rule—and everything in a poster must lead the eye

*San Francisco Unified School District*

*Board of Education,
Rochester, New York*

189

to the message. Color should be chosen accordingly, with the strongest colors used for important places. Simplification is the answer to good poster design, not a pictorial theme with a mass of detail.

Cut paper is a satisfying technique for children to use in making posters. Cutout letters are simple and plain, and poster papers offer a wide choice of colors. Letters may be shifted around until the best possible arrangement is found. Then, if a light pencil line has been drawn around each letter, the child knows exactly where to put it when it is pasted on the poster.

A quick type of freehand lettering which a skillful fifth- or sixth-grade child can master is done with a disposable felt pen available with inks of various colors. These pens never present the problem of dripping color on a poster, as frequently happens when a paint brush is used. Guide lines should be drawn lightly in pencil on the poster and the letters spaced in the same way before using the felt pen. This tool is not suitable if heavy, bulky lettering is used.

The function of a poster is to present an idea so clearly that there is no doubt of its message. Good spacing, strong lettering, and dramatic color fulfill this function and are the bases upon which evaluations should be made.

Making posters is further discussed in Chapter 10 under methods of printing in the silk screen section.

LINES, ANGLES, AND SPACE

An interesting and different way for children to learn more about line direction is to make a three-dimensional design which will graphically demonstrate how crossing lines make unusual angles and shapes. Only the simplest materials and tools are necessary: a wood frame from which the glass has been removed; a supply of yarn, twine, and string of different colors, textures, and weights; thumbtacks to anchor the material used for stringing the design, scissors, and a hammer.

The yarn, or whichever material is used, is strung back and forth around thumbtacks which have been partially, but firmly, inserted along the inner edge of the frame so that they will not pop off. A thumbtack is also used for tying on and tying off the yarn when stringing the frame. Yarn is tied on and off many times in the course of completing a design when colors and textures are frequently changed to give variety.

190

It is a wise procedure for the children to string up a skeleton pattern in one-color yarn on the frame before the final stringing is undertaken. Adjustments of line directions can then be made by changing the position of any thumbtack, or by adding others. The pattern must be checked to ensure that the openings provided are not too small. When more yarn is added to complete the design in the final stringing, the open spaces may substantially diminish in size or even disappear. Should this happen, the individuality of the design is destroyed. The result should be an openwork pattern, which, with imagination, could be likened to asymmetrical latticework. One should be able to see through the design. Before starting to string the colored yarns, remove any thumbtacks not used. After completing the stringing process, hammer the thumbtacks firmly into the frame. Add fine wire for hanging.

When the framed design is hung on a wall, the shadows help create a delightful feeling of penetration of space. This art activity is quickly accomplished and emphasizes two elements of design: line direction and space forms.

There are two other more simple activities which provide experience with lines, angles, and space. Both are done on chipboard, one with soft twine and chalk, the other with yarn and all-purpose white glue.

Cut a piece of chipboard of the desired size for a background. Cut a number of separate pieces of soft twine long enough to cross the board in any direction and with enough extra length to enable a child to hold the ends of the twine firmly with his hands. Color each piece by rubbing it over a piece of chalk just before using. Then, while one child holds the twine by each end on the chipboard, a classmate picks up the twine at the center and lets it snap back on the board. Where the twine is lifted, a line of color is left. Although there is no sharp edge to the line, the chalk gives it a pleasing quality. Continue making lines in this manner at various points on the chipboard, using different colors to form whatever design the child has in mind. When completed, lightly apply a plastic spray to the surface to keep the chalk from smudging.

Another way of doing much the same thing is to glue lines of colored yarn to a chipboard background. Using the nozzle of a container of all-purpose white glue, draw a line of glue on a piece of paper. Holding a piece of yarn with both hands, dip it into the glue. Then, still holding it taut, lay the yarn on the background and press it gently into place. Some pieces of yarn can be glued side by side to give variety to

191

*Courtesy of Mrs. Hook Sutherland, Los Angeles*

the width of the lines. When the design is completed, turn it over and glue the ends of the yarn to the chipboard.

Either of these activities could precede the major technique described earlier if the teacher feels that a pilot experience would clarify the children's understanding of angles, lines, and space. But these pilot activities should not be undertaken with the intention of making a design to copy; this would destroy the creativity of the three-dimensional experience.

## THE PAINTING ARTS

Painting is probably the most popular of all the arts with children. Through it they find expression for their observations and imaginations.[6]

Two kinds of paint are used in the elementary school: opaque tempera paint and transparent water colors. Tempera is a powdered pigment that has to be mixed with water before it can be used.

Tempera is an excellent paint for elementary grades. The colors are beautiful. Tempera is easy to handle and so inexpensive that it can be generously provided. It is appropriate for both individual and group work.

A full color palette of tempera has twelve colors for school use: red, orange, yellow, emerald green, deep green, blue, turquoise, violet, brown, black, white, and flesh. Purchasing more colors than the primary colors saves money and time. Brown and flesh are used so much that it is more efficient to buy them prepared than to mix them continually. Deep green and turquoise are so useful that it is a mistake not to have them on hand.

In primary grades the teacher mixes all the paint for the children; otherwise a great deal of pigment is wasted as well as the children's time, which is more profitably spent in painting. A few drops of alcohol will speed the mixing of red, orange, and violet—colors that are less soluble than the others. A good way to mix double colors, like blue-green, is to combine the two pigments first and then add the water. Pastel color such as pink is made by starting with white and then adding red by degrees. Many times a large amount of a special color must be mixed for a particular purpose, such as painting the cartons for an Indian pueblo. If all the color is mixed with water at the beginning of the project, when there is only a little painting to do, it will probably turn sour before the painting is completed. It is better to add water to portions of the dry color as needed, and keep the rest in readiness for future use.

Children in the upper grades find they need grayed colors. Grayed colors are made by one of two methods: by combining opposite colors, and by using black. There are three pairs of opposite colors: red and emerald green, blue and orange, and yellow and violet. Since the best way for children to learn about grayed color is to mix it, time should be arranged for them to make experiments. First, mix two grayed colors for each of the pairs: by adding some green to red, then red to green; orange to blue and blue to orange; violet to yellow and yellow to violet. Second, make a set of grayed colors by adding black to each of the six colors and compare the difference. Grayed colors made with opposites will be found to be more subtle and alive than those mixed with black.

It is good to have a supply of small jars, cut-down milk cartons, and baby-food cans for mixing. It is quicker and cleaner to use     193 a new container for each mixing. Every color should be well stirred before painting. Many color pigments sink to the bottom of the container when left unused for a time.

Good brushes are very important. Half-inch and three-quarter-inch bristle brushes with a fairly long handle are used for tempera. In the trade, the brush is called an easel brush. Easel brushes should be provided for every color. When painting, brushes should be held easily but firmly. To clutch a brush tightens up action; to hold it too loosely results in lack of control and indecisive work. The best place for holding an easel brush is about where the ferrule and handle come together. Drips may be overcome, in time, by teaching the children to wipe off the brush

*Arlington County Public Schools, Arlington, Virginia*

against the edge of the container before painting. Nevertheless, a drip or two is no major calamity in primary grades, for they are inevitable with young painters. In upper grades, where children are expected to have better control, drips are indications of sloppy painting habits. A paper towel is handy in every grade for wiping off the handle and bristles when they become soaked with paint.

Good work habits are important for good painting. Brushes should never be left in paint overnight. They should be washed at the end of the day, placed upright in a jar, and left to dry. This preserves the bristles and keeps the wood from rotting so that the ferrule loosens and falls off. Each child should feel responsible for taking care of his own painting, for work left on the floor is likely to be stepped on and spoiled. In order to avoid such accidents, places should be provided where paintings can be hung to dry. They may be pinned on the bulletin board or hung up with clothespins on a long piece of string. Besides taking care of their pictures, children should take care of their clothes. In primary grades aprons are provided for children to wear, and teachers in upper grades should encourage children to bring something suitable from home to wear. A man's discarded shirt with the sleeves cut off serves very well as an artist's smock.

Painting may be carried on in several ways: at a floor or table easel, on a table, on the floor, and on paper fastened to the blackboard or the bulletin board—in short, any place which allows for freedom of action for the child. Suitable papers are wrapping, natural and colored newstock, and Manila. Colored construction papers are attractive, particularly black, which gives stunning results when brilliant colors are used. Tempera will cover cardboard, cartons, wood, and processed materials like Celotex. Tempera is a most useful paint.

Tempera painting is a direct technique requiring no predrawing with pencil or chalk and no copying of pictures. A teacher may ask, "How do I teach easel painting?" There is no definite answer. Creative work is not taught like the multiplication tables. The teacher can only provide the motivation, circumstances, materials, time, and appreciation that make a happy, creative experience possible for children. Evaluations of painting are based on the maturation of the group. It is right and proper for a young child to have a strip of blue across the top of his paper for the sky and to have the sun in a corner if this is the way he wants it to be. For the teacher to criticize his natural way of working is to run

195

*Elementary Training School, San Diego State College*

the risk of upsetting the balance, color, and repetition in a composition and to impose adult standards on the child's work. Evaluation at every level is based on the significance and effectiveness of what is said.

*Water-color* paintings[7] have a sparkle, transparency, and freshness that excel any other medium children use. Painting with water color requires more practice than other techniques, but when children become accustomed to it, they prefer it to anything else. It is often reserved for middle and upper grades because of the pleasure the children derive from being given a new art material.

The latest water-color box contains seven whole pans of color. A palette that has proved satisfactory for classroom use is magenta, orange, yellow, green, blue-violet, turquoise, and black. Practically any color a child would like for his painting can be mixed with this palette. Red is made by mixing magenta and orange; ultramarine blue from turquoise and blue-violet. Grayed colors are made by mixing opposite colors, which in this color assortment are magenta and emerald green, yellow and

196

blue-violet, and red-orange and turquoise. Time given to mixing colors improves color quality and develops appreciation for fine grayed color. When mixing water colors, the best method is to mix on the brush by taking both colors directly from the pans. Handsome color cannot be mixed by flooding the lid of the paint box with water and adding color. Besides being a wasteful method, the result is weak.

A good brush is essential for water-color painting. A No. 10 camel's-hair brush is the best choice except when sable brushes can be afforded. Brushes should be held with ease about the middle and fairly upright so that water and paint will flow to the ends of the hair. A brush is a flexible tool and will respond to every movement of the hand. Variety in brush strokes adds to the quality of water-color painting and can be learned with a little practice. Turning the brush in different directions as it is used will change the width of the stroke. Texture is achieved by slightly wiping off the brush on a paper towel before painting. Loading a brush with two colors gives delightful results.

There are ways of approaching water color that will help children to do good work. Large, free painting is more likely to occur when adequate working space is provided. A good procedure in a classroom where children sit at small desks is to send the children to paint in groups at a large worktable, perhaps the library table cleared of its books. Other ways to encourage a free technique is to devise easels so that children may stand as they paint. One method is to place a large piece of stiff cardboard against the ends of the legs of a chair up-turned on a table. Another is to make stand-up-easels to use on a table by joining two pieces of plywood with hinges. Two children may paint at this type of easel. Also, paper may be taped to the blackboard, an apple box standing on end being used as a table to hold paint box and water jar.

Once the mechanics of preparing for a water-color lesson are organized, everything will proceed smoothly, and a committee can take over for the teacher. Before school or during a recess period preceding the lesson a water-color box, a brush, a container of water, paper, and a paper towel or a piece of absorbent tissue should be put at every child's

198    *Los Angeles Board of Education*

place. A bucket for emptying water containers and a pitcher of water for refilling them during the course of the lesson are great conveniences. A newspaper on the top of the desk is not recommended because it hampers freedom of movement by making an unstable working surface. If any paint gets on a desk, it can be cleaned off at the end of a lesson with a damp sponge. Every child helps at the close of the period by cleaning his own paint box. In damp weather it is well to leave the boxes open on a table to dry before closing the lids. Brushes are pointed and when collected are put handle down in a jar. Under no circumstances are brushes ever left with the hair standing in water.

Water-color painting may be done on wet or dry paper. Both Manila and white water-color paper are used. The paper should not be soaked with water; a quick wash is enough. This technique is called wet-on-wet painting and gives rich color blendings and soft edges as long as the paper remains moist. Painting on dry paper has sparkle and freshness; brush strokes are definite and contrasts are strong. Scrubbing with the brush and repainting areas are fatal to good results. It is equally bad practice to draw a picture with a pencil and fill in the outline with paint. If a child feels he must have some guide lines, teach him to block in the large areas of his composition with a brush and a light color. There is always a time, a critical time, when a painting is at its best, and that is the time to stop.

In evaluating water-color painting, children should look for originality, rich color, contrast, and a free and loose technique. Water color should still retain the quality of wetness even when dry.

## Finger Painting

Finger painting is the most relaxing of all the art experiences for children.[8] There is an informality about it that releases tensions and an ease that relaxes muscles. A better name might be hand painting, because the motions are not confined to the fingers; the hands and even the wrist and lower arm are brought into play.

The paper must be of good quality. It should have a slick surface and a strong body so that it will not tear when it is wet. Shelf paper, if it does not have a plastic coating, is good. Also, the paper should be white or finger-paint colors will not be clear and brilliant.

There are different methods of wetting the paper for       199

*Arlington County Public Schools, Arlington, Virginia*

finger painting. One way is to dip a big sponge in a bucket of water and sponge the paper. Another is to submerge the paper in a shallow pan of water such as a baking pan. To do this, hold the paper by two corners and draw it through the water. If there is a sink in the room the problem is more efficiently solved.

Prepared finger paint can be purchased. Bottled laundry starch or starch cooked by the teacher from dry starch to which a small portion of soap flakes is added when the mixture has cooled can be used. To the starch, the children add their choice of tempera color. A neat way to distribute the color is from a shaker made from a jar with holes punched in the top. Darker colors are best for painting because the contrast with white paper is greater. Several colors may be used with beautiful results.

When working with finger paint, children should always wear aprons and roll up their sleeves. A good way to clean the hands when there is no sink in the classroom is to wipe off the paint on a damp bath towel. This will prevent finger paint from being smeared on the

200

doorknobs and woodwork on the way to the lavatory. Children should be cautioned to keep their hands away from their faces when working.

Greater freedom of motion in finger painting is possible when children stand to work. Double motions should be encouraged so that both hands are used together or alternately. This is fine exercise for the left-handed child and will automatically train and exercise his right hand, particularly if the teacher makes a game of it with primary children. Dual hand motion is helpful for the right-handed child as well, and will aid him in overcoming some of his natural awkwardness when using his left hand. A good working surface for finger painting is oilcloth. It is smooth and waterproof. The daily newspaper is not good because the creases will show up in the finished painting.

Designs, landscape, ocean and shore lines, marine gardens, deserts, and clouds all give opportunity for sweeping arm movements and unique finger textures. Children are inventive with finger paint and have many suggestions to give each other. Rhythm patterns made to music are fun to do. Tempo and mood are quickly caught by the children as they paint. When thoroughly dry, finger paintings are improved by pressing them on the wrong side with a warm iron.

Finger painting is good for booklet covers and decorative papers for craft problems.

## The Drawing Arts

The drawing arts include colored chalk, crayon, charcoal, and a very little pencil work in the upper grades. Drawing should be used, considered, and evaluated as a sincere and important art expression, natural to children.

Good drawing depends not only upon skill and sensitivity to line but also upon observation. Outline drawings by young children will often reveal amazing powers of observation. A four-and-a-half-year-old boy demonstrated this one evening at home when he picked up a pencil and, on the inside of a used envelope, drew his house, the family television cabinet, and the characters of the show he had just watched, "Beanie and Cecil."

Although *colored chalk* is dusty, it is nevertheless a splendid drawing material for children in every grade. Chalk comes in a wide range of colors and in large and small sizes. It is responsive to pressure

201

*Courtesy of Mrs. Lloyd Lounsbury, San Diego*

and may be blended and shaded, as well as used sharply. When used heavily, the full power of the colors is obtained. Chalk is good for easel and flat work, for individual and group activities, and as a quick material for covering large surfaces like murals and backgrounds. Chalk drawings are protected by a coat of plastic fixative; the kind available in a self-spraying container is the best to use.

When working with chalk, the direct approach, without predrawing in pencil, is the most effective. If some sketching is necessary, do it with chalk. It is a superior material for music rhythms because it is so easy to handle that rapid drawing is possible. Children can keep up with the tempo of the music when using chalk and still have changes in color.

Chalk can be used on any paper which does not have a smooth surface. Newsprint, Manila, colored construction paper, and wrapping paper are all acceptable.

*Wet chalk* is misleading because it is the paper and not the chalk that is wet. The moisture of the paper acts as a binder for the chalk and sharpens the colors. The paper may be wet in any of the ways described for finger painting but it must not be too wet or it will tear when the drawing is done. Wet chalk is not an easel material; it should be used flat on a table or on the floor. Newsprint, newspaper, or oilcloth is used to protect the table or floor.

Bottled *laundry starch* is a better binder for chalk than water. It prevents the chalk from rubbing off of the paper; hence no fixative is needed. One precaution to take when using water or starch is to handle the paper carefully while it is still moist. After the chalk drawing has dried, the paper can be handled normally without tearing.

Vibrant *unit designs* in colored chalk can be made very quickly with leftover pieces of colored chalk. Interesting results are largely dependent on a sensitive choice of colors. Children have an instinctive reaction to color and use combinations that an older person would hardly

*San Diego City Schools*

dare to use. Using the broad side of the chalk, start with any color and at any place on the paper. Rub blocks of color on the paper, frequently changing colors to develop variety as the work proceeds, but not so often that the result is chaotic. When an interesting asymmetrical shape emerges, stop work. Covering the entire paper defeats the purpose of this art project, which is to compose a free-floating design. Any kind and size of paper can be used. Using standard size paper for all drawings and paintings can, in fact, be tiresome. This project offers a good opportunity to clear the paper box by using leftover pieces. Use a spray on the work after it is completed. If laundry starch is preferred to fix the chalk, paint it on Manila paper before starting the chalk work.

*The* Louisville Courier-Journal and Louisville Times *and Louisville Public Schools*

*Board of Education, City of Chicago*

An imaginative use of color and a direct approach to the work results in attractive color patterns with style and spontaneity. There just cannot be teacher direction in an art activity such as this.

*Colored crayons*[9] have many uses in the art program, but they have been overemphasized by some teachers. Too much crayon work limits children's art experiences to an unwarranted extent. It also depletes the vitality of creative work. When wisely used, crayon has a contribution to make and a function to fulfill that belongs to it alone as an excellent drawing tool.

Crayon is not an easel material, nor is it appropriate when large surfaces must be covered, such as backgrounds. Crayon is best as an upper-grade drawing technique where children can handle it properly.

Unfortunately, crayon is constantly used in the primary grades for coloring outline drawings and following directions in workbooks and on mimeographed work sheets. A study[10] has shown that there is a

205

decline in children's creative ability where this sort of material has been extensively used in class.

Good crayon work has brilliant color when applied heavily enough to give character to the composition. A light crayon technique is insipid. Compact, fairly small drawings are charming, for crayon gives strong dark and light contrasts and is good for drawing details. Why not take a box of crayons along on a sketching trip?

*Crayon etching*[11] is an interesting new method for making line drawings. Cover the surface of an average-sized sheet of Manila paper with a coat of crayon in a light color—yellow, light green, turquoise, pink, orange, white. A solid color may be used or a combination of several colors, if preferred. Over this put a second coat of black or purple. Draw the picture by cutting through the top layer of crayon with a sharp-pointed tool. The colors underneath will be revealed in the lines of the drawing. Crayon etchings are striking when mounted on large white mats. Designs, abstract patterns, landscapes, and flowers have a delicacy which is unusual in children's work. Why not save this technique for the upper grades where children are skillful in freehand drawing? (See mounted crayon etching, Chapter 12.)

A variation of crayon work called *crayon resist*[12] is a combination of India ink or tempera paint with crayon. The crayon must be put on heavily or the method will not work as expected. When the drawing is completed, paint over it with India ink or a dark tempera color. The colors in the drawing will become brighter against the dark background. Another way is to paint a simple texture pattern over the crayon drawing with a partly dry bristle brush and tempera paint. This last method is more subtle in its effect than a solid background and adds a pleasant quality of roughness to the picture.

A fun-time art activity for younger children that quickly achieves results is making a *crayon texture* surface pattern. It involves no more than finding several fairly flat objects and materials with a textured surface. These could be wire screening, scouring cloth, corrugated paper, coarse sandpaper, a large piece of bark from a tree, a cheese grater from mother's kitchen, or a heavily veined leaf picked up on the way to school. In short, whatever can be found in the natural environment is appropriate. As children are great searchers, each will enjoy finding his own materials. The teacher may give a child a clue or two, then let him carry on from there by himself. After the materials have been assembled, put them on a

*Board of Education, Newark, New Jersey*

*Long Beach
Public Schools*

207

worktable in a scattered arrangement and lay a piece of paper on top of them. With the flat side of a piece of crayon, rub over each unit vigorously with a color. The result will be a scattered design of unusual and surprising surface patterns. It is fun for children to see the interesting and varied types of design that result from this method of using a crayon in a new way.

*Charcoal drawing* is another technique best reserved for upper-grade children. Successful results depend to a considerable degree upon the quality of the charcoal and paper provided. For good drawing, vine charcoal and charcoal paper are needed. When finished, the work needs to be sprayed with a fixative.

Charcoal is efficient for outdoor sketching, and paper fastened with tape to a heavy piece of cardboard is a good drawing board to take along. When sketching out-of-doors, children are looking for mass, not details. Contours should be simple and strong, not weak and fluttery around the edges. Outdoor sketching offers a fine opportunity for drawing buildings. Children greatly enjoy the novelty of going outdoors to work.

A recent, truly effective art medium developed for drawing is the disposable *felt pen* available in inks of the following colors: black, blue, brown, red, orange, yellow, green, and purple. Its use is best reserved for the upper grades where children have a more mature approach to drawing. The ink dries instantly and is waterproof. While a felt pen is primarily intended for linear drawing, it can be used to fill in small areas in a design with solid color. Or, to enrich the effect, some free brush painting with water color can be added when the design is completed.

Lines are drawn with the broad side of the pen; if narrower lines are needed, the tip of the pen is used. A felt pen is not as flexible as a paint brush. The pen is a direct and precise tool that in itself is effective. Drawings made with a felt pen are crisp and sharp.

A felt pen can be used on any paper or on chipboard. Children can practice on newsprint to get the feel of working with the pen. Several designs can be drawn during an art period. This provides the children with an opportunity for self-evaluation. Each child can select his best piece of work and discard the rest. Children should stand while drawing; this gives them greater freedom in making the pen strokes because they can use both their hands and arms.

After gaining experience in the handling of a felt pen, children can prepare multi-colored backgrounds for over-drawing. Preparation should be made the previous day in one of three ways: a collage of colored papers can be made, a shaded wash of water color can be painted on paper, or a finger painting can be used for the background. All three techniques are attractive for over-drawing.

Nicolas Sidjakov, who illustrated the children's book, *Baboushka and the Three Kings*,[13] used a felt pen for the illustrations and won the Caldecott Medal in 1960 for this work. This medal is awarded for the best illustrated children's book of the year.

For added experience in design, drawing with a felt pen provides practice and attractive results.

*Pencil drawing* is a poor technique for elementary school children. It is better to err by never using a pencil than to use it indiscriminately, as too often has been the case. Ordinarily schools do not provide drawing pencils; the hard pencil that is used for written work is very difficult to handle. The constant erasing which children are prone to do in pencil drawing does not further the direct and positive approach so much more successful in children's work.

Pencil drawing is appropriate for lettering, cartoons, and sketches to be used on stencils for illustrating a school newspaper. A pencil is an efficient tool; in fact, the only one that should be used. Boys like to make cartoons and will have an admiring audience when their work appears in the school paper. An E. G. in a lower corner of a cartoon can be shown to the family at home with modest pride.

*Pen and ink* drawing has no place in the elementary school art program.

## WAYS TO USE PAPER

There are a number of practical and imaginative ways to use paper. The assortment of papers now available gives opportunity for choices of color, design, and texture. Projects may be developed with paper sacks, strips of paper, and papier-mâché; paper sculpture provides still another way of using paper. This variety offers a range of experiences which are adaptable to the different maturation levels of children.[14]

### KINDS OF PAPER

Children work with papers which are glamorous and others which are as plain as a paper sack. Manila, white water color, bogus, colored tissue, poster, and construction paper are available in school stock rooms. Other kinds of paper may be salvaged or ordered. Cellophane, corrugated, gift wrappings, metallic, wood-grained, and marbleized papers are needed for some things. Scraps of paper from discarded greeting cards and merchandise wrappings should be saved. Textures of papers differ and add interest to finished work. The combination of decorated and plain papers, different in color and in texture, provides opportunity for making art decisions.

TOOLS AND PASTE

The most essential tool for paper work is a good pair of scissors with sharp points. There should be a pair for every child. Many uses are found for pinking shears and sometimes a pair of small manicure scissors is useful. A helpful tool is a stapler. There are three kinds: a staple gun for very heavy work, a desk stapler for general use, and a hand stapler for small work. A paper punch is handy and a paper cutter essential. Even when a paper cutter has a safety guard, no child should be permitted to use it.

For problems of pasting, wallpaper paste and all-purpose white glue are necessary. All-purpose white glue neither wrinkles, puckers,

*Indianapolis Public Schools*

*Galveston Independent
School District*

stretches, nor discolors paper. Two other aids in working with paper are glitter glue and cellophane tape. Glitter glue is useful at Christmas time for putting glitter on decorations. Paint the glue on the paper and sprinkle the glitter over it. Tiny seeds and shells can be attached to paper and cardboard in the same way. Cellulose tape is a quick way to join papers and is particularly helpful in primary grades where as little pasting as possible should be asked of children.

USING PAPER SACKS

Two articles that children enjoy making from paper sacks are masks and animals.

A *mask* may be made to wear over the head for a Halloween party or to carry on a stick in a parade. For a head mask, slip a sack over the child's head and mark the place for eyes, nose, and mouth with chalk. The child begins making the mask by cutting out holes for the eyes, nose, and mouth. Next, paper hair and big ears are pasted on.

211

*San Diego City Schools*

The sack is decorated with tempera paint; the more fearful the effect, the better pleased the children will be. To make a stick mask paste on eyes, nose, and ears and stuff the sack with paper.

Are paper sack *animals* fun to make? Second- and third-graders think so. Wild animals are more interesting to make because of their distinctive characteristics and bright colors. There is a basic pattern that can be used to make almost any animal and, while some guessing may be needed at times to identify species, on the whole children do very well.

Collect a lot of shredded packing paper and bring it to class before starting the project. A great deal is needed if many animals are to be made. Each child must have four mailing tubes to use for the legs of his animal, a large paper sack for the body, and a smaller one for the head. A few extra sacks are needed for other parts of animals.

A teacher may start the project of making paper sack animals by demonstrating the method to a group and then choosing leaders

212

from the group to help the other children, being always ready and willing herself to give special aid when needed. Start the animal by stuffing the large paper sack with shredded paper until it is firm and well packed. Fold over the ends of the sack and glue them together. Make the head from the small sack in the same way. Fasten the head to the body with long pins or paper fasteners, or sew it in place with a darning needle and soft cotton string. Punch four holes in the body for legs. Push the ends of the tubes into the body, checking to see that all are the same length. Glue the legs to the body with strips of paper an inch wide and six inches long. Part of the strip is glued to the tube and part to the sack. When enough strips to hold the legs in place have been glued to the body, the leg will be firmly attached. Cut a tail and ears from an extra sack and glue them in place. Paint with tempera.

A tube is used for the trunk of an elephant. Cut slits along the tube part way through the cardboard. Bend the tube into a curve. While a child holds the tube in position, glue a strip of paper on the inside of the curve and another strip on the underside of the curve. Punch a hole in the head, put in the trunk, and glue in place with paper strips. Make a neck for a giraffe from a tube and fasten it to the body. Make a head from a small paper sack and add ears and short horns. Once the project is under way, children are able to make animals with very little supervision by the teacher.

*Barnyard fowl* may be made by stuffing sacks, twisting the ends together for the neck, and adding comb, beak, and wings cut out of colored paper.

USING PAPER STRIPS

Paper strips over a foundation of clay, wire, or rolls of paper may be used for making people and animals, as well as for the masks described previously. The technique is adaptable and can be used for large and small projects.

*People* and *animals* made from paper strips are wrapped over a wire skeleton. Use three wire coat hangers or building wire, type T W No. 12. Building wire bends easily and is strong. Children have no difficulty using it. For the figure of a person make long arms, a body, and very long legs by bending a long piece of wire without cutting it until the skeleton is completed. This gives a double wire for all parts, with loops 213 at the ends of the arms and legs. Bend the legs sharply to make hips, and the ends of the legs to make feet. Make a loop for the head and fasten one end to the body for the neck. Pad the head and body with newspaper as follows. Cut a long piece of newspaper six inches wide. Fold it into a narrow strip. Fold one end over a shoulder and tape in place. Wrap the strip under the opposite hip, up and over the shoulder above, across and under the opposite hip, and finish by bringing it up to the shoulder where it started. Tape in place. Wrap around the body with folded strips until it is sufficiently padded. Fill the wire loop for the head with a wad of newspaper and tape in place. Make a nose from a sliver of wood and glue to head. Wrap strips of paper towel dipped in paste around the whole figure and head. Paint the body, face, and hair, or glue on yarn for hair. Dress the figures in cotton goods and cloth. Make shoes if the clothing does not cover the feet. Nail the feet to a wood base with staples. This is a useful type of figure for small-scale construction units. The same method

214

*Detroit Public Schools*

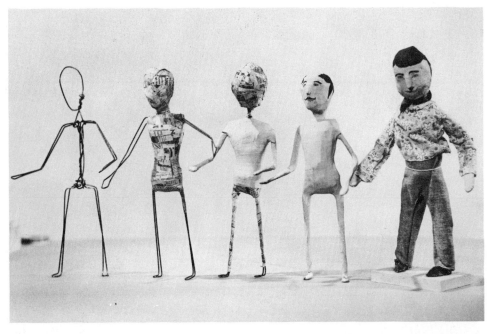

*San Diego City Schools*

using lighter wire may be employed to make small figures for dioramas.

Make the wire frame for an animal in the same way, padding it well. Animals may be wrapped with strips of colored crepe paper, which requires pasting only at the ends of the strips. Paint or paste on the bodily characteristics of animals. Animals made this way are good for farm, zoo, and circus units.

Foundations may be made of strips of newspaper folded tightly and tied together with string. The foundation is covered with strips of paper dipped in paste as previously described. A good film to show the class is *How to Make Papier-mâché Animals*.[15]

### PAPIER-MÂCHÉ

Papier-mâché has a few uses for which it is particularly well adapted. It is good for the heads of hand puppets, fruits and vegetables for markets, small figures of people and animals, and the extra (and often small) things needed for dioramas. When thoroughly dry and rubbed with sandpaper, papier-mâché will have a fairly smooth surface.

215

*Department of Education, Baltimore, Maryland*

The following recipe for making papier-mâché will serve all purposes which may arise in a classroom. Tearing up the paper for the pulp is always the children's responsibility.

### Papier-mâché

Tear into fine pieces one and a half sheets of newspaper. Paper should not be folded. Cover with boiling water and stir until mixture becomes a pulp. Mix two heaping tablespoons of flour with cold water. Add one cup of boiling water. Add the flour and water mixture to the paper pulp.

### PAPER SCULPTURE

Paper sculpture[16] is a term descriptive of the new trend toward bulk and three-dimensional form in cut-paper work. Certainly the flat, plastered-down cutouts seem passé compared to the newer approach

216

which gives depth and structure to the finished work and gives children more opportunities for creative expression. This is the time for a class to draw liberally upon its storehouse of fancy papers so painstakingly collected.

Paper sculpture demands imaginative thinking in the use of a pair of scissors, for many things can be done with scissors in the hands of clever children. Every technique previously mentioned for cut-paper murals can be successfully used on individual projects as well. Parts of a cut-paper design or composition can be made to stand out from the background if a folded paper spring is pasted between them and casts a shadow. When sharp folds have to be made, lay a ruler against the line to be folded, score the paper with a scissor blade, and bend the paper against the ruler. Scoring gives a smarter and neater fold than bending with the hands. Use a stapler whenever possible. All-purpose white glue should be available for pasting.

Paper sculpture can give variety to the long-established custom of making Christmas decorations for the classroom. Candles, trees,

*San Diego City Schools*

angels, and decorations for the tree are better looking if they give the impression of roundness of form.

One clever project for paper sculpture is another version of the decorative mask. Make a hollow cylinder, a·rectangle, or a three-cornered form of construction paper. Cut out, bend, and fold paper to make a nose and hair and paste in place. Make a hat, crown, or exotic headdress to cover the opening. Decorative details cut out and pasted to the mask can be made of different kinds of paper. The color film *Paper Sculpture*,[17] mentioned in Chapter 2, provokes a lively interest in paper sculpture.

Paper sculpture contributes to mural work, bulletin board arrangement, room decoration, and poster making.

## THE PHYSICALLY HANDICAPPED CHILD

The problems of physically handicapped children are many and complex. National organizations, educational groups, and specialists are studying these problems and continuously evaluating theory and practice. Fortunate are those children living in districts where a school staffed by specially trained teachers has been established. In such schools the best methods are used to help children overcome their physical handicaps and the consequent emotional disturbances that make adjustment difficult. Special schools are equipped with every kind of chair, table, and technical device for the welfare of handicapped children. Such schools have an abundance of the proper materials for them to use, materials which have been carefully selected with regard for the physical limitations of individual children.

Art makes a contribution to the rehabilitation of handicapped children. It is a basic part of the individual program planned by the teacher for each child. Individual instruction is necessary, for even if several children with similar handicaps are able to work together, the performance of no two children is ever the same, and no group approach could possibly fit the needs of all. Individual instruction is thus imperative since the goal is to rehabilitate the children so that as many as possible will return to a regular classroom. Nevertheless, many are never able to do this.

The value of art experiences is basically therapeutic, and, 218  because these experiences are creative within the limits of the children's

San Diego City Schools

abilities, the work is rewarding to handicapped children.[18] Children are given every opportunity to be imaginative and to make choices of color, of materials, and of the tools approved for their individual use. Handicapped children lack neither original ideas nor inspiration, but the sad fact remains that for many execution requires closer supervision and more teacher help for a longer period of time than normal children require. This depends largely upon the nature and extent of the disability. Because an art activity is concrete, it tends to provide a motivation for many handicapped children to complete what they have started and not to give up when they become discouraged. Finished art work wins approval and appreciation from the other children and the family at home, both sorely needed by these children. When pride of accomplishment has been fairly won, the spirit and strength of a handicapped child is encouraged toward continued efforts.

A contribution of equal importance is the sociability that art provides, for, like all children, handicapped children are happiest when they have interests in common with other children. Cooperative activity has been found to aid in stimulating speech. Inability to express themselves orally is one of the most frustrating afflictions that many of these children endure, and a vital personal experience will often stimulate a child to talk spontaneously and successfully. Since the handicapped child has pitifully few meaningful personal experiences in his life to share with others, those that are possible should be developed to the fullest degree.

219

When a handicapped child is able to return to a regular classroom situation, the teacher who receives him has three sources to turn to for advice. The best source is a conference with the principal and teacher of the special school the child attended. They will be able to give her the personal information that she needs in order to guide his work more effectively. They can suggest what activities are the best for him and the kind of materials and tools he is able to use. Sometimes all that is needed to make the regular school supplies suitable is a small adjustment of some sort. A child may be able to paint very well at the easel provided a sponge is attached to the slender handle of the brush so that he will have something to grasp. Another child may be able to use scissors by the simple device of taping the thumb hole on the scissors to his thumb. Many of these children find it helpful when drawing and painting to have the paper held in place with a couple of sandbags or a piece of masking tape.

A second source of help is the literature in the field. The best current material is found in the bulletins published by national foundations devoted to specific disabilities, such as The Society for Crippled Children and the Muscular Dystrophy Association. The writings of specialists will assist a teacher to understand the nature of the child's disability and what he may be reasonably expected to accomplish. This information will help the teacher to select the kind of work to give in order to avoid any retrogression in progress that might come about through lack of information.

Another source of literature for the teacher is the individual writings of teachers of handicapped children which are published in professional and general periodicals. One teacher in the Midwest wrote a very sensitive article on her experiences in working with deaf children. The article, "Art Is Our Language,"[19] effectively shows the joy that art experiences gave to the children in her class.

And, last, the art consultant, or supervisor of the schools, can help by suggesting a variation of a prescribed program of art activities which will help a handicapped child to feel that he is making progress, thus overcoming any boredom that an endless repetition of the same problem inevitably develops.

Every teacher who works with handicapped children realizes that there is a long life of restricted activity ahead for them, and that the years of childhood may well be a critical period for developing a reservoir of interests. Although, in their creative work, many physically handicapped children may see the vision but are blocked in performance

220

by difficulties beyond their control, this is not so for aesthetic enjoyments and appreciations. Music, literature, and art can be brought into their lives. Many publications on art are available which will help a child to build an art background that, when he is adult, may become the equal of anyone in his community.

Appreciation of his efforts and opportunities for creative expression within the possibilities of his performance can be vital forces in the continued progress and happiness of the physically handicapped child. Intelligent guidance at a special school, at home, and when he returns to a regular classroom leads to the cultivation of every talent that a handicapped child may possess and will enrich his life immeasurably.

## THE GIFTED CHILD

In the primary grades many children seem to be gifted in art. A child with a special talent is not as noticeable among younger children because nearly all are lavish in their expression and confident of their ability. This complete faith in themselves leads primary children to undertake, and very successfully, most difficult compositions. In creative work they will display an amazing visual memory, which adds to their confidence and independence. As young children mature, there seems to be a gentle tapering off of the exuberance that marked their years in primary grades, and the difference between the child with average ability and the child with superior ability begins to be recognized in upper grades. Even so, children's rate of growth and changing interests always affect their art expression to such a degree that in one year a child's output may seem to be quite ordinary and in the next year quite superior. However, within the school population there are children with marked art ability who need careful guidance and wise counsel.[20] Most gifted children are characterized by a strong drive for accomplishment and a yearning to achieve which seem greater than similar drives in other children. A child gifted in art can become so engrossed in creative work that even though the recess bell may ring or lunchtime may come, he cannot be diverted from his task until he has done what he must do.

Probably the wisest approach a teacher can take with such a child is to expand his art program. She can provide a wide range of independent experiences that offer the challenge of new materials. She can encourage him to go outdoors for an hour of sketching. She can place

221

beautifully illustrated books and art portfolios on the reading shelves in the classroom for him to enjoy. She can help him to develop an interest in art history by borrowing books from the library, such as Hillyer's *A Child's History of Art,*[21] and, for the competent reader, Craven's *The Rainbow Book of Art.*[22] She can stimulate his perception of beauty by borrowing from the audio-visual department of the school district filmstrips such as *Learning to Look*[23] for him to study, and providing a table viewer[24] for his use. She can investigate what the community has to offer in Saturday classes for children and can make the necessary arrangements for him to attend.

Fortunately, there is an awakening interest in gifted children[25] on the part of the public and educators. To meet more adequately the needs of these children, Saturday morning classes for selected children are rapidly becoming a part of the school art program. The classes are often held in special art rooms in a secondary school where equipment and facilities are superior to those available in the average elementary school classroom.

Children who wish to or are recommended to attend special art classes are screened by a committee which includes the child's past teachers, his school principal, and the art supervisor. Identification of a gifted child should not be the responsibility of one person; a broader overview of his creative work is required. Some questions to which the committee might try to find the answers are: Is the child perceptive of beauty? Does he have strong visual imagery? Has he acquired a degree of skill in his work? In addition, a selection of examples of his work should be considered. It would also be helpful to the special art teacher if a short resumé of his past school life is prepared for the committee. At best, an appraisal of the talents of a candidate is not infallible. The classes should not be used for "encouragement" as some teachers would wish.

It is very important that a gifted and broadly trained teacher be appointed to special classes. These children are seeking instruction from an expert who is creative and who is a leader in art. Saturday classes have enjoyed remarkably good attendance. Gifted children are eager to learn and a joy to teach.

Classes for the gifted in art should not be overcrowded. The special needs of the gifted child require time for conferences with the teacher and plenty of space in which to work. About twenty children in one class is probably ample. Otherwise, the goals of individual guidance and accelerated experience cannot be achieved.

The basic needs of the gifted child are, in reality, not so different from the needs of all children, and perhaps the greatest service a teacher can contribute to his future success is to keep him unspoiled. No teacher can be quite sure to what degree a child may possess talent; time only will reveal the depth and breadth of his gift. In the meantime, he is hungry to see, feel, and experience examples of fine creative work. His aesthetic responses are quick and sensitive, for he has an art maturity above and beyond his years.[25]

## REFERENCE MATERIAL

1. *Make a Mobile.* 16mm. film, 10 min., sound, color; produced by International Film Bureau, Inc.

   Lynch, John. *How to Make a Mobile.* New York: Thomas Y. Crowell Company, 1953.

2. Weise, Harvey. *Clay, Wood and Wire.* New York: William R. Scott, Inc., 1956. pp. 31–33.

   Lord, Lois. *Collages and Construction.* Worcester, Mass.: Davis Publications, Inc., 1958.

3. Krasz, Mariska. *Adventures in Stitches.* Rev. ed. New York: Funk & Wagnalls Company, 1959.

   *Art Teaching Guide—Hawaii.* Honolulu, Hawaii: Department of Public Instruction, State of Hawaii, 1960.

4. Lord, Lois. *Collages and Construction.* Worcester, Mass.: Davis Publications, Inc., 1958. pp. 12–29.

5. *The Loon's Necklace.* 16mm. film, 11 min., sound, color; produced by Encyclopaedia Britannica Films, Inc.

6. *Painting* (Primary). Filmstrip, approximately 35 frames; produced by McGraw-Hill Book Company, Inc.

   *Beginning of Picture Making.* 16mm. film, 9 min., sound, color; produced by International Film Bureau, Inc.

   *Picture Making in the Gang Age.* 16mm. film, 9 min., sound, color; produced by International Film Bureau, Inc.

7. *Water Coloring.* (Primary) filmstrip, approximately 35 frames; produced by McGraw-Hill Book Company, Inc.

   *Painting With Water Colors.* (Intermediate) filmstrip,

223

approximately 35 frames; produced by McGraw-Hill Book Company, Inc.

8. *Finger Painting Methods.* 16mm. film, 8 min., sound, color; produced by Coronet Instructional Films.

*Finger Painting.* 16mm. film, 5 min., sound, color; produced by International Film Bureau, Inc.

*Finger Painting.* Filmstrip, approximately 34 frames, color; produced by McGraw-Hill Book Company, Inc.

*How to Make a Starch Painting.* 16mm. film, 13 min., sound, color; produced by Encyclopaedia Britannica Films, Inc.

9. *Sketching With Crayon.* (Intermediate) filmstrip, approximately 35 frames, color; produced by McGraw-Hill Book Company, Inc.

10. *Workbooks and Art Education.* Vol. 3, No. 1. Kutztown, Pa.: Eastern Art Association, 1952.

Jefferson, Blanche. *Teaching Art to Children.* Boston: Allyn and Bacon, Inc., 1959. pp. 256–261.

11. *Birds and Etching.* 16mm. film, 5 min., sound, color; produced by International Film Bureau, Inc.

12. *Crayon Resist.* 16mm. film, 6 min., sound, color; produced by International Film Bureau, Inc.

13. Robbins, Ruth. *Baboushka and the Three Kings.* Berkeley, Calif.: Parnassus Press, 1960.

14. *Cutting and Pasting.* (Primary) filmstrip, approximately 35 frames, color; produced by McGraw-Hill Book Company, Inc.

*Paper Craft.* (Primary) filmstrip, approximately 35 frames, color; produced by McGraw-Hill Book Company, Inc.

*Making a Mask.* 16mm. film, 6 min., sound, color; produced by International Film Bureau, Inc.

15. *How to Make Papier-mâché Animals.* 16mm. film, 12 min., sound, color; produced by International Film Bureau, Inc.

16. Becker, Edith. *Adventures With Scissors and Paper.* Scranton, Pa.: International Textbook Company, 1959.

Hughes, Toni. *How to Make Shapes and Forms.* New York: E. P. Dutton & Co., Inc., 1955. (Sec. on paper.)

Johnson, Pauline. *Creating With Paper*. Seattle, Wash.: University of Washington Press, 1958.

Johnston, Mary Grace. *Paper Sculpture*. Worcester, Mass.: Davis Publications, Inc., 1952.

17. *Paper Sculpture*. 16mm. film, 6 min., sound, color; produced by International Film Bureau, Inc.

18. Dolch, Edward William. *Helping Handicapped Children in School*. Champaign, Ill.: Garrard Press, 1948. (Chap. V, "Crippled Children," pp. 120–150.)

Baker, Harry J. *Introduction to Exceptional Children*. New York: The Macmillan Company, 1945.

19. Bilger, Grace. "Art Is Our Language," *Junior Arts and Activities,* Vol. 37, No. 1 (Feb., 1955), pp. 28–32.

20. Lindstrom, Miriam. *Children's Art*. Berkeley, Calif.: University of California Press, 1960. pp. 48–54.

21. Hillyer, V. M. and E. G. Huey. *A Child's History of Art*. Rev. ed. New York: Appleton-Century-Crofts, Inc., 1951.

22. Craven, Thomas. *The Rainbow Book of Art*. New York: Harcourt, Brace & World, Inc., 1956.

23. *Learning to Look*. 6 filmstrips, color; 1 recording; produced by Filmscope Inc.

24. Standard Viewer Model 200. Standard Projector and Equipment Company, Inc. Contact local or district supply company for audio-visual equipment. (For filmstrips only.)

25. Witty, Paul (ed.). *The Gifted Child*. American Association for Gifted Children. Boston: D. C. Heath and Company, 1951. (Chap. XII, "Experience With Children Gifted in the Arts.")

*Educating the Gifted*. A Book of Readings edited by Joseph L. French. New York: Holt, Rinehart and Winston, Inc., 1959. "Some Guide Lines for Action," pp. 145–48.

## READER PARTICIPATION

Organize a program of art activities for any grade level that will balance the strengths of both group and independent work.

Devise efficient ways for storing art materials and children's work.

Prepare sample portions of all the art materials which are new to you.

Devote a practice hour—more time if possible—to each of those art activities which you have never experienced. Do not be concerned with your art performance, rather, try to get the feel and responsiveness of the material as you use it.

What differences may be made in the approach to the teaching of physically handicapped children? of gifted children?

# 10

# *Furthering Art Experiences*

Every art program is broadened when crafts and allied art activities are included. New materials are introduced, new techniques developed, and the children are given an opportunity to increase their skills in handling tools. Good design is simple and free of nonessentials, regardless of the material used.

## WORKING WITH CLAY

Three-dimensional form can be expressed creatively by children in no better way than working with clay.[1] The value for children is that they will not only see but feel three-dimensional form as they model it. Clay is plastic, responsive, pleasant and cool to touch, and economical to provide. There is something so basic in its manipulation that children have deep feelings of satisfaction in the experiences of patting, rolling, squeezing, thumping, pulling, and kneading clay. Besides the pleasure and release children find in clay, it encourages ambidextrous use of the hands. Using the "other" hand is done more readily in modeling than in any other art technique, with the possible exception of finger painting. The muscular exercise in the clay process is helpful in developing stronger hands and fingers, yet the plastic nature of the material prevents strain and fatigue. The relaxation that clay gives the nervous and overstimulated child cannot

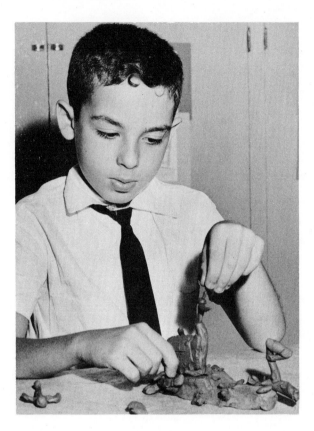

*Elementary School, District of Toa Baja, Puerto Rico*

be overemphasized. Many a teacher has skillfully dispelled the temper tantrum of an emotionally disturbed child with a ball of clay.

Clay is an earth material, and results are more dynamic when the earth qualities of sturdiness, strength, and bulk are preserved, and children do not strive to reproduce the delicacy of porcelain or the fineness of china. Interesting surface modeling that shows the imprint of fingers and tools gives character to children's work and should not be washed away with a wet sponge or rubbed smooth with sandpaper. Bold, strong expression is the most desirable outcome of clay modeling in the elementary grades.

### GLOSSARY OF TERMS

Using the correct vocabulary for clay work will assist both the teacher and the children, particularly in the upper grades. As the need

228

arises, the correct terms should be learned. These are some useful terms:

| | |
|---|---|
| *Bat* | A flat, level slab made of plaster that is used to absorb the moisture from wet clay, particularly in drying tiles. |
| *Biscuit* | Clay ware that has been fired once. |
| *Bone dry* | As dry as clay can become without applying heat. The ware is light in color and is fragile. |
| *Cone* | A ceramic temperature gauge placed in a kiln during firing. The cone melts down when the temperature in the kiln reaches the melting point of the cone. Cone numbers are equivalent to pyrometer temperatures as follows: No. 08 = 1733° F., No. 07 = 1787° F., and No. 06 = 1841° F. |
| *Core* | A clay form over which a slab of clay is modeled. |
| *Engobe* | Color pigments added to slip used for painting decoration on clay. Engobe and colored slip are essentially the same. |
| *Firing* | Baking the clay object in the kiln. |
| *Glaze* | A mixture of powdered chemicals and water which is applied to biscuit-fired ware. The term is also applied to the glasslike surface which is the result of firing the raw mixture in the kiln. |
| *Green ware* | A term applied to unfired clay models. |
| *Kiln* | A furnace or oven in which pottery is fired (pronounced "kill"). |
| *Leather hard* | Clay which is partly dry. The color of the clay is still that of moist clay, but the clay is firm and cannot be modeled. |
| *Score* | To make marks or scratches on moist clay with a tool; a step in welding two pieces of clay together. |
| *Sgraffito* | Decoration produced by scratching lines of a design through a surface layer of engobe which reveals the clay below. |
| *Slip* | Clay that is mixed with water to the consistency of cream. |
| *Slip painting* | Decorating with engobe, also called colored slip, by painting directly on clay. |
| *Stacking* | Placing clay work in kiln before firing. |
| *Stilts* | Small pieces of equipment to put under glazed ware during firing in the kiln; namely, buttons, triangles, pins, and the pieces called stilts. |
| *Texture patterns* | Designs pressed or scratched into moist clay by a variety of small articles such as nails and combs. |

229

*Underglaze*    Commercially prepared color used for decorating raw clay.

*Waterproofing*    Sealing a bowl that is porous and sweats after firing. The bowl is heated and a candle rubbed over the inside.

*Wedging*    The process of conditioning clay for efficient use and removing air pockets.

*Welding*    The process of joining two pieces of clay together securely with slip.

KINDS OF CLAY

There are several kinds of clay that can be used in the elementary grades, but three in particular are basic for a well-rounded series of experiences. These are white or buff modeling clay, red modeling clay, and terra cotta. The white and red modeling clays are the most frequently used; terra cotta gives variety to children's work in the upper grades.

Terra cotta is a mixture of red clay and 10 to 20 percent of medium coarse grog or brick dust. The addition of grog or brick dust strengthens the clay body and lessens the hazards of firing. Terra cotta has a rough texture that is attractive for many articles, such as Indian bowls and animals.

Clay may be purchased in either of two forms: a dry powder, usually called clay flour; and prepared clay ready for use, called either moist or pugged clay. Without a doubt, moist clay is the more efficient for school use, and the slight additional cost is negligible when compared to the efficiency of having clay ready when it is needed.

QUALITIES OF CLAY

Good clay should be workable, plastic, and fine in texture, and it should dry well. Workable clay will neither stick to the hands nor crumble and fall apart when used. Plastic clay can be rolled in a coil and bent into different shapes without cracking. Fine texture in clay, except terra cotta, which is a rough clay, is determined by the satin smoothness of clay flour and moist clay when rubbed between the fingers. Good clay dries in a reasonable length of time, not only on the surface but within as well. Atmospheric conditions affect the time it takes clay to dry.

230    If after mixing a trial batch of clay it is not workable

or plastic, the next batch of clay can be improved by adding to the clay flour up to 40 percent talc and up to 5 percent bentonite. When clay flour is coarse, there is nothing to do except order a finer mesh clay next time. Moist clay can have the same defects as clay flour, and these defects can be remedied only by buying from another manufacturer.

## PREPARING CLAY

Clay flour is not difficult to prepare. The only disadvantage of mixing clay is that it requires wedging by the children. Moist clay is delivered ready to use and only needs a little wedging to make it easier to handle.

In general, the following proportions are successful, but, since clays differ, experience in mixing may lead to smaller or larger amounts of water:

For twenty-five pounds of clay flour add five quarts of warm water and one-quarter cup of vinegar.

For fifty pounds of clay flour add ten quarts of warm water and one-half cup of vinegar.

For one hundred pounds of clay flour add five gallons of warm water and one cup of vinegar.

Put the clay flour into a crock large enough to hold the amount to be mixed. If talc and bentonite are added, mix the ingredients into the clay flour with the hands. Pour in the water and vinegar, but do not stir or mix it into the clay. Allow the mixture to stand for sixty hours in the crock with the cover on. Check for moisture from time to time and add a little warm water if necessary. Clay which has matured for this length of time is easier to wedge. Vinegar in the water tends to neutralize the alkaline content and makes the clay less drying to the hands. Terra cotta is prepared in the same way.

## WEDGING THE CLAY

The purpose of wedging clay is to make it more plastic, to force out any air trapped in pockets, and to secure a uniform distribution of moisture. Clay that is not sufficiently wedged will be crumbly and stick to the hands. Air pockets cause a piece of work to break when fired. Clay is

231

hard to model when some parts are soggy and wet, others powdery and dry.

There are two methods of wedging—dropping clay and smearing clay. The first method is more practical for lower grades and is done by dropping a piece of clay onto the wrong side of a piece of oilcloth from a height of about two feet above the table. After a number of such drops, exert force by throwing the clay down hard. Twenty times should be enough for wedging. If all the members of the class are wedging at one time, the teacher might count so that the children will wedge in unison and so speed the operation. The stimulating activity of wedging clay excites some children, so it is a good plan to wedge just before the recess period and let the class work off its high spirits on the playground.

The second method of wedging clay, by smearing, is a quieter activity, but it takes stronger hands and more skill than are required for dropping. Pile a portion of clay on the front edge of the wrong side of a piece of oilcloth. Push small quantities of clay across to the opposite side of the oilcloth with the heel of the hand. Switch the oilcloth around, and do the same thing. Repeat this two or three more times. Pressure should be exerted downward on the clay as it is pushed across the oilcloth. This squeezes together any air pockets in the clay, thus expelling the air.

If the clay work is to be fired it must be tested for the presence of air pockets regardless of how the wedging was done and even if prepared moist clay is used. From a piece of fine wire and two short sticks make a cutter for testing clay. Wind the ends of the wire around the sticks and use them for handles. Cut through the clay with the wire. If any air pockets are present they will show in the cut surfaces of the clay and prove that more wedging must be done. When the clay is put together again to wedge, reverse one part so that the two cut parts are not joined together. It is wise to test the clay several times with the wire if there is any doubt about the efficacy of the wedging.

Wedging clay is a good habit for children to form and it is good practice to do a little before starting work. Terra cotta requires less time spent in wedging than other clays because the grog makes the clay porous and permits air to escape freely during the firing.

STORING CLAY

Clay must be stored in such a way as to retain its moisture. Crocks and garbage cans with lids always in place make good containers.

It is helpful to cover the clay with a wet cloth. When clay begins to dry out, holes can be poked in it with a smooth stick and some water poured in the holes. Moist clay is packed in plastic sacks or cartons. Clay may be safely left in sacks, but should be removed from cartons and stored in a crock. No clay should ever be stored in a hot, dry place or near a heater.

RECLAIMING CLAY

Leftover and discarded pieces of clay are reclaimed by wrapping them in damp cloths and setting them aside for a few days. When the clay is sufficiently wet it may be put back in the clay crock and used again.

PRESERVING UNFINISHED WORK

Children's incompleted work must be kept moist until finished. Partly completed work may be wrapped in a damp cloth between working periods and put away on a cupboard shelf. However, if a piece of work must be kept for a long time, wrap a piece of plastic over the damp cloth and fasten the plastic together with clothespins to keep it as airtight as possible. A small piece of work can be kept airtight in a coffee can with the lid on.

DRYING CLAY WORK

Proper drying is important for successful clay work. The thin edges and small parts of clay work dry faster than the body of the work and often crack and fall off. To avoid this, moisten the parts lightly with a paint brush dipped in water. Do this several times during the drying period until the danger is past.

Cracks sometimes appear around the base of a bowl where the sides and bottom are joined together. This frequently happens when a bowl is left on a table to dry and may be prevented by setting the bowl on stilts. By doing so, air can circulate under the bowl as well as around it and the drying will be more even.

Children often hope to shorten the tedious drying period by putting their work on a heater. This is unwise because the heat will dehydrate the surface clay while the inner clay remains moist. Because of

233

the more rapid shrinkage of the surface, cracks will appear and parts will fall off. It is best to be patient and not try to hurry the process.

The body of an animal has a tendency to sag from the weight of the water in the clay. To overcome this, put a piece of wadded-up paper under the body while it dries. Another device for supporting extended parts of an animal, such as a giraffe's neck, is to brace the neck under the head with a stick or pencil. The stick can be kept from slipping by embedding the end in a wad of clay. Supports should be removed as soon as the clay is firm enough to hold its shape.

WELDING WITH SLIP

Slip is used when two parts of a piece of work are to be joined. The process is called welding. The slip must be made of the same kind of clay used for the rest of the work. Mix clay and water together to the consistency of thick cream. With a sharp pencil score the two parts

*San Bernardino City Schools*

to be welded, apply the slip, and press the parts together. Smooth the joining so that it will not show when dry. Do not handle the parts until the welding has set, and then carefully until the clay is bone dry.

## MENDING CLAY WORK

Mending is a difficult job to do and the teacher will have to do it for primary children. Bone-dry clay is impossible to mend and leather-hard clay will often break again when in the kiln. There are two things to remember about mending clay: use as little water as possible, for too much water will wash away more clay; and mend with moistened clay shavings scraped from some place on the piece to be mended.

A crack in a bowl must first be widened a little with a knife to make enough space for pressing in the moistened shavings. Make a tiny hole at the end of a crack and fill it with moistened shavings. This will keep the crack from becoming any longer. Smooth the surface of the crack carefully and put the bowl aside to dry. A chip which has broken from the rim of a bowl cannot be put back in place; instead, the area must be rebuilt with shavings.

## FIRING CHILDREN'S WORK

It is always a question as to how much of children's work is material for firing. For one thing, much that is done in every grade is exploratory and not of enough value to be made permanent. Also, it is a rare exception when primary work survives firing. Nor is there any necessity to fire work made for small-scale construction units, dioramas, or similar needs. In fact, if for these purposes clay is left unfired and painted with tempera, the result is more colorful and fits in better with the rest of the work. Pottery and tiles must be fired, and it is good to fire figurines and other modeling done in upper grades where children are skilled in the techniques of welding and wedging clay.

### Kilns

Every school should have a large, permanently installed electric kiln. An additional, small, movable kiln on a platform with rollers is a valuable teaching aid. The movable kiln can be rolled into a classroom and plugged into an electric outlet. (See illustration.) This will serve two purposes: a small amount of work can be fired promptly, and the class can have the highly educational experience of observing a firing. Children need this experience to understand what firing means. It is exciting for them to remove the plug and look through the peephole and see what is happening inside the kiln. This is the dramatic and concluding step in the cycle of working with clay.

### Methods of Firing

Traditionally, clay that had been glazed was always fired twice, first for biscuit and next for glaze. However, if one of the recently developed glazes is used, only one firing is required. This saves teacher-time spent in stacking the kiln twice. Consult a local ceramic supply dealer for the best glaze to purchase. Some brands are not always available in every area. Glaze should be painted heavily on the clay when the work is to be fired only once. Handle the work carefully when putting it in the kiln, taking care not to brush off any of the glaze. Use stilts.

### Preparing Cones for the Kiln

Insert a number of cones of each temperature into small lumps of clay several days before firing; otherwise, the cone will topple over when the clay shrinks in the heat of the kiln.

### Stacking the Kiln for Two Firings

Divide the children's work into two groups, green ware and glazed ware. Before completing the stacking of the kiln,[2] place cones on a shelf opposite the peephole. Use cone Nos. 08 and 07 for green ware; cone Nos. 08, 07, and 06 for glazed ware. Every inch of space can be used in a kiln provided no work touches the side walls where the electric elements are installed. Work should be about one-half inch from the walls. Green ware, both plain and decorated with engobe, can be stacked by putting the heavy pieces on the bottom and the lighter pieces on top. Little objects can be placed wherever one is able to find a spot for them in the kiln.

When stacking glazed ware, each piece must be placed individually on a stilt to prevent the glaze from fusing to the floor or a shelf of the kiln. Pieces of glazed work must be placed about an inch apart or they, too, will fuse. Glaze is essentially liquid glass and will fuse to whatever it touches.

236

*Stacking for a Single Firing*

Follow the same directions as given above, putting the unglazed ware on the bottom and lower shelves of the kiln and the glazed ware above. Place three cones opposite the peephole: Nos. 08, 07, and 06.

*Prefiring and Firing a Loaded Kiln*

Prefiring children's clay work is a necessary operation for the safety of the stacked work. Prefiring drives out any moisture retained in the clay and glaze. Prefiring will often, but not always, prevent an explosion in the kiln during the firing period. Pieces of children's work, when improperly wedged or welded, will explode in the kiln. This destroys other children's work adjacent to them. Prefiring will also dry out the glaze. Of course, no clay work is ever put into a kiln until after a period of slow drying in the classroom. This drying period can *never* be omitted.

To prefire a loaded kiln, prop open the lid slightly. If the kiln is large and has more than one switch, turn on the lower switch late in the day and let the kiln heat during the night. Early the next morning, turn on all the switches and fire the kiln until the required temperature is reached. (Make sure the lid of the kiln is closed.)

To prefire a small kiln, prop open the lid and turn on the switch. Let the kiln heat for an hour or two, close the lid and fire. The more work fired in any size kiln, the longer the firing time will be.

Watch the cones during the firing period. After the first cone, No. 08, goes down, check the remaining cones about every twenty minutes. Remember that electric heat builds up very fast toward the end of the firing period. When all the cones are down the firing is completed. Check the pyrometer at this time to see if the temperature coincides with the cone numbers. If not, reset the pyrometer to correspond with the cones. A cone is the more reliable indicator of conditions inside the kiln. Keep a record of the firing time for future reference.

The kiln can be opened when the temperature has dropped to 200° F. Some pieces of work may still be too warm to handle.

*Care of the Kiln*

From time to time, drops of glaze will spot the floor and shelves of the kiln during a firing. This can cause trouble in a subsequent

237

firing unless the spots are removed. Remove the spots by painting the floor and sides of the kiln with kiln wash. Then the drops of glaze can easily be picked off with a spatula. The kiln wash may be purchased in powdered form. Mix it with water until the mixture is fairly thin.

### DECORATION

Children nearly always want to decorate their finished clay work. Decoration[3] should be adapted to the clay in choice of design, space to be filled, and technique. Decoration should in no way detract from the structure or function of the basic clay form. Appropriate and well-designed decoration adds to creative work and provides new experiences for children in using tools and color. Children can effectively make four types of decoration: painted designs, incised designs, sgraffito, and texture patterns.

### Painting with Tempera and Water Color

Decoration with tempera and water color is a quick and easy way to add color to clay work. The color should be painted on while the clay is still moist. When the clay is thoroughly dry, it may be covered with a coat of plastic spray, which prevents color from rubbing off. This method can never be fired.

### Painting with Engobe (colored slip)

Decorating with engobe is also called slip painting because the underglaze color must be mixed with clay flour and water before it can be used. This type of decoration is one of the basic techniques. The work must be fired twice, once for biscuit and again for a transparent glaze. Prepared engobes under various trade names are now available for school use. They are more expensive than mixing the color at school because underglaze color is potent and a small quantity makes a lot of slip.

Underglaze colors which are successful when fired are black, green, royal blue, turquoise, yellow, rose, red brown, chocolate brown, and, of course, white. Engobe is prepared as follows:

One teaspoon of underglaze color pigment

Two tablespoons of white or buff clay flour
(moist clay must be dried out before measuring)

A few drops of glycerin

Mix the dry ingredients together and add water until the mixture is the consistency of thick cream. Glycerin is added to make the slip flow more smoothly. Use the same clay for mixing slip as is used for the clay piece.

Clays and colors vary in different localities, and it is wise to run a sample test through the kiln before mixing enough engobe for the class. The proportions given above should make a rich, dark color. Lighter values may be obtained by adding more clay flour. Remember that no pigment is a true color before it is fired and glazed.

Engobe should be painted on semimoist or leather-hard clay with a camel's-hair brush. Do not paint too heavy a coat or it will flake and fall off in the kiln.

*Incised Designs*

Surface patterns and unit designs are drawn on semimoist clay. Plan the design first on paper because incised lines are difficult to

*Beverly Hills Unified School District*    239

eradicate on the clay. Use a pencil with a sharp point for drawing on the clay. When leather hard, the clay may be burnished with the bowl of a spoon or a marble. This gives a soft satiny finish to the clay when it is fired.

Incised designs are made more attractive by adding a color. Engobe may be painted solidly on enclosed areas or in very simple patterns of dots and lines. Bands of color may also be painted next to the incised lines.

## Texture Patterns

Handsome texture patterns may be made with an assortment of miscellaneous items pressed into moist clay or scraped over the surface. The head of a screw or a nail, the end of a paper clip, or a pencil without an eraser, a small bolt, and a piece of a comb are a few of the things to use. Simple repeated patterns and borders are effective. Press deeply enough into the clay to leave a clear-cut impression. Practice making impressions on scrap clay before working. This is a time when an opaque glaze may be used in the firing.

*San Diego City Schools*

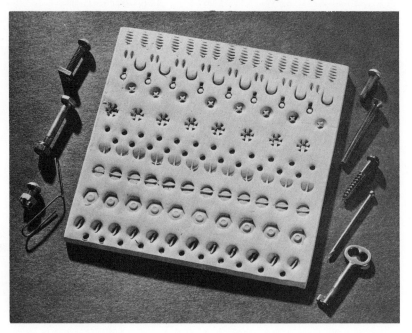

240

*Sgraffito*

Sgraffito is a combination of two methods, painting and incised lines. The color of the engobe should be in contrast to the clay, white or a light color on red clay, and dark colors on white clay. Paint on a thin coat of engobe when the clay is semimoist or leather hard, keeping the brush strokes in the same direction. Paint a second coat over it in the opposite direction. Plan the design carefully before starting to incise the lines because once a line is made it cannot be changed. Incise the design through the top coat of color with the sharp point of a pencil or an orange-wood stick. The color of the clay beneath will be revealed in the lines. The clay piece must be fired.

*Mottled Decoration for a Bowl or Tile*

The surface of a piece of clay work can be mottled with one or more colored slips by using a small, fine-grained sponge. Dip the sponge lightly into a saucer of engobe. Daub, pat, or press the sponge lightly over the surface of the clay. If a decorative pattern is desired, it can be made in three ways. Cut a paper stencil, hold it on the clay and sponge the engobe to the bowl. Or, cut a pattern out of paper, place it on the clay and sponge over and around it. The third technique is to first sponge the entire surface of the clay and, with free brush work, paint a black linear design on top of the engobe. Remember, mottling cannot be done on bone dry clay.

Mottled decoration is homely unless covered with a transparent glaze. Engobe colors do not mature until after a firing.

*Embossed Decoration*

An embossed design is attractive on a fairly large bowl but is too bulky for small bowls. Older children can handle this technique easily. Roll out a thin slab of clay. Next, draw a number of simple designs on paper—squares, circles, leaves, fish, or similar units—and cut them out with scissors. Try the patterns on the bowl for size and arrangement. Select those to be used for the decoration, and lay them on the thin slab of clay. Using a sharp knife dipped in water, cut around the patterns chosen. Cut as many units as needed to make the design. Apply slip to a unit, position the unit carefully and weld it in place. Smooth the edges of each unit of the decoration so that when glaze is later applied, it will smoothly

241

cover the whole surface of the bowl. A colored glaze is usually preferred because of its decorative effect.

### THE CLAY PROGRAM

Clay projects for children are divided into two categories, modeling[4] and pottery.[5] Children need helpful guidance by the teacher in order to develop self-confidence in handling new tools and equipment. Modeling and pottery offer opportunity for individual expression in form and decoration.

*Modeling Shows Development*

Early clay experiences reflect lots of imagination on the part of the child. A visitor to a kindergarten one day before Thanksgiving noticed two formless lumps of clay arranged on a piece of colored paper. The work was identified as "Two Dead Indians. Made by Dale." This is

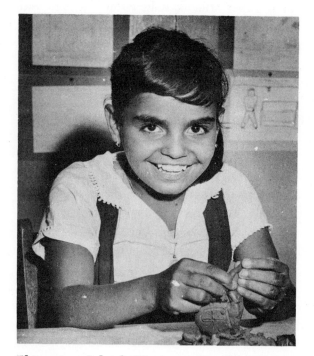

242    *Elementary School, District of Toa Baja, Puerto Rico*

representative of children's early manipulative experiences with clay. Beginning clay experiences are similar to the exploratory period in drawing and painting, for children are again discovering the nature· of a new material. The manipulative period in clay can last a long time with some first-grade children. However, the majority of children soon start making the seemingly endless number of snakes, worms, and baskets of eggs that so delight them.

From these exploratory experiences will develop the small-scale modeling of the things children know—trains, trucks, boats, and tea sets, produced by the dozen each year.

Primary children's work often breaks and falls apart after it dries or when children play with it, but the satisfaction of working with clay stays with them. As time passes and children mature, they become dissatisfied if everything they make comes apart or breaks. This provides motivation for instruction in welding with slip in order to make a sturdier and better piece of work.

There are two natural methods of modeling figures and animals. One method is to make the different parts—head, body, arms, legs—separately and weld them together. The other is to start with a ball of clay and pull and squeeze out the different parts of the body. Children should be encouraged to continue work in the way most natural to them as long as the method satisfies them. Big, chunky, short-legged figures of people and animals are natural with children and best because they are sturdy and representative of the natural quality of clay. Action and movement are always more expressive than static form.

Children's personalities are expressed in the surface modeling of their work, and it is a pity to destroy this individuality by sponging the clay with water or rubbing it down with the fingers. Texture marks left on clay show the directness of approach that is natural for children's work and that reveals their primitive response to clay. Clay modeling is one of the most rewarding, releasing, and satisfying of the art experiences for children. They can make clay come alive when encouraged to be creative and not allowed to copy a model. There is concrete evidence of maturation in the progress that children show in modeling from their first immature experiences to the skillful work of sixth-grade children. This development can only take place when children are provided with sufficient opportunity to model in every grade.

Modeling which will not be fired may be painted with

243

*Detroit Public Schools*

tempera or water color if some decoration is desired. Modeling which will be fired may be painted with engobe, biscuit-fired, and fired again with a transparent glaze. If preferred, an opaque color glaze may be used instead of decorating with engobe.

The base of all clay models should be leveled by rotating the model on medium-coarse sandpaper until the surface is smooth. After this is done, scratch the child's initial into the clay. When the work is to have a color glaze it is well to add the initial of the color to be glazed.

## Pottery and Related Projects

Children need techniques and processes in pottery[6] which must be correctly executed if their work is to be successful. Pottery is very different from modeling, for while originality and creative thinking are as important, pottery cannot be successful unless the skills are learned. Explanation of step-by-step procedure and demonstration of techniques are essential for establishing good habits of independent work.

The more lengthy discussion of pottery as compared with the discussion of modeling is no reflection on the significance of the model-

244

ing experience, but is necessary to assist the teacher to identify problems in order to do two things: select the most appropriate projects for the maturation of her group; provide proper materials and equipment.

TEACHER GUIDANCE FOR TYPICAL CLAY ACTIVITIES

### Making a Candle Holder and a Pencil Holder

A candle holder and a pencil holder are two very simple projects for first-grade children.

*Materials:* any kind of clay, dextrin, tempera paint

*Equipment:* newspaper, oilcloth, medium-coarse sandpaper, water, a candle, and a pencil

*Procedure:*

PREPARING THE CLAY: Make a ball of clay and work a teaspoonful of dextrin into the clay with the hands. The dextrin will harden the clay so that it will not have to be fired. Dextrin is not recommended for general use. Clay treated with dextrin can never be used again after it hardens. Dextrin may be purchased from ceramic supply stores.

MAKING THE HOLDER: Slam the ball of clay down on the table to make a flat surface for the base. Poke a hole with a candle or several holes with a pencil. Make the holes a little larger by rotating the candle or pencil. Otherwise, when the clay dries and shrinks, the holes may be too small.

DECORATING THE HOLDER: While the clay is still moist use tempera. When it is dry, spray with a plastic or paint on clear lacquer.

LEVELING AND INITIALING THE BASE: When the clay is bone dry, rotate the bottom of the holder on sandpaper and initial the base with the child's name.

### Making a Thumb and Finger Bowl

A small bowl shaped by using the thumb and fingers is suitable for primary grades.

*Materials:* red, terra cotta, or natural clay

*Equipment:* newspaper, oilcloth, medium-coarse sandpaper, water

*Procedure:*

MAKING THE BOWL: Take a portion of clay and shape it    245

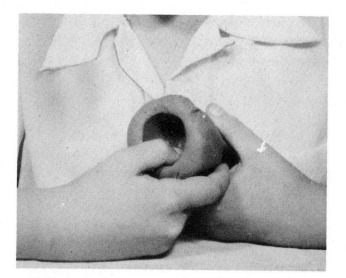

*San Diego City Schools*

into a ball. Work the thumb and fingers into the center of the ball until the walls of the bowl are formed. Keep the walls thick. Any shape of bowl may be made.

DECORATING THE BOWL: While the clay is still moist, paint on a decoration with engobe.

LEVELING AND INITIALING THE BASE: When the clay is bone dry, rotate the base of the bowl on sandpaper and initial with the child's name.

FIRING: Apply glaze and fire as preferred.

### Making a Free-Form Bowl

A free-form bowl is an adaptation of the thumb and finger method described above. While the clay is still moist and pliable, place the bowl in the palm of the hand. Holding the bowl in position with the thumb, press the fingers against the side of the bowl. A pleasing new shape will result. Complete the bowl as previously described. This is also a good upper-grade technique.

### Making a Coil Bowl

A coil bowl is a primitive type of pottery and is suitable for the Mexican and Indian units.

*Materials:* red or terra cotta wedged clay, slip, engobe, or tempera for decoration

246

*Equipment:* newspaper, oilcloth (wrong side), paring knife, water, medium-coarse sandpaper, small sponge, pencil, small can

*Procedure:*

MAKING THE BASE: Place a lump of clay on the oilcloth. Shape the clay into a round base about one-half-inch thick. Make a circle

*San Diego City Schools*

247

on the clay by pressing a can, cooky cutter, or jar onto the clay. Cut around the circle with a paring knife. Score around the base with a pencil and apply slip.

MAKING THE COILS: Shape a lump of clay into a fat sausage and roll gently with the hands, moving gradually toward the ends to stretch the clay into a long roll. The roll should be about one-half-inch thick and soft enough so that it will not crack when bent.

MAKING THE WALLS: Fit the coil around the scored edge of the base. Cut off the surplus coil. Weld the coil to the base and weld the ends together. Always work with one hand inside the bowl opposite to the hand smoothing the clay on the outside. This will keep the bowl in shape and prevent the walls from getting too thin. Score along the top coil and apply slip. Roll a second coil and weld it in place. Continue until the bowl is the desired height. Make an outward flare by putting each coil toward the outer edge of the coil below. Make an inner curve by putting each coil toward the inner edge of the coil below. See that the walls are about one-half-inch thick. Three coils are the most that can be added at one time; otherwise the walls will sag. Cover the unfinished bowl with damp cloths and continue work the following day.

FINISHING THE BOWL: After the bowl becomes firm, smooth any sharp edges on the rim with a sponge and the fingers.

DECORATING THE BOWL: If the bowl is not to be fired, paint designs with tempera; otherwise use engobe. Burnish the bowl by rubbing the clay with the bowl of a spoon or a marble.

LEVELING AND INITIALING THE BASE: When the bowl is bone dry, rotate the base on sandpaper and initial with the child's name.

FIRING THE BOWL: Glaze and fire as preferred.

### Making a Ripple Bowl
A ripple bowl is shallow and graceful.

*Materials:* red, terra cotta, or natural wedged clay, scrap clay, materials for decorating

*Equipment:* newspaper, oilcloth (wrong side), water, rolling pin or dowel rod, paring knife, medium-coarse sandpaper, small sponge, two pieces of lath twelve inches long or two rulers

*Procedure:*

DESIGNING THE BOWL: Draw and cut out a paper pattern

for the bowl. Circles and broad ovals are effective for this type of bowl.

MAKING THE SLAB: Place a portion of clay on the oilcloth and flatten it down with the hands. Put a lath on the oilcloth on each side of the clay. Roll the clay crosswise and lengthwise down to the level of the lath. If the clay cracks, make the slab into a ball, add a little water, and roll a new slab.

*San Diego City Schools*

MAKING THE BOWL: Place the paper pattern in the center of the slab and cut around it with a knife. Remove the excess clay and use it to make seven or eight balls about the size of marbles. Space the balls around the edge of the clay about two inches apart. Make extra balls if necessary. Lift up the edge of the slab and put the balls in position under it. The clay between the balls will fall naturally into place and make a ripple which gives the bowl its unusual shape.

FINISHING THE RIM: Smooth the rim with a sponge and the fingers so there will be no sharp edges.

DECORATING THE BOWL: Both painted and textured designs are attractive. Use engobe for painted decoration. Texture patterns must

249

San Diego City Schools

be done when the slab is moist and on the oilcloth. A color glaze may be used on unpainted clay or over a texture pattern.

LEVELING AND INITIALING THE BASE: When it is bone dry, rotate the bowl on sandpaper and initial with the child's name. If a color glaze is to be used, add an initial to indicate the color choice.

FIRING THE BOWL: Glaze and fire as preferred.

*Making a Bowl in a Hammock*

A hammock bowl can be an attractive free form.

*Materials:* red, terra cotta, or natural wedged clay, scrap clay, materials for decorating

*Equipment:* newspaper, oilcloth (wrong side), water, rolling pin or dowel rod, clothespins, paring knife, medium-coarse sandpaper, small sponge, two pieces of lath twelve inches long or two rulers, cheesecloth or muslin, a carton or kitchen bowl

*Procedure:*

PREPARATION OF HAMMOCK: Cut a piece of muslin or cheesecloth to go over the top of the carton or bowl, leaving a hangover of about four inches on all sides when in place. Use clothespins to fasten

250

the cheesecloth or muslin to the rim of the carton or bowl. This cloth serves as a hammock or sling to shape and hold the clay while it is drying. Roll out a slab of clay on the oilcloth. Cut out a paper pattern of the desired shape for the bowl. Place the pattern on the clay and cut around the edge with a paring knife dipped in water. Remove the extra clay and place the slab in the center of the cloth hammock or sling. Depress the clay gently in the center to form the bottom of the bowl.

FINISHING THE BOWL: Remove the bowl from the hammock when the clay is firm. Smooth the edges of the rim with a moist sponge or with wet fingers.

DECORATING THE BOWL: Both painted and textured designs are attractive. Use engobe for painted decoration. Texture patterns must be made when the slab is moist and on the oilcloth. A color glaze may be used on unpainted clay or over a texture pattern.

LEVELING AND INITIALING THE BASE: When the clay is bone dry, rotate the bowl on sandpaper and initial the child's name. If a color glaze is to be used, add an initial to indicate the color choice.

FIRING THE BOWL: Glaze and fire as preferred.

### Making a Tray

A small tray may serve many useful purposes. If made of white clay it can be glazed with a color. If made of red clay, a clear glaze would be used.

*Materials:* red, terra cotta, or natural wedged clay, scrap clay, materials for decorating

*Equipment:* newspaper, oilcloth (wrong side), water, rolling pin or dowel rod, paring knife, medium-coarse sandpaper, small sponge, two pieces of lath twelve inches long or two rulers

*Procedure:*

DESIGNING THE TRAY: Draw and cut out a square or rectangular paper pattern.

MAKING THE SLAB: Place a portion of clay on the oilcloth and flatten it down with the hands. Put a lath on the oilcloth on each side of the clay. Roll the clay crosswise and lengthwise down to the level of the lath. If the clay cracks, make the slab into a ball, add a little water, and roll a new slab.

MAKING THE TRAY: Place the paper pattern in the center

of the slab and cut around it with a knife dipped in water. Remove the excess clay and use it to make four thick rolls of clay. Place them under the edges of the slab to lift the clay up to make the sides for the tray. The sides should flare outward, rather than be perpendicular. Square sides would cause the clay to crack where the sides turn up. Put slip on the inside of the corners and pinch them tightly together on the outside. Apply slip to the bits of clay left over from making the corners and weld them to the outer side of the tray.

FINISHING THE TRAY: Smooth the edges with the fingers or a damp sponge. Dry the tray on a bat if possible.

DECORATING THE TRAY: Both painted and textured designs are attractive. Use engobe for painted decoration. Texture patterns must be made when the clay is moist and on the oilcloth. A color glaze may be used on unpainted clay or over a texture pattern.

LEVELING AND INITIALING THE BASE: When the tray is bone dry, rotate the bowl on sandpaper and initial with the child's name. If a color glaze is to be used, add an initial to indicate the color choice.

FIRING THE TRAY: Glaze and fire as preferred.

### Making a Compote

A compote has three legs and two handles. It is appropriate for the Mexican unit, but can be made of natural clay and decorated for other purposes.

*Materials:* red and terra cotta for the Mexican unit, or natural clay, slip, scrap clay, engobe, talcum powder

*Equipment:* newspaper, oilcloth (wrong side), water, rolling pin or dowel rod, paring knife, two pieces of lath approximately twelve inches long or two rulers, medium-coarse sandpaper, a piece of cheesecloth, small sponge

*Procedure:*

MAKING THE CORE: Place a mound of scrap clay on the oilcloth for making the core of the bowl. Model the clay into a pleasing shape. Make the sides flare outward toward the base so that the rounded top is smaller than the base. Smooth the sides and make the shape as symmetrical as possible. Cover the core with a double layer of cheesecloth and sprinkle with talcum powder.

252              MAKING THE SLAB: Place a portion of clay on the oilcloth

and flatten it down with the hands. Put a lath on the oilcloth on each side of the clay. Roll the clay crosswise and lengthwise down to the level of the lath. If the clay cracks, make the slab into a ball, add a little water, and roll a new slab.

MAKING THE BOWL: Lift the slab and place it over the cheesecloth on the core. Gently press the clay into position. Trim the excess clay from around the edge with a knife. Be sure the edges are the same thickness as the sides of the bowl; otherwise the edges may crack.

PUTTING ON THE LEGS AND HANDLES: Make a fat coil and cut it into three equal lengths for the short legs and two lengths for the

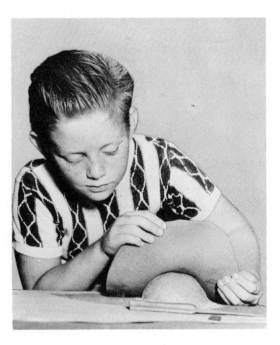

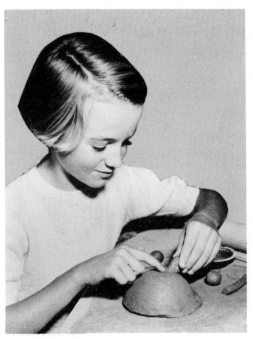

*San Diego City Schools*

handles. Taper the lower end of each leg. Score the top of the legs with a pencil. Score the places where the legs will be attached to the bowl. Apply slip to both scored areas. Press the legs onto the bottom of the bowl. Shape the pieces of coil for the handles and attach to the sides of the bowl at the base as described for the legs.

REMOVING THE BOWL FROM THE CORE: Allow the clay to become firm by leaving it on the core for several hours. Inspect the bowl occasionally to be sure it does not crack. Mend cracks immediately by smoothing them together. Lift the bowl off the core.

FINISHING THE RIM: Smooth around the rim with a sponge and the fingers so that there will be no sharp edges.

DECORATING THE BOWL: Make several designs for the inside of the bowl and select the best. Paint the decoration on the inside of the bowl with engobe. Black and white are the most effective on the red clays.

LEVELING AND INITIALING THE BASE: When the bowl is bone dry, gently rotate the ends of the legs on sandpaper and initial the bottom of the bowl with the child's name.

FIRING: Glaze and fire as preferred.

*San Diego City Schools*

*San Diego City Schools*

### Making a Planter

A planter is made over a core. Terra cotta is a good clay to choose. It blends harmoniously with both the earth in the planter and with the sturdy type of plants most suitable for the planter.

*Materials:* wedged clay or terra cotta, talcum powder

*Equipment:* newspaper, oilcloth (wrong side), water, rolling pin or dowel rod, paring knife, two pieces of lath about twelve inches long or two rulers, two blocks of wood eight by two by two inches, medium-coarse sandpaper, a piece of cheesecloth, metal-edged ruler, small sponge

*Procedure:*

Designing the Planter: On separate pieces of paper draw a number of interesting shapes of the size the planter is to be and select the best.

Making the Core: Place the drawing on the oilcloth and put a mound of clay within the outline drawn on the paper. With the hands shape the sides of the core even with the drawing. Make the sides

255

flare outward toward the base so that the top of the core is smaller than the base. Make the top of the core flat. To do this, put a block on each side of the core. Scrape the top of the core down to the level of the blocks with the metal edge of a ruler. Smooth the sides of the core and do not lose the changes of contour. Lay a double thickness of cheesecloth over the core and sprinkle with talcum powder.

MAKING THE SLAB: Place a portion of clay on the oilcloth and flatten it down with the hands. Put a lath on the oilcloth on each side of the clay. Roll the clay crosswise and lengthwise down to the level of the lath. If cracks appear, make the slab into a ball, add water, and roll a new slab.

MAKING THE PLANTER: Lift up the slab and place it over the core. Gently press the clay into position. Trim the excess clay from around the edge with a knife. Be sure the edges of the planter are the same thickness as the sides, for thin edges may crack.

REMOVING THE PLANTER FROM THE CORE: Allow the clay to become firm by leaving it on the core for several hours. Make a hole in the top of the slab, later the bottom of the planter. If a commercially prepared potting mixture is to be used in the planter, no drainage hole is necessary. Inspect the bowl occasionally to be sure the clay does not crack. Mend cracks immediately by smoothing them together. Remove the planter by taking hold of the cheesecloth and lifting the bowl off the core.

FINISHING THE RIM: Smooth around the rim with a sponge and the fingers so that there will be no sharp edges.

DECORATING THE PLANTER: A texture pattern of grooves on the sides with a fork or a comb is one suggestion; but other texture patterns can be made.

LEVELING AND INITIALING THE BASE: When it is bone dry, level the base by gently rotating the planter on sandpaper and initial with the child's name.

FIRING: Glaze the inside of the planter and fire. By putting the glaze inside, the seepage of moisture from watering the plants is minimized. If the same color glaze is allowed to drip down over the edge of the bowl, an interesting effect is achieved.

### Making Tiles

Making tiles is an activity for upper grades. It is appropriate as a related art project for the Mexican unit.

256

*Materials:* red, terra cotta, or natural wedged clay, engobe

*Equipment:* plaster of Paris bats, newspaper, oilcloth (wrong side), water, rolling pin or dowel rod, two pieces of lath twelve inches long or two rulers, medium-coarse sandpaper, paring knife

CAUTION: Tiles must never be made unless enough bats for drying them are available. Tiles warp and are useless unless properly dried.

*Procedure:*

DESIGNING THE TILE: Cut several squares of paper the size that the tile is to be and draw designs on each. Select the best for the tile.

MAKING THE SLAB: Place a portion of clay on the oilcloth and flatten it down with the hands. Put a lath on the oilcloth on each side

of the clay. Roll the clay crosswise and lengthwise down to the level of the lath. If cracks appear, make the slab into a ball, add a little water, and roll a new slab.

MAKING THE TILE: Place the pattern in the center of the slab and cut around the edge with a knife. Remove the excess clay. Place the tile on a bat and check for accuracy with the paper pattern. Smooth the edges and corners with the fingers.

DRYING THE TILE: Dry the tile between two plaster bats. Bats with tiles between may be stacked on top of each other so that each tile will be between two bats.

DECORATING THE TILE: (a) Painted design: remove the tile from the bats when it is leather hard and paint the design with engobe. (b) Incised design: draw the design with a sharp pencil before putting the tile between the bats. (c) Sgraffito: remove the tile from between the bats when it is partially leather hard, paint the surface with engobe, and draw the design with a sharp pencil. (d) Texture: press the pattern into the clay before putting the tile between bats.

TRANSFERRING DESIGNS AND GUIDE LINES: Designs and guide lines may be transferred to tiles in the following ways: (a) Draw the design on paper with ink. Place the paper on the moist tile and gently roll with a roller. When the paper is removed the drawing is imprinted on the clay. The lines will burn out in the firing. (b) By using a piece of foolscap paper transfer guide lines for a surface pattern to be made with texture tools. Cut out a square of paper, lay it on the tile, and gently roll it. When the paper is removed the lines will be on the tile but will burn out in the firing.

LEVELING AND INITIALING THE BASE: When it is bone dry, rotate the tile on the sandpaper. Do this thoroughly so that the tile will not rock when fired. Initial with the child's name.

FIRING: Glaze and fire as preferred.

### Making a Trivet

A trivet serves a useful purpose, particularly when used to hold a hot dish.

*Materials and equipment:* newspaper, oilcloth (wrong side), water, rolling pin or dowel rod, two pieces of lath twelve inches long or two rulers, medium-coarse sandpaper, paring knife, clay

*Procedure:*

DESIGNING THE TRIVET: Cut several triangles of paper, rather like a flatiron in shape. Select the best for the trivet.

MAKING THE SLAB: Place a portion of clay on the oilcloth and flatten it down with the hands. Put a lath on the oilcloth on each side of the clay. Roll the clay crosswise and lengthwise down to the level of the lath. If cracks appear, make the slab into a ball, add a little water, and roll a new slab.

MAKING THE TRIVET: Place the pattern in the center of the slab and cut around the edge with a knife. Remove the excess clay. Roll three balls of clay for the feet and weld them to the corners of the triangle. Turn the clay piece over and very gently press down on each corner in order to flatten the feet. Make a handle of clay and weld it to the short side of the trivet. Smooth the edges and corners with the fingers.

DRYING THE TRIVET: Put something under the trivet to prop it up to keep it from sagging while drying. A trivet will require a long drying period because it cannot be put between plaster of Paris bats.

DECORATING THE TRIVET: Any type of decoration can be used. If an incised or textured pattern is chosen, make the pattern before adding the feet to the trivet.

FIRING: Glaze and fire as preferred.

## Making Animals for Fun

A simple and entertaining art project for making caricatures in clay is to model the body of an animal over a balloon.

*Materials and equipment:* a slab of clay, slip, a medium-sized balloon of round or oval shape, a sharp instrument, a knife or other modeling tool

*Procedure:*

MAKING THE BODY: Blow up the balloon. Roll out the slab of clay as described in earlier projects and wrap it around the balloon, carefully sealing the edges with slip. The tied-off end of the balloon can be completely sealed over in this operation, if desired.

MODELING: Model the head, legs, and tail of the animal separately; weld each part to the body with slip. Let the clay dry until it is about leather hard. Then carefully puncture the animal on its underside with a pin or other sharp instrument, thus popping the balloon. With a knife or modeling tool carefully cut out a small hole at the point of puncture and extract as much of the balloon as possible. This operation provides an escape hatch for air that is trapped inside the balloon, thus preventing a possible explosion of the piece when it is fired. After the balloon has been removed it is usually possible to depress certain parts of the animal to more nearly conform to its normal shape. A side can be flattened so that the animal will sit more firmly, or a neck can be pressed into a more refined shape to alter the bulkiness of the creature being caricatured.

FIRING: Glaze and fire as preferred.

Some animals that lend themselves to this treatment in clay are the pig, rabbit, and beaver, and fowl such as ducks, penguins, and owls.

This approach to animal modeling is suitable for upper-grade elementary children who are capable of this type of clay activity and can catch the humor inherent in the work.

## MOSAICS

Mosaics have always been an important art form. Rio de Janeiro is famous for its sidewalks, and European churches of the Byzantine

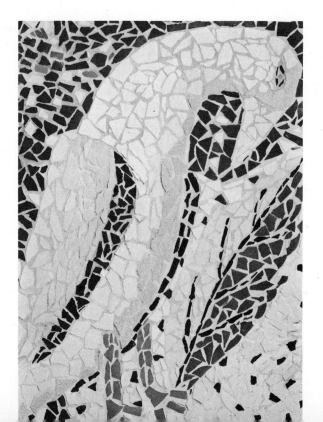

*La Mesa-Spring Valley
School District, Calif.*

260

period are noted for their wall decorations depicting Biblical and ecclesiastical history.[7] Mosaics have an important place in the elementary school art program.[8]

In school, several materials can be used to make a mosaic. The most important of these is tesserae. Tesserae is an Italian word meaning fragments of marble, glass, tile, and the like. Any kind of subject can be used for a mosaic—people, houses, birds, animals, geometric forms. Preliminary drawings should be strong in design and simple to execute.

Mosaics made of *paper* are a quick and instructive introduction to mosaics made of tesserae. Initiate the work by collecting colored paper, not only school paper, but also magazine advertisements and business brochures. These two sources provide some of the loveliest colors the children can have.

Start by drawing a design or picture on paper. If a firmer background is desired, trace the drawing onto a piece of cardboard. Cut the colored paper into small squares and rectangles and arrange them on the drawing, working for beautiful color combinations. When an unusual shape is required for a part of the mosaic, trim a square to fit the area, keeping the sides straight. When satisfied with the arrangement, fasten the pieces of colored paper to the background with all-purpose white glue, then fill in the background areas to complete the mosaic. It is best not to have any of the colored pieces overlap because this will be impossible when using tesserae. However, the pieces may touch each other or lie slightly apart so that the background is visible. A couple of coats of clear lacquer painted over the mosaic will protect it and add highlights.

Making a mosaic of *tesserae* follows much the same procedure as for making one of paper. After the drawing has been traced on a piece of plywood cut to fit the composition, the class is introduced to the interesting new experience of making the tesserae from clay. Roll out a quarter-inch slab of clay and cut it into small squares and rectangles. Dry the pieces slowly and thoroughly to prevent warping, sand the tiles, and put them in the kiln for the biscuit firing. Two firings are recommended because of the sanding. Paint colored glazes on the biscuit ware, then fire again. It is better to have too many glazed tesserae than too few. (But children can trade colors and share the tesserae.)

The next step is to arrange the tesserae on the plywood backing. They may be placed touching each other or slightly apart so that channels the depth of the tesserae become a part of the mosaic.

261

*La Mesa-Spring Valley School District, Calif.*

In the course of making the arrangement some odd-shaped tesserae will probably be needed. To cut a tile the desired shape, use tile cutters and a cutting box. A cutting box is a safety precaution to protect children from flying pieces of tile. To make a cutting box, remove one side of a wood or heavy cardboard box. Bind a piece of heavy glass on all four edges with masking or adhesive tape. Cover the open side of the box with the glass. By looking through the glass, a child can use the tile cutters efficiently inside the box.

Fasten the tesserae to the plywood with liquid casein glue or all-purpose white glue. If there are channels in the mosaic, fill them with grout or cement. Should any of the filler adhere to the face of the mosaic, it can be wiped off with a damp cloth.

An attractive way to complete a mosaic is to frame it in a wood molding.

An outstanding example of interschool cooperation through an art experience was the planning and execution of a tessera mosaic for an outside wall of a new elementary school building in Bart, Pennsylvania. The project is described and illustrated in Chapter 8.

*Other materials* for making mosaics have become popular. Combinations of beans, seeds—sesame, bird seed, packaged flower seed, seeds gathered from fields—shells, gravel, pebbles, uncooked and dry cereals, and different kinds of rice can result in muted and subtle color patterns.

Another material that children like is crushed eggshell. Wash the shells in soap and water and put them in a mild vinegar and water solution overnight. Spread out the shells to dry, and crush them the following morning. Save some pieces of shell for white accents and dye the rest. Commercial dye, ink, Easter egg dye, tempera, and water color can be mixed with hot water for dyeing. To obtain different shades

*Montclair State College*

263

*Elementary Schools,*
*Solana Beach,*
*California*

of a color, remove some of the eggshells from the dye from time to time. This will result in a gradation from light to dark values. This is a learning experience for children because most of their work, and particularly that with colored papers, uses colors of full intensity. By dyeing eggshells and removing them from the dye at intervals, the children gain an experience in color value which is less common than their experience with colors of full intensity.

When using delicate materials like eggshells for a mosaic, apply the glue to the area to be covered, sprinkle the material over it and gently pat in place. Shake off anything that has not adhered to the paper.

Mosaics offer children a rich experience in color and an opportunity to learn more about design.

## SAND CASTING

Sand casting can be done equally well by primary- and upper-grade children. What are the supplies? Not many: plaster of Paris to which vermiculite, coarse brick dust, sand, and color pigments soluble in water can be added for texture and color; a wood box lined with oilcloth and partially filled with moist sand; a hook for hanging the casting if it is to be hung on a wall; and whatever a child wishes to use for decorative interest, provided it is a firm material, such as shells or pebbles.

With a spoon, carve out the shape to be cast in the sand, put the decorative pieces in place, and pour in the plaster. Teachers who have not mixed plaster of Paris before can follow the procedure described on the following page.

*San Diego City Schools*

*Plaster of Paris*

Pour some water into a bowl and sprinkle plaster of Paris on top, increasing the amount as it absorbs the water. When all the required plaster has mixed with the water, add the materials suggested for texture and color. Sprinkling is better than stirring the mixture because stirring creates air bubbles. For uniform consistency, submerge the hand into the plaster mixture and press out any lumps. When the plaster of Paris begins to set, lift the bowl and tap it sharply on the the bottom. This causes any air pockets formed in the plaster to rise to the top, resulting in a smoother, air-free, pouring mixture. A teacher must estimate how much plaster of Paris is needed for a given amount of water or use a full box of plaster according to the accompanying directions. It is much better to make the mixture as needed because plaster of Paris hardens very quickly and may set before the children are ready to use it. Plaster of Paris is ready to pour when about the consistency of thick starch.

Insert the hook when the plaster is partially set. When the plaster is firm, lift the sand casting from the box.

Sand casting is a good opportunity for free carving. Many things can be carved on the surface of firmly packed sand—animals, starfish, fish, geometrical designs—and depressed decorative areas can be added for interest. Depressions are reversed when the casting is removed from the sand and form raised patterns on the casting. The texture and shadows of these relief patterns soften the flat, cold appearance of plaster of Paris.

The great advantage of this type of carving is that mistakes are easily erased with a sweep of the hand, and a fresh start can be made. Some sand will always adhere to the casting; this adds texture and again softens the appearance of the surface of the casting. Indented designs in a carving are made by depressing the sand, either with a finger tip, the end of a pencil, a small block or disk of wood, a conical object, or any other similar instrument. Because the finished designs in sand casting are reversed, the children are in for a surprise when the plaster cast is removed—and the surprise is usually a pleasant one.

Sand casting is simple; it is excellent for primary grades.

## PLASTER CARVING

Carving can be dangerous for children, and most certainly so when hard wood is used. Soft pine is rather difficult to handle and balsa wood is almost impossible to carve because it splinters easily, but plaster is safe and easy to carve. Carving is usually the choice of boys.

After adding vermiculite to the plaster, mix it and pour into a milk carton which has been rinsed with a solution of liquid soap. When dry, the plaster block easily comes out of the carton. Plaster may be carved with a kitchen paring knife, tenpenny nails sharpened into different shapes, or with a Boy Scout knife.

As a child carves, he should look at his work from all sides to maintain a proper relationship between proportions. Texture patterns may be added by incising the surface of the plaster with a nail or any other suitable sharp tool. If the children are mature, they will like carving abstract shapes, and their results are often most interesting. Carvings of this kind are an additional experience in three-dimensional abstract forms.

## METHODS OF PRINTING

Printing offers a comprehensive sequence of experiences for children. There are methods of printing suitable for the maturation of children from the first to the sixth grade. All printing should be done on a thick newspaper pad.

### FINGER AND SPONGE PRINTING

Printing for primary children is easy, quick, and a pleasant new activity. Finger printing is no more than dipping the tip of a finger in tempera paint and pressing the color on paper. When several colors are used, a nice scatter pattern is made. Sponge printing moves along as rapidly as finger printing. Cut a fine-grained sponge into small pieces. Moisten the sponge slightly and rub it over a pan of water-color paint or dip it in tempera paint. Press the sponge on the paper. The amount of pressure will determine the shape and size of the spot. A separate sponge

267

must be used for each color. Finger and sponge prints are suitable for book covers and mats. Mats look very nice on primary tables under a vase of flowers or a figurine.

STAMP PRINTING

Stamp printing with wood or potato stamps follows naturally after finger and sponge printing. Odds and ends of soft wood such as pieces of dowel and spools are used for the printing. Besides a potato,[9] a carrot or a turnip can be used for a stamp. Cut a slice off the end of the vegetable and cut a design on the end. Several stamps may be made to use in one pattern and are attractive when printed in different colors. Place a thick newspaper pad under the paper before printing. A narrow strip of paper may be laid on the paper to guide the placement of the stamps.

268

Another method of stamping a design on paper is to use chipboard. Cut pieces of chipboard into different widths, probably under two inches. Each piece must be long enough for a child to hold comfortably. Apply tempera paint to the bottom edge of the stamp with a brush. Choose a paper for stamping that is fairly absorbent, such as the Manila and colored paper stocked by schools. Have a different stamp for every color to be used so that each color will keep fresh and clear. At first the pattern will be scattered, but as the child works he will enlarge it by choosing different-sized stamps and by changing colors. Repetition of a dominant color will give unity to the design. Besides pressing the stamp on the paper, the child may drag the color on with the stamp. Also, the stamp can be twisted onto the paper with different arm movements, giving a different shape to the color when printed. There are other ways of varying the printing process which the child will discover for himself after he starts work.

When finished, chipboard printing can result in compact and colorful surface patterns.

## LINOLEUM PRINTING

Linoleum printing[10] is the most difficult of the printing processes. For this reason upper-grade children do it more efficiently. Linoleum tools, interesting subjects, and good organization are necessary for a successful experience.

A cutting board is a safety device for cutting linoleum. Boards are easy to make and a few in the classroom would speed the process of cutting for children. Make a board from a piece of wood six by nine by three-quarters of an inch. Nail a narrow strip of wood across one end of the board. Turn the board over and nail another strip across the opposite end. Put the board on the table so that the under strip catches the edge of the table. The top strip keeps the linoleum from slipping while it is being cut. Instruct the children always to cut away from themselves when using a linoleum tool.

Only linoleum purchased at an art supply house will make a good print. Other linoleum does not have the necessary cutting depth or proper surface. It is not necessary to mount the linoleum on a block of wood. Put a coat of white tempera paint over the linoleum and lay it aside until later.

269

*San Diego City Schools*

      Start by making a pencil drawing on a piece of paper the same size as the piece of linoleum. When the drawing is completed, paint all the parts black which are to be cut away on the linoleum. This will show the child how his drawing will look after it is printed and give him the opportunity to make any changes he thinks necessary. Carbon the back of the paper with a soft pencil. Trace the drawing onto the linoleum. Using the drawing for a guide, wipe off the white paint on the linoleum from the corresponding areas which are black on the drawing. This will make it clearer to the child when he starts to do the cutting.

      Only good linoleum tools should be used for cutting. A wide and a narrow U gouge and a V liner are needed. Razor blades and penknives are dangerous for children to use. Put the linoleum on the cutting board and start gouging away the largest areas. This will give the children experience in handling the tool before cutting the fine lines with the liner. Texture patterns give interesting accents when printed. It takes time to cut the linoleum and children should not feel pressed for time or the tool will slip and spoil all their good work. Wash off the white paint when the cutting is completed.

Any kind of absorbent paper may be used for printing, but the best is a paper towel. It is highly absorbent and has an interesting texture.

Do the printing on a large table and have everything laid out in advance: a newspaper pad, printing paper, inking block, ink, and roller. Use a piece of glass or marble for the inking block. Put a small quantity of ink on the block and smooth it over the block with the roller. Water-soluble ink comes in several colors and is preferred to printer's ink in elementary grades. Place the printing paper on the pad. Ink the linoleum with the roller and put the linoleum on the paper. Press down on the linoleum as hard as possible. Or put the paper on the cut and rub over it with a block of wood, a roller, or the bowl of a spoon. Several prints will have to be made before the child learns how much ink to use and how much pressure to exert. Many prints can be made from a linoleum block.

Surface patterns may be printed on paper or fabrics. Use a strip of paper to assure correct placement of the block. It is rewarding to see how handsome a very simple design becomes when it is repeated

*Beverly Hills Unified School District*     271

*Board of Education,*
*City of Chicago*

many times in a pattern. Printing on fabrics requires textile inks; otherwise designs on tea napkins, handkerchiefs, and place mats will wash out when laundered.

GLASS PRINTS

Glass prints are naïve and childlike. They are quick to make and primary grade children have fun doing them. Only three prints can be made from the original. The technique is simple. Spread the ink on a piece of glass with a roller. Draw a picture or design on the glass with the tip of a finger or the eraser end of a pencil. Put a piece of newsprint over the ink and smooth the paper very gently with the hands. Lift off the paper and what will the child find? A delightful impression of the drawing he made on the glass. Nicely mounted, glass prints make a delightful gift to take home.

ROLLER PRINTING

Roller printing is fast and successful. It holds a surprise for the child because he cannot foresee what the result of his work will be until the first printing has been made.

272

There are several ways to make a roller. One very easy way is to use an eight-inch tall glass jar. Other ways are to use a thick piece of doweling at least two inches in diameter, a firm mailing tube, such as is used for mailing photographs, or an old rolling pin.

The first step in roller printing is to prepare the roller. If a glass jar or a mailing tube is used, pull or soak off the label. Then the procedure is the same as for any roller. The pattern to be printed is a design made by gluing a length of heavy and absorbent soft twine, or pieces of felt, or a combination of twine and felt pieces, to the jar in whatever design or pattern the child may choose.

Extra fast drying, water-resistant glue must be used. All-purpose white glue cannot be used; it would dissolve when the printing is done with tempera or poster paint because it is water soluble. The water-resistant glue comes in tubes and is the same as that used for airplane models.

Using the nozzle of the tube as a drawing tool, trace the design on the glass jar, running the glue just ahead of the twine and press-

*Courtesy of Mrs. Herbert Berlier, San Diego*

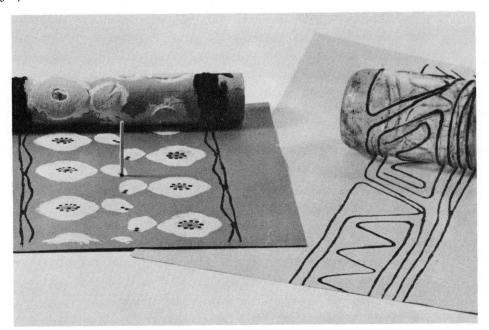

ing the twine firmly in place on the glue. Any kind of linear design can be made by laying the glue down in curves, angles, or straight lines. If solid areas are to be a part of the design, glue pieces of felt to the roller. These pieces of felt can be cut in geometrical designs, such as circles and triangles, in the outlines of animals or birds, or in whatever shape strikes the fancy of the child.

There is just one caution to keep in mind. Leave ample space at each end of the roller for the child to place his hands when rolling out the design. Otherwise his hands, clothes, and paper will be smeared needlessly with paint. After the roller has been prepared, set it aside for a day so that the twine and felt will thoroughly dry.

The advantage of using a mailing tube or rolling pin is that if a child wishes to he may sketch his design on the roller before gluing on the string or felt pieces. Even if he does do this, he cannot fully visualize his design before it is rolled out, so a surprise still awaits him.

Before starting to print, the child should decide on the color of paper and paint he is going to use. The paper can be Manila, cutting paper, or any absorbent paper that will print well. Water-color or tempera paints should be used. A small, wide brush makes it possible to paint with one stroke several lines that are close together; this will shorten the time required for painting.

Paint the twine and pieces of felt as fast as possible so that they will remain moist until the printing is done. Different parts of the design, such as the felt pieces, can be painted in different colors. After allowing a little time for the twine to absorb the paint, apply a second coat to provide more moisture. Make a trial printing by rolling the jar over a piece of newsprint. Repaint if the trial print is not satisfactory. In printing, remember to move the roller forward only. Never roll back over a design already printed. When the trial print is satisfactory, make as many prints as desired. If the string or felt dries out, repaint.

If, after the trial printing, the child finds that he wants to add an accent to his design, he can do so very easily. It can be done by making a little wood stamp and painting it with whatever color he chooses for the accent. Dots can, for example, be made with the end of a matchstick. Press the stamp onto the print already made. Stamp printing superimposed on roller printing will result in two-color prints when the string or felt has been painted with only one color.

274 After his first printing, should the child find that his design

is incomplete, he can glue on extra pieces of felt or another length of string, and allow them to dry overnight. He can evaluate his own work, or join in the evaluation of the work of the group.

A child greatly enjoys doing this type of printing and relishes its unexpected outcomes. To think of ingenious ways of using his print can be a challenge to him. He might, for example, wish to delight his mother with a place mat or decide to print some invitations for a party.

## OFFSET PRINTING

Another type of printing is done with a gelatinous roller called a brayer. A brayer has a soft and impressible surface; when inked, this surface picks up any design it is rolled over. The inked brayer is then rolled over whatever paper is to be used. The imprint on the brayer is printed on the paper. This process is called offset printing.[11] To ink the brayer, roll it over some printer's ink on a flat, hard, non-absorbent surface.

## STENCILING

Stenciling[12] does not offer a wide range of opportunities for expression. As a short-term activity, it can further experience in design. The approach must be creative, for stenciling can easily become trite and monotonous. However, as a change of pace in a year's art program, stenciling serves a useful purpose and many children enjoy it very much.

Undertaken as a design problem, stenciling can produce varied and distinctive results. By overlapping stencils, using colors well, and varying the number, size, and shape of each stencil, surface patterns of interest and individuality can be achieved. There is something satisfying to many children in the mechanics of repetition which stenciling provides, as do all printing methods.

Upper-grade children can handle a number of stencils competently. Each unit must be very simple in shape because it has to be cut out of the stencil paper. Nature forms and geometric shapes can be simplified and modified. The texture and color of the paper on which the stenciling is done can be an asset to the finished work.

The discarded backs of typewriter stencils can be salvaged from the school office. They can be cut into fairly small pieces and each piece used for a single stencil unit in the design. It is the manner in which

275

these individual units are combined when stenciled that makes a finished piece of work smart or ordinary. A unit is drawn on each piece of stencil paper. In the elementary grades, sharp scissors should be used to cut out the stencil—never a razor blade. In the upper grades a stencil knife may be used. A pair of sharp-pointed manicure scissors is helpful when cutting inside curves.

When stenciling a fabric, a textile paint must be used and the manufacturer's directions followed explicitly. Otherwise, for paper work, tempera paint and crayon have equal value. Choose a stiff brush for painting. Stroking a loaded brush over a paper towel a couple of times removes some of the moisture from the bristles and produces a textured effect rather than a solid color when the stencil is removed. A line of colored crayon drawn around the edge of the cut-out and rubbed onto the paper with the eraser end of a pencil will give much the same effect. Color can also be applied solidly.

Surface patterns developed by stenciling are crisp and have a style of their own.

### SILK SCREEN PRINTING

Silk screen printing is a simple way for children to make prints, greeting cards, and posters. It is a quick and efficient process.

276

When lettering is necessary, it does not present the problem that occurs in block printing because there is no reversal of either design or lettering.

Silk screen printing may be done in either of two ways. One method is based on the principle of crayon resist, and the other is similar to stenciling. For the first method, use a pair of round or oval embroidery hoops for the framework. Standard organdy, theatrical gauze, tarleton, or any other material which will keep its tension and not become soggy when wet, and through which the design to be traced can be seen, can be substituted for silk. Even an old handkerchief can be used, providing there are no holes in it. It is best to experiment with different materials, because some will prove satisfactory and others will not.

Before making the screen, draw around the inner side of the inner hoop on a piece of paper. This will define the area for the subsequent drawing.

To make the screen, put the fabric over the inner hoop and slip the outer hoop in place, pulling the fabric as tautly as possible. If the outer hoop has a screw-type fastener, screw it as tightly as possible to take up the slack of the fabric.

A squeegee takes the place of a brush in spreading paint on the screen. Cut out several small pieces of cardboard and fold them in two. A child will probably use two for each printing. The open ends of the folded cardboard can be fastened together with a staple. The folded edge is used for spreading the paint. These squeegees are disposable at the end of the project.

Draw the picture or design in the oval or circle that has already been made. Before crayoning, the child must decide which would be more effective printed in color—the picture or design, or the background. If lettering is to be used, as on a greeting card, do the lettering on the drawing. However, lettering is not too suitable for small children to attempt.

Place the inner hoop, fabric side down, on the drawing. Trace the drawing with crayon on the inner side of the fabric, bearing down heavily. Every so often, hold the screen up to the light to see if all areas to be covered are crayoned sufficiently to make them as opaque as possible. However, it is the slight variations that give the printed work a charm of its own in unexpected texture patterns.

When ready to do the printing, have the children put on their smocks and cover their desks or the working tables with newspaper. This is a messy project.

277

The paint to be used should be either a prepared silk screen paint or a substitute such as poster paint or dry tempera mixed to the consistency of poster paint. It is absolutely necessary to add a commercial binder to the paint. This binder is a colorless, jelly-like substance and is available at a paint store or a silk-screen supply house. Use about equal parts of the binder and paint. The teacher will have to experiment to get the right consistency for printing. The importance of using a commercial binder cannot be overemphasized.

To print, place the prepared screen, fabric side down, on the paper to be used. Place about a teaspoonful of the paint mixture at the top of the screen. Then with the folded edge of the squeegee, spread the paint across the screen, being careful to cover the whole surface of the fabric. Carefully lift up the embroidery hoop; a reproduction of the printed drawing can then be seen on the paper. It is best to have one child hold the paper while another carefully lifts up the hoop. As in crayon resist, the paint slides off the crayon, but penetrates the fabric wherever there is no crayon.

The results of this type of screen printing are attractive,

*Courtesy of Mrs. Herbert Berlier, San Diego*

and children of every age are pleased to learn an easy way to reproduce a number of copies of their original work.

The second method, which is based on stenciling, may require a small commercial screen and squeegee; these commercial devices are best used in the upper grades. Regular stencil paper should be used; a substitute paper such as the backs of office stencils tends to curl and will not give satisfactory results.

Cut a piece of stencil paper the exact size to fit in the frame of the screen. Draw the design or picture on the stencil paper with a pencil and add any lettering that is to be used. Cut out the areas to be printed. After careful instruction by the teacher, responsible upper-grade children can use a small X-acto knife for cutting out small parts. But a razor blade is never safe. Put the stencil in the frame and secure it in place with a strip of gummed craft tape. This will prevent paint from seeping through any openings between the stencil and the sides of the frame. Place the screen on a piece of paper of the same size or slightly larger, apply the paint, and spread it across the stencil with the squeegee. Upper-grade children can make a two-color print by drawing and cutting a second stencil to add additional parts and a second color to the print. When this is done, print the lighter color first; then, where overlapping colors are desired, the darker color will cover the lighter color first printed.

A pair of hoops can be used for a one-stencil print. Cut the paper the exact size to fit the inside of the inner hoop. After cutting the stencil, slip it into the hoop frame. Should paint seep out around the edges of the stencil, the circle can be trimmed later.

Silk screen printing eases the burden of upper-grade children who often have the responsibility of making many posters. Lettering need not be stenciled. After printing, lettering can be added freehand with a felt pen by the most skillful child in the class.

Stencils produce colors that are flat and unshaded compared to the shaded colors of crayon resist. But stencils can be used over and over, and crayon resist wears out after a few printings. Each has its function and each fulfills a different art need.

## Weaving

Weaving, like clay modeling, is a primitive craft and integrates naturally with the Indian and Mexican units. Weaving was a highly

*Beverly Hills Unified School District*

prized skill in early American life and contributes to the pilgrim and pioneer units in the social studies. Besides the values of correlation, weaving is a craft that offers fine independent experiences for children.[13]

### MANUFACTURED LOOMS

There are three types of manufactured looms generally used in the elementary grades: the jiffy loom, the waffle loom, and the harness loom.

The jiffy loom, which is for weaving pot holders, is excellent for primary grades. The construction of the loom eliminates the difficulty encountered by young children in establishing and maintaining an even tension. The weaving material is a jersey loop. The loops are like big rubber bands and the jersey gives them an elasticity that makes them easy for young children to use. Attractive patterns can be developed by the choice of colors used and their combination on the loom. There are

280

never two pot holders alike in a class; and there is seldom, if ever, a child who fails to have a successful experience.

The larger, adjustable waffle loom derives its name from the pattern of the table mats made on it. Although classed as weaving, the waffle loom does not use the weaving process of over-and-under warp threads. The looms are strung up with cotton or raffia according to the directions supplied by the manufacturer. Mats are attractive in color and texture and make a welcome and durable gift for a child to take home.

An excellent culmination for weaving in the elementary grades is the opportunity to weave on a harness loom. Harness looms can be purchased in table models and in twenty-four inch four-harness floor models. Although stringing up the warp is too difficult for children and must be done by the teacher, the children can successfully weave simple patterns such as the Doric, the herringbone, and others. Since hand weaving was one of the important crafts in our early culture, weaving has a significant historical meaning for children. Cotton thread and roving are suitable materials to use. Once under way, weaving proceeds rapidly, and mats, scarves, and other small articles are completed in a reasonable length of time.

*Beverly Hills Unified School District*

*San Francisco Unified School District*

TEACHER GUIDANCE FOR MAKING LOOMS

The box loom is the simplest kind to make because the basic construction is already done. Any sort of box will do; one as small as a cigar box, or as large as an apple box. An uneven number of brads for stringing the warp are nailed across the top edge of each end of the box. The size of the brads and the space between will depend upon two things: the size of the box, and the weight of the weft to be used. A thick weaving material like roving requires a wider space between the brads than is needed for a knitting yarn.

When a loom is made from a large box like an apple box, a narrow piece of wood must be sawed off both sides to make them lower than the ends of the box. This is done before the brads are nailed in place. Draw a line two inches from the edge on both sides of the box. Put a pencil mark two inches from each end. Draw lines from these marks to each top corner of the box. Using a coping saw, follow the line to cut off the wood. Smooth the edges with sandpaper. Lowered sides on the box make weaving easier for the children.

282

A table loom can be made like a frame. Horizontal cross-pieces are added to brace the loom. One-by-two-inch soft finished pine is the best wood to use. Cut two endpieces and two crosspieces of pine the correct length for the size of the frame to be made. In addition, cut as many additional pieces of wood the same length as the endpieces as seem necessary to brace the frame. Lay the endpieces on the worktable and put the sidepieces on top, making four corners. Nail the frame together. Lay the braces on the sidepieces and nail in place. Turn the frame over and nail the brads across each end. An uneven number of brads must be used. Weaving is easier for children when the brads are spaced about an inch apart. String the loom with carpet warp.[14]

SUGGESTIONS FOR WEAVING

Before commencing to weave, it is good practice to assemble the materials to be used for the weft and plan the color pattern by

*Board of Education, Rochester, New York*

making a crayon drawing. Put it on paper the same size as the weaving area of the loom. A pattern assures a more pleasing piece of work.

Commence weaving by putting in several rows of the warp thread at each end of the loom. Push the warp up tightly against the brads to make a firm band at each end. Weave the weft at both ends of the loom alternately by putting in a strip of color at one end and repeating it at the other end of the loom, doing this until the weaving is completed. This method makes possible a more uniform pattern. When a design unit is to be woven in the center, such as a diamond, put the design in first and then proceed with the rest of the weaving, interlocking the weft with the central unit.

Small rag rugs make a good group project for an integrated art experience with colonial or pioneer kitchen construction units. Colored cotton goods, both prints and solid colors, or muslin dyed different colors by the children are torn into strips and woven on the frame type of table loom.

Wools, rovings, and cotton yarns are appropriate for the simple looms which children make and use. These materials provide a variety of textures and offer opportunity for imaginative combinations of both colors and yarns.

THE SECRET OF GOOD WEAVING

The secret of good weaving is to keep an even tension. This takes time to learn to do. An even tension overcomes the "hour glass" shape that is seen in much of children's weaving and that is caused when the weft is pulled tighter than it should be as the weaving proceeds.

## REFERENCE MATERIAL

1. *What Will Clay Do?* 16mm. film, 12 min., sound, black and white; produced by Tabletopper Productions.

2. *Stacking a Kiln.* 16mm. film, 10 min., sound, color; produced by Indiana University.

3. *Craftsmanship in Clay: Decoration.* 16mm. film, 10 min., sound, color; produced by Indiana University.

4. *Clay Modeling.* (Primary) filmstrip, approximately 35 frames; produced by McGraw-Hill Book Company, Inc.

5. Duncan, Julia Hanlin, and Victor D'Amico. *How to Make Pottery and Ceramic Sculpture.* New York: Simon and Schuster, Inc., 1947.

6. *The Child as Potter.* 16mm. film, 20 min., sound, color; produced by Coast Visual Education.

   *Pottery Making.* (Intermediate) filmstrip, approximately 35 frames, color; produced by McGraw-Hill Book Company, Inc.

7. Bovoni, Giuseppe. *Ravenna Mosaics.* Greenwich, Conn.: New York Graphic Society, circa 1956.

   Kollwitz, Johannes. *Mosaics.* New York: Herder Art Series, circa 1954.

8. Sister Mary Magdalen, I. H. M. *Mosaics for Everyone.* Los Angeles, Calif.: Immaculate Heart College, 1958.

   *Mosaics for All.* Filmstrip, approximately 35 frames, color.
   I. "Easy ways—inexpensive ways."
   II. "Greater richness through variety in tesserae and cements."
   Produced by International Film Bureau, Inc. (Coordinated with *Mosaics for Everyone.*)

   *Mosaic Experiments.* 16mm. film, 20 min., sound, color; produced by International Film Bureau, Inc.

   *How to Make a Mosaic.* 16mm. film, 10 min., sound, color; produced by Tabletopper Productions.

9. *Potato Printing.* (Intermediate) filmstrip, approximately 35 frames, color; produced by McGraw-Hill Book Company, Inc.

   *How to Make Potato Prints.* 16mm. film, 12 min., sound, color; produced by International Film Bureau, Inc.

10. *How to Make a Linoleum Block Print.* 16mm. film, 14 min., sound, color; produced by International Film Bureau, Inc.

11. *Print With a Brayer.* 16mm. film, 8 min., sound, color; produced by International Film Bureau, Inc.

    Weiss, Harvey. *Paper, Ink and Roller.* New York: William R. Scott, Inc., 1958.

12. *Stenciling.* Filmstrip, approximately 35 frames, color; produced by McGraw-Hill Book Company, Inc.

285

13. *Weaving.* (Intermediate) filmstrip, approximately 35 frames, color; produced by McGraw-Hill Book Company, Inc.

14. *How to Make a Simple Loom and Weave.* 16mm. film, 16 min., sound, color; produced by Encyclopaedia Britannica Films, Inc.

MAGAZINES

*School Arts,* Davis Publications, Inc., Worcester, Mass.
*Arts and Activities,* The Jones Publishing Company, Skokie, Ill.

## READER PARTICIPATION

Try some clay modeling.

Draw a design for a greeting card and silk screen it using the crayon resist method. You may be surprised and really want to send some of your cards to friends when Christmas comes.

Make a paper mosaic in preparation for later presenting the making of a tessera mosaic for your class. If you are really ambitious, make a tessera mosaic for the top of a coffee table in your home. It will not take as long to do as you may think.

Discuss craft activities with a group of children to ascertain where their natural interests lie. Explore their previous craft experiences in school and do not repeat the same project in your class.

# 11

# *Evaluation*
## *Sets the Goal*

Evaluation of children's creative work is more effective when the approach is constructive and builds self-confidence than when it is critical and tears down good feeling. Constructive evaluation interprets art principles at the time when there is possibility for immediate application and when explanations are in terms familiar to children. Evaluation has for its goal the growth of children, not a perfected art product.

## PURPOSE OF EVALUATION

Before rewarding outcomes are to be expected from evaluation, the children must believe in its value. Their attitude is basic to the success of evaluation. Children usually believe in things which have proved helpful, about which they feel confident, and for which they have neither fear nor unhappy associations. There was a time when evaluation of creative work was chiefly criticism, and it was thought good practice to hold up before the class the paintings from a lesson and to look for mistakes. Happily, this point of view has passed, and the present emphasis in evaluation is upon building self-confidence, preserving the creative approach, adapting the interpretation to the maturity of the children, and helping them to become independent. Besides the educational purposes of evaluation, there is a practical side to be considered. Without evaluation, children

287

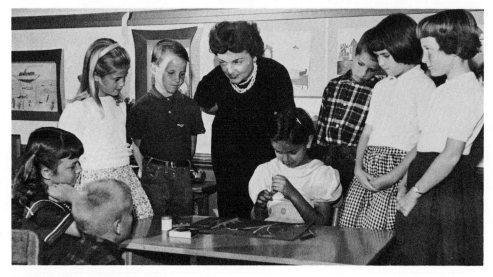

*Santa Barbara City Schools*

tend to feel that their art work is not recognized and that art does not have the same status in the program of studies as have other subjects.

## SINCERITY IN EVALUATION

Successful evaluation rests upon the sincere recognition of ability. When children trust their teacher, her opportunities for leadership in evaluation are unlimited. Without trust, evaluation can deteriorate and become a period of insincerity for the children rather than a time of fuller understanding of themselves and of art. When, throughout the day, and in every area of instruction, the children have a confident experience, evaluation is no longer a strange and potentially unhappy experience.

Children are appreciative of their teacher's recognition of the work of their classmates. When the teacher has an opportunity to present the talent of a child to the group in a natural and informal way, she demonstrates her respect for children's efforts and her appreciation for an art skill. Even though the children do not realize it they will have experienced evaluation through a sharing of skills. Evaluation, when an intrinsic part of the day's work, strengthens the child's feeling of recognition. Properly handled, children unconsciously identify themselves with the well-earned recognition given to their classmates and friends.

288

## EACH TO HIMSELF

Art evaluation has no measuring stick except as each child is measured against his own growth, his past production, and his present realization. An evaluation should not destroy the quality of child art, which is indeed subjective and elusive to define. Could it be that its essence is close to some spiritual quality of personality that makes each child what he is? Once a teacher has sensed the quality of child art, she will see it again and again as she studies and enjoys the creative work of children.[1]

Children's work changes in character from year to year, as do the children themselves, for it is inevitable that as children mature they will work differently. The delicate situation that arises for the teacher is to maintain the quality that is intrinsic to child art and not let it be overshadowed by an emerging concern for techniques which is natural as children mature. With skillful teacher leadership, the balance can be kept between child art and growth in skill.

## WHAT TO LOOK FOR IN AN EVALUATION

First and before everything else in creative work is the honesty of the expression. A cog in logical thinking has slipped when a teacher permits or, worse still, encourages children to copy. Any teacher would reprove a child who claimed authorship to a poem, story, or song that was not his own work. Should not the same be true for art? Originality as it applies to children's art work is not intended to mean evidence of an unusual talent or even an outstanding piece of work, but a true piece of work, each child's own work. In creative work children draw upon many things within their experience, things they have seen or heard or read, as well as what they imagine. This is a natural process and the way everyone works. When all these varied experiences have been united in their thinking, children evolve an image of color and form which they proceed to express in painting, modeling, printing, and crafts. This synthetic result, stimulated from many sources, may be called, for want of a better word, originality.

When children copy the work of others, the synthesis has been done for them. The ideas have already been translated into material form, and the problem has been solved: the colors chosen, the shapes determined, and the mood expressed. The skills demanded of the child in copying add nothing to his experience as compared with what he gains when he must rely upon himself. The simplest, crudest art expression that is a child's own work has more value for him than the most perfect copy.

Lowenfeld writes that copying, among other detrimental effects, ". . . conditions the child to adult concepts which he cannot produce alone, and which therefore frustrate his own creative ambitions."[2] Once children have acquired the habit of copying, the best, and perhaps the only way to stop the practice, is by strong motivation which will so stimulate them that copying will be forgotten in the greater satisfactions of original work. Children become copiers largely when they have not been led to see that they have a wealth of ideas within themselves, or when they have known only failure and insecurity in creative work. These limitations of experience develop habitual copiers, and it may well be through no fault of their own.

### EVALUATION FOR INTERPRETATION

The interpretation of art structure—color, form, line, contrast, pattern, composition—through discussion and demonstration is of value to children when interpretation is useful to what they are doing and given in words they understand. Unless a functional and immediate application is possible, lip service may supplant learning, and a rule take the place of feeling. Art is not a skill subject, and any emphasis in the wrong direction could easily destroy natural feeling and make the art experience an exercise to fulfill a rule, thus killing the joy of creativity. Consequently, it is wiser that interpretation of art structure shall emerge naturally from the projects and activities of the class.

Children instinctively use line and color, dark and light, with power and demonstrate repetition, subordination, balance, rhythm, and proportion continually in their work. This child has a particularly fine sense for color; that one, an unerring feeling for rhythm. A gifted child seems to possess them all, and no child is so deprived but that he has something upon which a teacher may build.

### TEACHER BACKGROUND

A teacher will want to refresh and broaden her background for her work in order to have more to give children when evaluating their work and also to establish standards for herself. Reading, enrollment in workshops, and seeing children's work other than that of her own class will aid her. Workshops help a teacher to understand the nature of materials and to appreciate through personal experience both the difficulties and the rewards that children meet. New teachers will benefit by attending school and museum exhibits of children's work. There are also collections of children's work reproduced in Kodachrome slides,[3] and a color film[4] which will give an overview of what is being done in other places. Often a new teacher is at a loss because she has had few opportunities to see paintings, craft work, and all the other activities of a full art program.

### INTERACTION IN EVALUATION

An evaluation period is a welcome relaxation for children. After the intense concentration that creative work demands, they need activity. It is good for the muscles when children are free to get up from their seats and move around. It is relaxing for the emotions for them to do a little chatting and talking among themselves and with their teacher. Interaction is good, very good, for the total art experience of children.[5, 6]

Through evaluative discussions children have practice in expressing opinions and a chance to become more articulate about art. It is encouraging to see the improvement that results in creative work and the progress made in better understanding of art values when there is a free give-and-take during an art evaluation. Perhaps the best outcome of all is the effect on the morale of children as they see for themselves that art work is recognized and find out for a fact that it does not disappear into a cupboard or vanish into a wastebasket at the end of the lesson.

### BEGINNINGS OF EVALUATION

Primary children are accustomed, during the sharing period, to talk over and enjoy together everything they do, and art is one of the experiences that provokes lively discussion. Many delightful sentence stories and short poems develop at this time and are often attached to the picture they describe. This pleases little children and gives added importance to their art work. Besides showing art work in the circle, groups of children may hold up their own pictures in some convenient place in the room, making it possible for the children to enjoy each other's work and to

291

comment on it. It need not take long to look over the day's paintings, giving opportunity for appreciation from the group and the added comments of the teacher: "How well Tom has done today." "Do see Bobby's big bear." "What a beautiful color Kathy used for her house. Please tell us how you mixed it."

### SUGGESTIONS FOR UPPER GRADES

Evaluation may be carried a step farther for drawing and painting in the upper grades by providing children with an opportunity to appraise their own work and draw their own conclusions. This can be carried out through group cooperation and a display of work. Two groups of children may exchange work with each other and when one group holds up the work of its classmates, the others remain in their seats to view their own work. Not only are children thus helped to become objective toward their work; but also weaknesses not discernible in close desk work become obvious from a distance. It is then evident, for example, that an important color lacks character because it is too light in value, or that a scattered composition needs to be unified.

Another good practice is to put up the work of the class for general evaluation. The separate pieces can be pinned to the bulletin board and identified by numbers cut from a calendar, or taped to the blackboard and numbered with chalk. This kind of identification makes an impersonal evaluation possible. Also, numbering is practical and focuses the attention of the children on the right picture without argument. Equally important, every child should be free to put up his own work before it is finished in order to see what progress he has made.

Older children react most favorably to evaluation and through it grow more objective in their point of view.

### GROUP PROJECTS AS A STIMULUS

Any type of large group work, such as a mural or a construction unit, gives children an excellent opportunity for a continuing experience in evaluation. First, the work is always in evidence. The children see the mural or the construction project as they come into the room in the morning and as they return from recess. They may pause for a minute or two at the noon hour as they go out to lunch or return to the room before the bell rings. These observances give opportunity to see what is done and what has to be done. And, second, so many children are working on a group project that the nonparticipants will be interested to see what their friends are doing, and since enthusiasm is contagious, the whole class will be drawn into the spirit of the activity. Spontaneous comments made by the children in little group discussions arising from natural interest quickly go to the ears of the committee members who are working together on the project. Are the costumes for the people in the crowded village square true for the time and the place? Are the distant hills in the background of the construction unit harmonious with the farm buildings in front of them? Will the lettering on the poster for the class play be as easy to read out in the hall where the light is poor? There is no other evaluation experience that is as democratic or as stimulating to the active participation of all the children in a class, and there is no other experience that as clearly presents relationships between color, form, balance, and dark and light pattern as does a large group project.

## STRENGTHENING AN OBJECTIVE THROUGH EVALUATION

When the members of a class have an honest attitude toward creative work and are vocal during the evaluation period, the teacher has strong allies for her campaign to eliminate copying. No copier in the group will want to lose status in the eyes of his classmates by having it discovered that his work is not his own, and discovered he will be. For the children themselves to disapprove of copying is the most effective way to combat this bad habit in a child.

## PRACTICAL OUTCOMES OF EVALUATION

One practical outcome of evaluation is for the children to select at this time the pictures or other examples of art work which will be used in their next display. The teacher can tactfully control any tendency on the part of the class to develop a star artist, one whose work is always exhibited to the exclusion of the work of other children. It is only right for every child to experience the satisfaction and pride of seeing his work placed on display not only once but frequently during the year. It is for this reason that teachers should change their classroom displays during the month so that equal recognition may be possible for all. In addition, exhibits for the hall and the central office may be selected during evaluation.

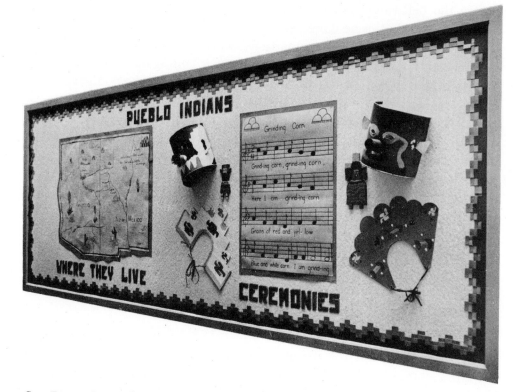

*San Diego City Schools*

DISCOVERING ART PRINCIPLES THROUGH A CAMERA CLUB

Another practical and novel experience in evaluation
occurred during one school year when a number of children in a sixth-
grade class formed a camera club. Clubs in elementary schools are not usual.
The children of this group were drawn together by their strong mutual
interest in photography, and a club seemed the natural way to solve their
problems. The teacher became a willing sponsor of the club, but under
no condition did she want to participate in the club in the role of a teacher.
Later, she did bring several books on photography from the public library
for the members to look at, but not until after the pattern of the club's
procedure had been well established by the children. She wanted the club
to develop in its own way. It was the children's club. She gave generous
encouragement and invited the members to use their classroom as a meeting

294

place after school hours. She did this because she sensed that a worth-while experience in evaluation and creative thinking was inevitable, and because, as an observer, she, too, could learn much from the group experiment.

At the first meeting of the club, the members stated their purpose simply: They wanted to take good pictures. They decided that each member should bring both a good and a poor example of his pho-tography to the meetings, and that the members would then talk over the pictures and see if they could discover how to improve their picture taking. As time passed, they found they could improve their camera work because photography always provided another chance to take a different picture of the same subject, applying their new-found knowledge.

Three of their many discoveries were: that a good picture did not always have to tell a story; that pictures which were either all dark or all light were monotonous; and that the background of a picture should not be the first thing to be noticed. Eventually they discovered that every picture had a quality of its own.

Choices in subject matter and in the way each subject was handled changed subtly as the year progressed. Many of the results were

*San Bernardino City Schools*   295

no longer snapshots: they were compositions. The children photographed subjects as simple as a pet parrot on his perch and as complex as the skeleton framework of a house under construction. The children began to see beauty in many things which, before, they had not been aware of.

Naturally a few children dropped out of the club before school ended, but for those who continued, there was little or no perceptible waning of interest. Club members cherished their work and kept it neatly in scrapbooks made for this purpose.

The teacher invited the club members to put up a display of their best pictures for the last night-meeting of the class parents. Great was the dismay of the child photographers when each found that he, himself, had to select his own best photograph. Despite pressure from the children, the teacher stalwartly refused to be drawn into the discussions; nor would she give any opinion whatsoever in the decisions being made by the children.

It is regrettable that this type of voluntary learning experience is so rare in a child's school life.

LOOKING BACKWARD

Many teachers have found it helpful to make some kind of organized collection of children's work to refer to as occasion demands. It is possible to keep flat work conveniently filed in portfolios and stored in the cupboard. It is easy to forget the individual progress made by every child in a class, and a sampling of his work provides the teacher with a quick review. Again, it is helpful to collect all the pictures from a lesson and several months later compare them with the day's work. A teacher can also show a child his own portfolio and let him see for himself how much better he is doing than earlier in the year. Often a disheartened child will find encouragement when he sees proof of his growth. For the gifted child, a portfolio of his work is essential in the event that he should be recommended for a special art class, such as is often sponsored by the school district for specially selected children.

OUTCOMES WHICH GIVE EVIDENCE OF GROWTH

Many teachers are hoping to define outcomes for an art program as precisely as is possible for a drill subject. This false hope should be set aside in favor of a more philosophical approach. The greater emphasis in any statement of expected outcomes should be on the aspects of the child's growing art consciousness rather than on skillful execution.

To recognize the importance of a child's natural endowment as part of expected performance is logical; it proves that the art program does not overlook individual talent but rather nurtures its growth.

### AN OVERVIEW OF SEQUENTIAL ART EXPERIENCES

Through a year of work every child should show some measure of progress. The teacher hopes he will strengthen his art understandings and become more independent in his creative work. No profile of growth for one child could ever be quite the same as that for another child. While every teacher must establish her own criteria for the expected performance in the elementary grades, she will find it of value to study educational literature[7] in this field.

### GENERAL OBSERVATIONS OF CHILD GROWTH

Opportunity to see a wide variety of art forms brings him emotional satisfaction and pleasure and fosters visual sensitivity.

Intelligent and understanding guidance gives him self-confidence in creative work.

Permissive classroom control allows him independence of thought and challenges his creativity.

Responsibility for supplies and materials teaches him good working habits.

Interest keeps him alert and working to his full capacity.

New and varied kinds of art materials offer him opportunity to experiment, investigate, and invent.

Good operational procedures in the classroom give him a comfortable and efficient working period.

Appreciation finds him eager to do his best.

### LEVELS OF EXPECTED PERFORMANCE

Any arbitrary grouping of children is always conditioned by maturation and differences in temperament. Nevertheless, research and

297

observation show that there is a pattern of growth which all children tend to follow.

### Age of Entering School through Five Years

A period of orientation.

THE CHILD

becomes accustomed to being and working with children and sharing materials and tools.

plays with art materials and tools before he realizes that they have a purposeful use.

scribbles, makes marks, or uses masses of color for an expressive purpose.

may fill or only use a small area of his paper depending upon his temperament.

is easily distracted when working.

makes progress slowly in the coordination of eye, hand, and art media.

chooses a color or colors which satisfy him and express his inner feeling.

uses several different kinds of art materials and tools; mainly, clay, tempera paint, chalk, finger paint, torn and cut paper, and paste.

cannot carry over to the following year all the progress made in his performance.

### Age Six through Seven Years

A period of fundamental learnings.

THE CHILD

is a doer with a short span of interest. Experimenting with materials and tools fills his initial need for expression.

tends to turn first to painting and drawing. Individual differences are evident as some children work boldly, others delicately.

begins by painting and drawing lines and masses in one color. Progresses to the use of more color and a hint of design emerges.

starts picture making. Symbolism prevails.

starts painting and drawing people very soon. Early efforts

298

bridge symbolism and realism. Figures are distorted and characterized by big heads and small bodies. Fingers are prominent.

moves toward better body proportions, but a big head continues to be typical. Is aware of different sizes of people.

puts sky and sun at top of paper, ground and picture content at the bottom in his compositions.

retains visual memories, making it possible for him to paint and draw pictures of great compositional complexity, provided the subject is representative of a personal experience.

recognizes the distinguishing characteristics of animals.

is expressive in many art media: cutting and pasting, building and construction, finger painting, and clay modeling.

can use approved tools for construction after instruction and with supervision.

cooperates in group projects.

can help take care of art materials and tools after working habits have been established.

## Age Eight through Nine Years

A period of enrichment.

THE CHILD

works on a large or small scale with equal confidence.

portrays figures that are better proportioned than previously.

perceives distinguishing characteristics of people and clothing. Adds many significant details.

paints and draws animals more realistically.

discards the static pose and develops action and grouping in pictures of people and animals.

develops richer backgrounds in compositions and intuitively achieves an interest center.

uses color, size, and overlapping to give a feeling of distance to landscape.

has a natural feeling for design and is equally expressive in small, precise, static repetition and in large, imaginative, free-flowing rhythm.

demonstrates ability to organize a group project. Takes his place with equal cooperation as a leader or assigned worker. Has initiative.

299

is more sensitive to color than heretofore. Starts mixing hues and values.

can integrate art with another subject.

is capable of using a variety of craft materials and is a careful worker.

becomes more objective in evaluating his own work.

### Age Ten through Eleven Years

A period of synthesis.

THE CHILD

has a good span of attention.

has a wide and varied interest in subjects for painting, drawing, and modeling.

can combine art media in imaginative ways.

draws with a degree of skill.

begins to understand, but cannot always graphically express simple perspective.

has interest and ability in the development of three-dimensional design forms, both static and mobile in character.

paints and sketches outdoors effectively. Is a keen observer.

is clever and original in the use of scrap and standard art materials.

has respect for good workmanship in crafts and endeavors to meet his goal.

is successful in printing techniques (not to be misconstrued as lettering).

requires instruction and practice in poster making.

seeks teacher assistance before an anticipated need arises.

uses results of personal research where proper and fitting to creative expression.

participates intelligently in evaluations. Tends to be overcritical of his own work and vacillates between satisfaction and disappointment.

notices classroom environment. Discusses arrangements and art prints on display.

profits aesthetically and intellectually from trips to art galleries and museums.

enjoys art portfolios and books that are placed on library table.

has been doing art work ever since entering school and is now ready to synthesize his skills and learning.

## SELF-EVALUATION IN TEACHING

As a teacher analyzes the needs of her class and sets its goals accordingly, by the same token she will want to assess her own growth. Does her work reflect the ideals that prompted her to become a teacher? Goals are not achieved in a short teaching experience, and progress toward their achievement is often not fully realized unless an objective analysis is undertaken. Self-questioning reveals whether there has been acquiescence to the status quo or a determination to keep striving for such key objectives as:

a freer approach to teaching,

an understanding but firm demand that every child do his best,

a more active participation in the art activities of the class,

a basis of mutual understanding in class planning,

a warm friendliness which encourages children to assume responsibilities voluntarily,

a purposeful basis for motivation,

a sensitivity in identifying emerging personality traits in children,

and a contagious enthusiasm for work.

In truth, evaluation guides both pupil and teacher growth in the art program.

## REFERENCE MATERIAL

1. Kuh, Katharine W. *Art Has Many Faces*. New York: Harper & Brothers, 1951. 185

2. Lowenfeld, Viktor. *Your Child and His Art*. New York: The Macmillan Company, 1957. pp. 12–14.

3. *Figure Drawings by Children*. Set of 52 Kodachrome slides 2″ x 2″. Dr. Konrad Prothmann.

   *The Child Expresses Himself Through Creative Art*. Set of 49 Kodachrome slides 2″ x 2″. Dr. Konrad Prothmann.

4. *Children Are Creative.* 16mm. film, 10 min., sound, color; produced by International Film Bureau, Inc.

5. Shane, Harold G., and E. R. McSwain. *Evaluation and the Elementary Curriculum.* New York: Holt, Rinehart and Winston, Inc., 1951. (Chap. III, "The Value of Evaluation and Its Function in Improving Elementary Education.")

6. Beverley, Felicia. "The Art Teacher and Evaluation," *Art Education Today.* New York: Bureau of Publications, Teachers College, Columbia University, 1945–1950. pp. 85–92.

7. Art guides and curriculum courses prepared by city and county school districts throughout the country.

## READER PARTICIPATION

Explain the subtle differences between evaluation and criticism.

Are there values for evaluation in group interaction?

Visit a kindergarten and a sixth grade successively and study the development and scope of children's growth in this span of time.

If possible, listen to an adult professional criticism and reflect upon it. What could happen when children are confronted with concepts and terms beyond their comprehension?

Study the goals, objectives, and expected outcomes of the art curriculum of several representative school systems and evolve your own set of values. Write them down.

The needs of children of superior intelligence are distinctive. Find new projects to challenge their talents and creative thinking.

Exhibits of children's art from foreign lands can often be borrowed from the Junior Red Cross. Have such an exhibit for your class to discuss and enjoy.

Experiment with an art material you have never worked with. Evaluate your experience and relate it to what children must often feel when in a similar situation.

Browse through a number of well illustrated art books for the pleasure it gives you. Forget about art principles, evaluation, and all formal approaches; let intuition be your only guide.

# 12

# *Let's Show Our Work*

Present-day schools are made attractive by the interesting and stimulating materials displayed. Exhibits of children's work are part of the school environment and overcome the impersonal formality and coldness of corridors and classrooms. Children are influenced by an orderly, well-arranged environment and respond happily to it. In addition to art work and general reference materials, flowers, plants, and attractive arrangements of toys, crafts, and textiles make the schoolroom a pleasant place for living and working each day.

## WHERE TO DISPLAY

While the classroom is probably the most important place to children, there are other locations in a school where art work may be effectively displayed. The entrance, corridors, cafeteria, auditorium, library, and teachers' lounge provide display areas. Through what he sees in exhibits a patron or parent visiting a school has evidence of the vitality of the program. School cafeterias offer opportunity for two kinds of art displays: wall exhibits, and table arrangements. Because of the large amount of wall space usually available, murals as well as pictures may be hung on cafeteria walls. The tables where the children eat their lunch are made more inviting by a fortnightly change of art arrangements in the center of each. All classes in the school can take turns in making the arrangements.

*The School Committee of the City of Boston*

*Public Schools, Kansas City, Missouri*

WHEN TO DISPLAY

There are occasions when exhibits are of particular significance. One such instance is American Education Week every November. Another school occasion is the regular meeting of the parent-teacher association. There are always individual and community interests that provide opportunity for showing the work of the children to school patrons.

EXHIBITS OUTSIDE OF SCHOOL

Children's work may find a way into community life through exhibits arranged at art galleries, museums, and county fairs. Another means of effectively reaching the public is a display in a downtown store window. A well-located exhibit of this kind will often reach members of the public who otherwise would never see the children's work for the simple reason that they never visit a school. A descriptive legend or caption always makes an exhibit, wherever it may be, better understood by the public.

*An Exhibit in an Art Gallery*

Every school district deserves a community art exhibit, something special, something on the grand scale. It should be displayed in an art gallery, if possible. Attractive invitations to the opening can be mailed in advance to parents, friends, civic leaders, administrators, supervisors of all subjects, members of the local Board of Education, club members, older citizens, and business people.

In a unified school district the art work of elementary school children and high school students is usually combined. Generally, the work is representative of a two-year span. This arrangement affords a wider variety in the work displayed. There is no feeling of disparaging the work of younger children; originality and beauty, not technique, are the criteria. To the delight of everyone, a first-grade painting is very apt to steal the show. An exhibit of the total art program forcibly demonstrates the inspiring scope of art education.

The Fine Arts Gallery in San Diego regularly schedules exhibits for the city and the county schools on alternating years. Crowds attend. An orchestra from one of the schools finds an appreciative audience, and the serving of refreshments from a handsomely decorated table en-    305 courages friendliness among the guests attending the opening reception.

A dramatic display in the gallery foyer will not only attract visitors to the place where the children's work is shown, but will invoke curiosity for the school exhibit.

A catalogue is a treasured memento for parents. The name, grade, and identification of the work of every child who participates in any way should be listed. Demonstrations of art techniques at the opening add interest. Visitors are delighted to watch a primary child as he finger paints at a low table, or a high school student as he throws clay on a wheel.

In arranging an exhibit, teachers' creative talents are worthily challenged. One goal in a big show is to carry the eye of the

*San Diego County Schools and the Fine Arts Gallery*

306

*San Diego
County Schools
and the
Fine Arts Gallery*

observer forward so that there is always something of interest ahead for him to enjoy. Another is to achieve variety without losing the unity of the total display. A way to minimize monotony on a long wall is to use dividers that project a few feet into the gallery. This provides additional wall space for hanging pictures and gives compactness to the display, which is partially enclosed. The dividers may be concrete blocks or a panel of strips of light wood. A clever teacher will find ingenious ways to use ordinary materials. Large plants add greatly to the decor of an exhibit.

Quotations from the writings of artists, poets, philosophers, and educators may be handsomely lettered on large cards and strategically

307

placed in the exhibit. A quotation from Goethe in the last exhibit of the county schools read: "The highest problem of any art is to cause by appearance the illusion of a higher reality."

Low areas for the display of crafts are needed. Appropriately placed blown-up photographs of art activities carried on in the classroom are informative. Visitors are interested to see what goes on in the classroom, as in a photograph of a child painting at an easel, or of a high school student stacking a kiln.

Yes, a community exhibit, in whatever type of accommodation a community can provide, requires work and a budget; but the results are worth every expenditure of energy and money.

### DISPLAYS IN THE CLASSROOM

A considerable amount of space is needed and some architectural problems must be considered when exhibits and displays are organized for a classroom. First, the room should be considered as a unit, not a series of unrelated spaces. Second, there should be variety in the arrangement or the results will be monotonous and lacking in emphasis. Everything in a classroom comes into the all-over design plan of room arrangement: children's work of all kinds, visual teaching aids, and table arrangements.[1]

Table arrangements are for both art enjoyment and reference work. Flowers, dried-weed arrangements, potted plants, and still-

308

*San Diego*
*City Schools*

life arrangements may be used. Aquariums, terrariums, and planters are attractive and will last a year with the minimum of care. Collections of rocks and shells, mounted birds, and other science materials are colorful. But, no matter how attractive a room may be, unless it is a functional workshop for children it is a failure. Pottery must not be where it can be knocked over and broken, or wall spaces so covered with displays that there is no space left free for the work of the day. A room that is too full of things is cluttered and confusing, and where confusion reigns, children act accordingly. A room that is full of leftover decorations from previous holidays is the worst of all. Santa Claus and every one of his eight reindeer should have departed when the children return to school in January.

### The Children's Part

Children enjoy taking part in arranging the room, with participation beginning in a small way in the primary grades. Perhaps it would be no more than deciding where to place the roses that Jim brought to school or how to display Vesta's painting of her new house. Upper-grade children have a genuine interest in and ideas about displays. After the teacher has made the basic plan for interest centers at the beginning of a year, the children may take part in subsequent planning and help with the work. Group planning of a bulletin board is as good and as practical an art experience as a class could have. Pinning up materials attractively will require the evaluation of spacing, color, variety, repetition, and all art principles that contribute to such a problem. These decisions are art judgments that are within the aesthetic appreciation of children and will, with skillful guidance by the teacher, become meaningful.

Color combinations may be varied with each successive arrangement. Colors have to be tried out experimentally in relation to woodwork and wall colors before a decision can be made. By having a part in the group planning, a committee of children will feel it to be an honor instead of a chore to stay after school and help the teacher in the work of putting up the display.

### Captions and Identifications

The identification of work on exhibit is important to the effectiveness of learning. This identification may be for subject matter areas, for interest centers, and for the work of individual children and groups, and includes table arrangements related to subject matter.

309

Captions are usually brief, and the lettering in them must be easy for children to read. In upper grades a wider variety of alphabet forms may be used than is appropriate for primary grades, where the form must be kept very simple.

Simple, block letter forms can be cut out of colored paper for use on bulletin boards. Letters may be put up with pins or a desk or wall stapler. Also, glass-headed pushpins are neat. Thumbtacks are usually shiny; moreover, they have a way of popping out of certain kinds of bulletin board material. When putting up the letters for a caption, it is always wise to use a ruler or a strip of paper as a guide, for even a slight deviation from the line looks much greater from a distance.

Manuscript writing on a strip of tagboard or paper is used in all grades and is particularly useful in primary classes. It may be done with a lettering pen and India ink or with the newer type of felt brush pen. Colored paper may be used for mounting this type of caption and is necessary when the paper is the same color or value as the bulletin board. Captions in cursive writing and painted with a brush, or cut out of paper,

*San Diego City Schools*

are smart and give accent to an arrangement. Chalk, too, can be used for script or manuscript writing. Cursive writing and block lettering may be combined if one or the other is dominant on the bulletin board.

A commercial type of alphabet recommended for school use is made of plaster of Paris. Fonts of upper- and lower-case letters may be had in smart modern designs. The letters are backed with a pin type of holder that is successful on bulletin boards. A complete font in a school is most convenient to have when captions have to be put up in a hurry or for permanent use on office or hall bulletin boards.

Whatever methods of lettering are chosen, one type should be dominant in a room. Too many different kinds and styles in a classroom will disturb the feeling of unity.

*Bulletin Boards*

Too large, too small, too high, too low, too narrow, too wide—these seem to be all too true of the average bulletin board. Yet teachers are clever in overcoming awkward proportions and placements.

Even though a great deal of material must be pinned up in every classroom, it can be done artistically so that it integrates with the room yet does not dominate the environment. No two arrangements of children's art or of reference materials need be the same. Nor, for that matter, could any two be alike, for the materials are never the same. Teachers can achieve dramatic and colorful effects by approaching new arrangements as an art problem. Some teachers like to get the material together, make a rough sketch on paper of how it might be combined, and     311 then try it out on the board. Others prefer to work directly on the board, temporarily pinning the material in place. A quick survey from across the room will suggest changes to be made for improvement in the arrangements. Then the material can be put up neatly and permanently.

Neatness is one of the most important requirements of a pleasingly arranged bulletin board. It is achieved by having everything straight and well secured in place. The eye is often not a sure guide, but a ruler can be depended upon. Two pins are not enough except possibly for very small items. A pin is needed in each corner. Otherwise, with the slightest breeze, the work will flap on the board like laundry on a clothesline. The essence of good display is a smart, well-put-together look.

A feeling for three-dimensional form, a bit of paper sculpture in captions, mats, frames, or wherever it seems to fit, helps to give variety and to add emphasis to an arrangement.

Different ways of mounting pictures, even though simple to do, are often difficult to explain in words. The methods used in the accompanying illustrations are easy to reproduce. The most useful papers for matting and framing are construction and corrugated papers. Poster and mat boards also make excellent mats.

The goal of a well-arranged bulletin board is to show work to its best advantage and to convey a clear message.[2]

*San Diego City Schools*

*A tear-out mounting is quick to make. A small hole is made in the center of a piece of poster or construction paper and gradually torn larger until it is the right size and shape to fit over the picture beneath.*

*It takes less than five minutes to make this mounting. Pin a piece of colored newstock to the bulletin board and pin the picture in place. Wrap four or five strands of colored yarn around the pins and letter the child's name in the corner.*

*Silhouettes can be cut from children's work and used in display. They give accent and variety to a bulletin board.*

*A double scroll frame of corrugated or construction paper is a permanent mounting quickly made. The ends of the picture are slipped under the rolls and pinned in place. It is easy to change pictures.*

A *turned back frame is made of light weight poster or wrapping paper. The picture to be framed is placed in the center of the paper and a pencil line drawn around the edge. Two diagonal lines are drawn between each pair of opposite corners. A cut is made with a razor blade along each diagonal line to within a quarter inch of the inside corner. This makes four flaps. Cut off the ends of the flaps about two inches from the points. The flaps are now turned or rolled back over the frame. On a square frame the flaps will be symmetrical, but not on a rectangular frame.*

*The corrugated frame and mat are permanent. The picture and the child's name can be changed every day.*

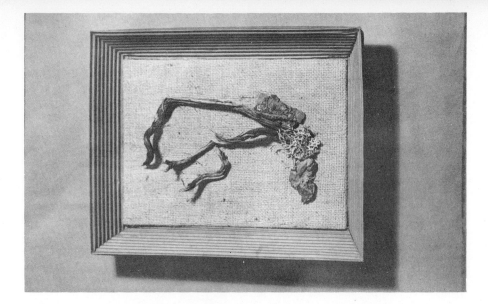

A deep edge frame adds a feeling of perspective to children's work. Each of the side pieces of this frame is a single piece of corrugated paper turned back at the outer edge and secured with masking tape. Both ends of each side are cut on an angle. The ends are brought together and fastened with a strip of masking tape on the back. The choice of corrugated paper seems appropriate for this three-dimensional texture design made of buckwheat roots, two kinds of lichen, and a couple of pieces of bark. The child gathered the materials while at the school camp and glued them to a piece of burlap stretched over cardboard when he was back in school.

The usual flat mounting of children's work can be made more interesting by cutting around the picture to make a background shape that is pleasing in contour. Simple free forms used with discretion can add individually to mountings.

A discarded wood picture frame makes a good permanent frame in which pictures may be quickly changed. The glass and backing are removed and the wood painted. The frame is hung on the bulletin board by either an inch brad or a strong pin at each upper corner inside the frame. Picture, mounting, paper, and child's name are fastened to the bulletin board.

A shallow box made of tagboard is used as the base for mounting this design. Narrow flaps are left on all four sides of the box and turned out when the box is fastened to the bulletin board.

A permanent frame can be made from any good sized piece of light weight wood. Half-inch laminated balsa wood is particularly good. The center opening is cut out with a jig saw. A narrow strip of corrugated paper is pasted along the outside and inner edges of the frame, or the latter may be painted a dark color.

A decorative edge makes a good once-in-a-while mounting for children's work. Used too often, it becomes tiresome. This mounting seems most appropriate with work that is delicate in technique, such as a crayon etching.

318

*A quickly made stand-out frame is cut from a sheet of construction paper a couple of inches larger on all four sides than the picture to be used with it. A center opening is cut out and the corners are creased together. The frame is placed over the picture and pinned or stapled in place. The corners should be pinched together occasionally to keep the frame from flopping.*

LET'S TAKE IT HOME

Rewarding as school recognition is to a child, it is taking his work home to an appreciative family that counts the most with him. There are ways that a teacher can help the child when this appreciation seems to be lacking, and one is through the parent conference.[3] If the matter is brought into the conversation tactfully, a teacher can help a parent to understand how very important the home's sharing in a child's accomplishment at school always is to the child. Teachers can sense the different attitudes of the families of children in the classroom, but try as they will they can never wholly compensate a child for the lack of warm approval from his family. The interest that a teacher may be able to stimulate in the

*Burbank Unified School District*

home through the parent conference is one of the most valuable contributions she can make to the greater security of the children in her class.

PARENTS GROW IN UNDERSTANDING

The increasing interest of parents in all phases of the curriculum affords opportunity for teachers to organize special meetings and workshops. One group of mothers was surprised one afternoon to find the first-grade room where they were to meet set up for finger painting. There was nothing to do but remove hats and gloves and set aside formality and go to work. The outcome? Several children later told the teacher that not only were their own finger paintings now hung up at home, but mother's too. Another teacher invited the mothers of her class to a workshop demonstrating an art technique. A demonstration? It started out that way, but soon the teacher had the mothers wedging clay and modeling. Each mother was her child for the afternoon and wore the name of her son or daughter pinned to her dress. Personal experience in some of the

320

activities of school makes parents more appreciative of their children's efforts and of their results.

Parents will willingly support an enriched school program when they understand what art is striving to achieve and, furthermore, will make art a vital home experience. There is no understanding that can surpass personal experience, particularly when it leads to the sharing of activity as well as interest. Happily, this happens in many families.

OPERATION CHRISTMAS CARD

Christmas was coming and the Worthingtons, as usual, were planning to make their own cards. With three children in the family many cards were needed, and the list was long. At a family council it was suggested that each member of the family submit a design and that the best one be chosen by vote. The linoleum block would be cut by father and all would have the fun of helping to print it. When the sketches were

*Courtesy of Mrs. George Worthington, San Diego*

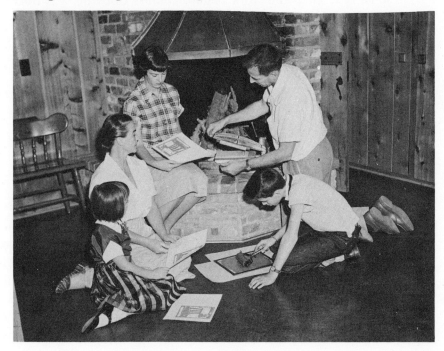

DIANE

the Worthingtons

*Courtesy of Mrs. George*
*Worthington, San Diego*

finished and all laid out on the dining room table, the family held a second council. By unanimous choice the drawing made by Diane, the youngest child, was chosen. Hers, it was felt, was the best of all. The colors to use were talked over, and it was decided that some cards would be green and some red. Then the work began. Diane's drawing was traced on the block and father tried to follow it faithfully. When Diane saw the first print she expressed her opinion frankly by saying, "The nose on my reindeer was much better than yours, Daddy. And, Daddy, I didn't have a star in my sky."

Friends were charmed with their cards and the family was proud of Diane. When art is a creative experience in a home, it is alive in the hearts of children.

AT HOME: THE LITTLE GALLERY

"Operation Christmas Card" can be carried further. A family workshop can be set up where children and their parents can experiment with, investigate, and enjoy art together.[4] Given the opportunity and motivated by their children's interest, parents are often agreeably surprised to discover that they enjoy creative work. Parental participation has great influence in the lives of children. Art escapes the four walls of the school building and enters into the home as a lively and compelling interest. Parents grow in their understanding of the goals of art education;[5]

322

by working with various art media, they discover the far-reaching influence art has on human development and psychological insight. Experience is indeed a mighty teacher.

Perhaps a space can be set aside in the home where a Little Gallery of both child and parent work can be displayed. In D'Amico's book, *Art for the Family*,[6] there are many illustrations of art work done by parents—many of whom had never done art work before.

### SAN DIEGO SPRING ANNUAL

A Southern California school district found that a publication representative of two correlated areas of creative work, writing and art, is one way of acquainting the public, particularly those citizens who have no children in public schools, with the accomplishments of children in their schools. The San Diego City Schools District publishes two booklets each year, *Creative Writing* for the elementary school program, and *Quest* for the secondary school program. The first issue of *Creative Writing* was

*A cow is just lovely*
*To give her milk away—*
*When all she ever gets to eat is*
*Hay!     hay!     hay!*

*San Diego City Schools*

323

published sixteen years ago. The first issue of *Quest* came later. These publications are distributed by the Office of the Superintendent to the waiting rooms of the offices of doctors, lawyers, and other representative people of the community. Here the booklets are picked up and read by many people who have no direct contact with the public schools. Many in a community have a sincere interest in their school system, but have no personal knowledge of what is being accomplished. The booklets are attractively printed paperbacks, and the content of current issues reflects the children's interests and learning experiences in these two subjects during the preceding year. The poem on the previous page and the delightful illustration of a man milking a cow[7] were the outcome of a primary grade visit to a farm.

## REFERENCE MATERIAL

1. East, Marjorie. *Display for Learning: Making and Using Visual Materials.* New York: Holt, Rinehart and Winston, Inc., 1952.

2. Burgert, Robert H. and Elinor S. Meadows. *Eye-Appealing Bulletin Board Ideas.* Dansville, N.Y.: F. A. Owen Publishing Company, 1960.

   *Bulletin Boards: An Effective Teaching Device.* 16mm. film, 11 min., sound, color; produced by International Film Bureau, Inc.

3. Bannon, Laura. *Mind Your Child's Art.* New York: Pellegrini & Cudahy, 1952.

4. *Art Begins at Home.* 16mm. film, 5 min., sound, color; produced by International Film Bureau, Inc.

   *Holiday Art.* 16mm. film, 5 min., sound, color; produced by International Film Bureau, Inc.

5. Lowenfeld, Viktor. *Your Child and His Art.* New York: The Macmillan Company, 1957.

6. D'Amico, Victor, Frances Wilson, and Moreen Maser. *Art for the Family.* New York: The Museum of Modern Art, 1954. Distributed by Simon and Schuster, Inc.

7. *Creative Writing.* Vol. VI. San Diego, Calif.: San Diego City Schools, 1950.

## READER PARTICIPATION

Keep a notebook of all the ideas for display which you may find on visits to schools, in store windows, and so forth.

Make a dummy bulletin board display, working for good organization of such unrelated materials as an office notice, a picture, a news item, and so forth.

Get several examples of different kinds of children's work and make an attractive mounting or background for each.

With paper and scissors experiment with making three-dimensional forms for holiday displays.

Prepare a pattern file of alphabets for use on bulletin boards.

Explore the possibilities in the community for an exhibit of children's creative work.

# 13

## *Interaction*
## *with the Community*

The school is integrated with the community and prospers with the cooperation of its patrons. Cultural and character values are strengthened by the endeavors of community leaders working for the welfare of children. The community makes a rich contribution to the school and is ever ready to do its share for the betterment of the school program.

### AN EFFECTIVE COMMUNITY-SCHOOL ART PROJECT

A large and most unusual, as well as creative, example of community-school group work is a mosaic that was undertaken in a rural school district centered in the township of Bart, Pennsylvania, where a new consolidated school building was to be built. This mosaic, truly a masterpiece of child art, had such an impact on those who saw it, that it was subsequently featured in *This Week Magazine,* the nationally distributed Sunday newspaper supplement.

The reason for making the mural was based on sound educational philosophy and astuteness on the part of educators; they recognized that the children needed a unified pre-enrollment experience before the new consolidated school was opened. The planning committee was well organized, and the goal to be achieved was high. Naturally, there were administrative details which the principal, teachers, art supervisor, and

326

architect had to solve. Throughout the project, a great number of children, teachers, and parents were closely associated.

The project, undertaken by children in grades three to eight, was to make a mosaic decoration twenty feet long and eight feet high for an outside wall of the new school building for the Bart-Colerain Unified School District. The enrollment in the new school would be made up of children from the several one- and two-room schools in the area.

A committee of children, composed of representatives from these one- and two-room schools, decided that an appropriate theme for the mosaic would be the children's activities throughout the year depicted against a background of the four seasons, starting with autumn on the left of the mosaic, and continuing through winter and spring to summer on the right.

Following discussions in each school, the children made preliminary sketches and paintings for the composition of the mosaic; from these, they chose the one to be developed in tesserae. Next, a full size,

*Bart-Colerain School, Bart, Pennsylvania*

327

multipaneled cartoon was drawn on sheets of kraft mural paper. The cartoon was then traced onto five plywood panels, ¾″ x 4′ x 8′, to which the tesserae would later be glued.

Of course, one of the basic problems was to match as closely as possible the colors available in commercial ceramic tile to the colors used in the cartoon. The children worked out a color code based on colors in a sample tile kit; the tiles required for each color were then ordered.

When the tiles were delivered, the children cut them into one-half-inch square tesserae, and stored them separately in labeled cartons according to the color code. To speed up this very slow process, hundreds of pieces of tessera were cut at home by eager children. Smaller tesserae of various shapes were later cut as required to fit into the design.

The tesserae were glued to the plywood panels with vinyl tile adhesive. Areas where the bolts would be placed and a one- and one-half-inch margin around the edges of each panel were left bare. These unfinished areas would be filled in after the panels were bolted to the wall, thus making an uninterrupted mosaic.

According to Kenneth Hoak, the district art supervisor, after one school had completed its assignment the parents transported the panels in trucks and station wagons to other schools so that the work could be continued by another group of children. Thus many proud children had a chance to participate in and fully appreciate the involved technique of making a large mosaic. When describing the project in a letter, Mr. Hoak stated that "our children became so enthused in working that it became necessary to open school and schedule several all-day Saturday sessions." For children to sacrifice their Saturdays to work on an art project is evidence of their genuine interest.

After the tesserae had been glued in place, the panels were laid flat on a school playground and the grouting was done. The panels were then ready to be installed by the contractor. When in place, the bare areas on the panels were filled in with tesserae and the final grouting was done carefully so as to make the joining of the panels as perfect as possible.

Because the art supervisor could not give his undivided attention to such a time-consuming project, Stanley Lipman, a sixth-grade classroom teacher, helped direct the work.

The mosaic strikingly showed the importance of inter-

*Bart-Colerain School, Bart, Pennsylvania*

action between the schools and parents in the community in bringing the project to a successful culmination. Such interaction is indicative of the American way of accomplishing a difficult undertaking. The project will have a lasting importance in the community, and no child will ever forget his part in the project.

This group project provided unity of purpose even before the new school was opened—and thus the educational goal was achieved. When the children were transferred to the new building, each could see for himself the part that he and his school had played in making the mosaic. This must have provided a warm spirit of friendliness and oneness among the children, a spirit which would inevitably lead to closer relationships of trust and acceptance of each other.

THE AMERICAN WAY

It is the American way of life to give serious thought to the needs of children. Communities are always alert to provide greater opportunity for children to grow in their understanding of the democratic way of life and to develop loyalty to American ideals. One way of realizing      329

*Girl Scouts of the United States of America*

this ideal is through the programs for children sponsored by the Girl Scouts, the Camp Fire Girls, the Boy Scouts, the Boys' Club, and the Junior Red Cross.

## Girl Scouts and Camp Fire Girls

Extensive, well-planned programs are maintained by Girl Scout troops and Camp Fire Girls' groups. Both provide opportunity for personal growth in art through varied activities. The work must be creative and her best effort if the girl is to earn a Girl Scout proficiency badge or a Camp Fire bead.

In the Girl Scouts, there are a hundred proficiency badges, twelve or more of which can be earned by girl scouts of elementary school age. Girl Scouts have found such crafts as weaving, basketry, and block printing to be rewarding and stimulating experiences. These are but three of the craft activities described in the Girl Scout manual, *Exploring the Hand Arts.*[1] The Brownies (ages seven to ten) are enthusiastic workers and show particular interest in crafts requiring plant materials, which they must find themselves. All kinds of burs, nuts, seed pods, and barks found in the woods are used for beads, buttons, and bracelets. Besides earning a badge in the crafts, a Girl Scout may follow a personal interest in drawing and painting and win an award through her good work. *American Girl,*[2] the official magazine of the Girl Scouts, encourages creative work in both writing and art through the department called "By You." The winning girl is proud to find her work published in her own magazine.

The Camp Fire Girls' groups have an active program in handcraft and art. The highest honor that a Camp Fire Girl may earn is that of becoming a torchbearer. Two categories in which this honor is awarded are handcraft and art. The qualifications are evidence of creativity and originality, plus proficiency in the handling of materials used.

Camp Fire Girls may earn honor beads in the creative arts.[3] Within this field there are nearly three hundred art projects for a girl to undertake. From such a comprehensive list a girl will find a project to meet her interest, and when it is accomplished, she is encouraged to undertake another. A program of this scope makes it possible for a girl to have an opportunity to use different materials and to learn new techniques. Such stimulation of creative endeavor leads to a widened interest in art and provides motivation for independent work on the part of the Camp Fire Girls who participate. The girls' own magazine, *The Camp Fire Girl,*[4]     331

*Camp Fire Girls, Inc.*

often gives directions for craft techniques which are helpful to the girl working independently on a project.

Many art projects are provided for the younger members of the Camp Fire Girls, the Blue Birds.[5] At some point in every meeting of Blue Birds, time is given to music and girls enjoy making maracas, humbuzzers, drummer traps, tomtoms, and box drums for their group sings. Meetings are lively when art and music get together.

*Boy Scouts and Boys' Clubs*

Art projects are one of the many important activities on the Cub Scout program.[6] Dens carry on a planned sequence of activity and exhibits are a part of Pack meetings. Credit in a handcraft may be earned more than once. This permits a Cub to explore a craft, if he likes, more thoroughly and to continue working in the craft of his choice. It is an accomplishment of a Cub to earn the ten credits he must have for a Gold Arrow and then the additional ten for a Silver Arrow. A Cub interested in any craft can achieve a proficiency in a technique in which otherwise he might only be able to make a start. This opportunity for a continuing experience is rewarding to the boy.

*Boy Scouts of America*

*Boys' Club of San Diego*

One of the popular projects of the Den is the yearly circus. In the project the ingenuity and imagination of the Cubs have full sway. Colorful costumes are planned and made, posters are prepared to advertise the event, and decorations for booths and sideshows take hours of time to plan and prepare. Nothing is too much trouble for a Cub to do to make the circus a success.

Den Mothers receive a chart each year which gives them suggestions for Pack programs. A typical year includes puppets, Christmas gifts, table decorations and place cards for the Blue and Gold banquet, masks and costumes for Jungle Tales, and Indian handcrafts. The culmination of the year's work provides opportunity for exhibiting handcrafts along with the entertainment developed by the Cubs for their families.

A visit to a Boys' Club will convince a teacher of the fine training in citizenship that these clubs provide for all boys who join. Boys find a wealth of activities to interest them after school and on Saturdays. Sports, games, dramatics, sings, and the arts and crafts workshop are evidence of a well-planned program. Each boy may choose his own activity, pursue it for as long as he wishes, and then go on to something else. Capable leadership in the workshop gives the boys instruction in techniques. Workshops are well equipped with facilities for working with wood and clay. Closely related to the art activities is the drama workshop where plays and puppet shows are produced. One group of ten-year-old boys carved large puppet heads from balsa wood and painted them with what might be said to be very "strong" colors. Since there were no girls around, there could be no argument about sewing the costumes.

Particularly in those communities where bad weather confines the boys to the club room, the craft workshop is indispensable. Good citizenship habits are reflected in the careful handling of tools and care of materials.

### The Junior Red Cross

The Junior Red Cross program is organized in elementary schools through a student council which elects a chairman and works under the guidance of a teacher-sponsor. Together they evaluate the numerous projects suggested by the Junior Red Cross and choose as many as they feel can be undertaken in a year. Among the projects frequently chosen are the making of soft toys, tray favors and menu covers, Christmas tree decorations, and holiday greeting cards. In all of these activities chil-

334

American National Red Cross

335

dren have the opportunity to express originality and to be imaginative in carrying out the work. Children are keenly aware of their responsibility to be good craftsmen, knowing that what they make should be a gift that is worth giving. The children's work is sent by the Junior Red Cross to many different places: to navy, army, and veterans' hospitals, to children's hospitals and homes, to old people's homes, and to any place that a need exists in the community. In addition, many soft toys are sent to refugee and orphaned children in Europe. This experience gives children a new insight into the lives of many people and reveals to them the significance of service to others. Children read reports of their activities in *American Junior Red Cross Journal*.[7]

The program of the Junior Red Cross carried on in elementary schools is a voluntary social service, and it contributes to the maturity of children through unselfish work for others.

### THE CAMP EXPERIENCE

A recent innovation in elementary education is to provide camping experiences[8] for children during their last year in the elementary grades. Organized with the help of many community agencies and parent leaders and supported by the schools, the camping experience is of great

*San Diego City Schools*

value for elementary school children. Although as yet this is not general practice, a number of school districts have found it to be administratively possible and a valuable extension of the total learning program. There are two types of art experience significant for children at camp, aesthetic appreciations and craft activities.

In the camping experience lies the opportunity for children to come close to nature under circumstances which provide skillful leadership and personal enjoyment. There are many children for whom a school camp may be the first, or the longest, experience of this kind in their lives. In a school camp the program is integrated with the school program and will be followed by evaluations in the classroom. Another advantage to children is that either their own teacher, or a teacher of another section of the grade whom they know, accompanies the group to camp. In this way the work at camp can be dovetailed with work in school and the learnings shared for the rest of the year.

*Aesthetic Appreciations*

Hikes and exploratory trips not only provide science learnings but deepen aesthetic appreciations. Children will see many things from a broader point of view. Examining a fern frond to find the spores inevitably attracts attention to the restrained and beautiful design of the frond; classifying a rock formation reveals color and pattern in its stratification; wood has texture, and stones are one color when wet, another when dry. In autumn, seed pods, acorns, and nut burs reveal intricate and fascinating design patterns, while in the spring there is the delicate color of pussy willows and early wild flowers. All year the grandeur of the mountains cannot help inspiring children. The beauty of the birds and the small furry creatures scampering among the trees become memories to cherish. To children who have not had rich nature experiences with their own families, the discovery of nature through the guidance of an appreciative teacher and camp counselor will open a new world to them. Later, in the classroom once more, the background of camp experiences will be reflected in creative work.

*Craft Activities*

Working in the arts and crafts shops is one of the most popular choices of the campers, and an indispensable activity when weather is bad and children are deprived of outdoor activities. An interesting part 337 of a camping art program is that children learn to find many of the materials they will use. Coarse and unrefined though freshly dug clay may be, it provides an adequate modeling material for camp use. The evaluation of samples from different clay deposits will determine which is the better clay to use and is, of itself, a worth-while experience. After some of the best clay is dug up, it is brought back to camp in buckets or sacks. The lumps are broken up and any particles of wood or small pebbles are removed. The camp counselor will know from previous experiments with the clay whether any talc or bentonite must be added. It is better for modeling if, after it is thoroughly wedged, the clay is allowed to stand overnight wrapped in damp cloths. If time permitted it would be an interesting experiment to fire the clay work in a pit in the same manner as was done by the Indians.

Plant material for weaving or making baskets and mats must be well soaked in water before it can be used. Grasses for sewed baskets need only a brief submerging, but tougher fibers like cattails, rushes, and willow sapling must be soaked for a number of days to become pliable enough to work with. This means that children cannot use the material, other than grasses, which they have collected themselves while at camp. A way to solve this problem is to allow the children to use materials prepared by an earlier group and in turn leave what they have collected in the workshop for later groups to use.

Interestingly shaped pieces of wood picked up along the trails are many times as fine in design as if they had been sculptured by an artist. The beauty and grain can be accentuated by sanding, brushing with steel wool, and waxing. The present interest in art arrangements of wood, dried grasses, and weeds makes a handsome piece of wood a welcome gift for a child to take home.

Soapstone may be one of the minerals available in the region of the campsite. It is an excellent material for children to use for carving. No special tools or equipment is needed.

Gathering materials for craft activities gives children greater respect for the supplies they have at school and spurs their imagination to devise new ways of using what they have found. The outdoor life, the natural beauty of the environment, the direct relationship between craft work and the raw material with which it is made make the camping experience rich in potentialities for a new approach to art experience.

*Government of the District of Columbia, Recreation Department*

PLAYGROUNDS AND RECREATION CENTERS

Playgrounds and recreation centers supported by funds from civic and private sources offer many children a haven of refuge that otherwise they would never know. In cities the recreation centers are centrally located and serve many neighborhood needs for children after school, on Saturdays, and in the evening. During the summer, camps in the country offer similar opportunities for creative work.

Centers have well-equipped workshops and provide all manner of art and craft opportunities which encourage children to develop leisure-time hobbies or help them to find a new art or craft interest. Instructors are present to help the children get started in making baskets, trays, mats, dolls, toys, or bags; in fact, a way is found to help any child in almost anything he might want to make.

Art exhibits and hobby shows are arranged during the course of the year for parents and friends to attend. Displays are put in downtown store windows which graphically demonstrate to the community the value of the experience. One of the finest services to children is provided when a community furnishes adequate facilities for developing art

339

interest and gives them the opportunity for enjoying happy companionship in doing creative work together.

SUMMARY

Opportunity for enrichment in the community gives children wholesome leisure-time experiences in the creative use of art materials and may establish an art interest that will continue into later life. The fellowship of children working together in groups makes the work a real and important experience and develops appreciation for craftsmanship. Children participating in Girl Scout, Campfire Girl, Boy Scout, Boys' Club, and Junior Red Cross activities have the privilege of the best community leadership possible and are held to ideals of citizenship that are worthy for every American child.

EDUCATIONAL PROGRAMS IN MUSEUMS AND GALLERIES

Museums and galleries provide opportunities for the extension of the school art program through their Saturday classes for children,

340                                                                      *The Cleveland Museum of Art*

*Portland Art Museum, Portland, Oregon*

small study groups, guided tours, special programs, and social activities.[9] The doors are always open to children, and every day many are seen walking about and becoming acquainted with the collection, looking for a favorite picture, or engrossed in the contents of an exhibit case.

A Saturday morning or afternoon spent in a museum studio or workshop appeals to children seeking opportunity to do creative work. Children look forward to Saturday with anticipation, knowing that at the museum a new art experience awaits them. It is not only gifted children who attend; just as many are children who are interested in art and find the time spent at the museum to be stimulating and rewarding.

Every child in a studio or workshop group, by the very fact of his presence, demonstrates a vital interest in art. What his creative performance may be is of relatively little importance when compared to what he gains through his natural and voluntary association with art.

*Study Groups*

At many museums and galleries small study groups are arranged for children. The children meet regularly in a cozy room furnished comfortably with small chairs and low tables. Appropriate reference materials, books, portfolios, and prints are available for the children to look at and for the use of the staff leader in group discussions. Among the many 341 subjects which are discussed and illustrated with color prints are clowns, animals, prehistoric paintings from ancient caves, and such appropriate items as foreign dolls and toys which the museum may own. Presented in a way that interests children and motivated by previous creative expression, study groups have a genuine appeal, and their membership remains largely the same year after year.

*Tours*

A tour in a museum, through its wealth of exhibit material, gives children experiences which invite return visits and a broader interest in art. A skillful storyteller on the staff or a well-prepared volunteer leader can open new worlds of art—mosaics, bronzes, jades—which will awaken intellectual as well as aesthetic response. The experience of becoming familiar with the masterpieces of art and the artifacts of historical cultures holds values which no teacher would willingly deny her class.

A feature that adds to the culmination of a tour is a game. In a gallery where games are always prepared for groups of visiting children, there are two modest prizes. The first prize is a small color reproduc-

*The Toledo Museum of Art*

tion of a painting by an artist represented in the gallery; the other is a postcard selected in the same way. One type of game that has been used is a modification of the old game "I spy." Besides its fun, playing the game seems to have real value as one means of motivating keener observation on the part of the children. To play, each child is provided with a clip board, a pencil, and a mimeographed copy of the game. It is amusing to watch the children scurry around looking for the answers to the questions. One of the popular games played before Christmas at a museum where there is a fine collection of Italian paintings is to find the right answers in the many paintings of Madonnas. The short period involved in correcting the answers is the best possible time for giving instruction. Observations and evaluations flow naturally from the children because of the motivation provided by the game. Answers are not just read off; children return to the picture to confirm their point, and lively discussion ensues when children disagree. Simple though both game and prize may be, to play it sends children away with the warm feeling that a museum is a friendly place.

There are occasions when principals and teachers of distant schools wish to bring large groups of children to a museum on a Saturday or a holiday. Very often the children will travel many miles by bus and private car from the communities where they live. The courtesy of the museum in sending advance information to the schools helps teachers to prepare themselves and their classes for what they expect to see and motivates upper-grade classes to do some reference work in art. Such books as *Famous Paintings*[10] and *The Rainbow Book of Art*[11] help children become familiar with some of the great names in art. This increases their anticipation of seeing paintings by masters represented in the books and owned by the museums. Children will have a better apperceptive basis for many of the exhibits if some preparation is done in advance in the classroom. A copy of the museum's illustrated catalogue will aid the teacher to build better understandings before the visit.

## Special Programs

Special events conducted by invited artists and programs given by a staff member are often arranged for large and small groups and are a pleasant culmination of a school or class visit. One program for several hundred children was a demonstration of clay modeling by a distinguished sculptor. Although it was not his intention to complete his life-sized head of Abraham Lincoln, the children watching refused to leave

343

*The Brooklyn Museum*

until the model was practically completed. Smaller groups can have privileges not possible for large numbers of children. A group interested in Chinese costumes in an eastern metropolis tried on a mandarin robe and hat from the museum's fine collection. The deep tone of an old temple gong carried them back centuries in time.

As was brought out in planning museum games, the importance of children's having a pleasant time at a museum should not be forgotten. A social activity also provides opportunity for the children to have a part in its success, and this children always love to do. One activity of this kind is carried out each year by two museums in the West where a Christmas party with a big tree in the foyer is featured each year. The decorations for the tree are made by children in the Saturday classes, and nothing not made by a child is allowed to hang on the tree. At other times children may enjoy professional entertainment of a type not ordinarily seen these days. Among such performances given for junior museum members are Chinese shadow puppets in the play *The Willow Plate* and a Punch and Judy show. The closer the association that a child builds up for the

344

museum in his city as a junior member, the more sure he is of continuing an active interest after his elementary school days are passed.

## Audio-visual Material

Another means of acquainting children with the treasures of a gallery may be achieved through the preparation of sets of Kodachrome slides with accompanying tape recordings. To keep this service compatible with the school program, teachers are invited by the gallery to serve on committees that select the pictures to be made into slides for different grade levels. The teacher committee also reads the script, usually prepared by an expert on the gallery staff, for the tape recording made to accompany each set of pictures. Both slides and tapes can be deposited with the school department of audio-visual education, the office of the art supervisor, or with the children's department at the gallery for circulation in elementary schools. A typical slide selection made for fifth- and sixth-graders was composed of beautiful portraits of children. Films and recordings for classroom use are best when limited to about twenty minutes. By having access to this audio-visual material, the teacher is relieved of the responsibility of hunting facts prior to her visit with her class to the gallery. Children get much more from a visit to a gallery when prepared in advance for what awaits them. This preparation also makes it easier for the member of the museum staff or for the volunteer guide assigned to conduct the children on their tour because the children will have an apperceptive background when seeing the original portraits.

Children attending schools located in a city or within reach of a fine arts gallery or art museum are indeed privileged. Besides attendance with their parents, children can participate in activities sponsored by the gallery, enjoy visiting exhibits with their class, and join a Saturday art class taught by a specialist.

### INTERACTION WITH A FOREIGN COMMUNITY

In today's world, people are striving to understand each other better. With this end in view, an affiliation has been established in San Diego with a "sister city" in Japan—Yokohama. Through the office of the mayor in each city, a Friendship Commission has been established with the purpose of sponsoring and furthering cultural and commercial relationships. One means of cultural interchange is the displaying of children's

345

work in both cities. In San Diego, the exhibits from Japan are displayed in locations where the general public will see them, as well as in the Fine Arts Gallery. The exhibit received from Japan in 1961, for example, was put in the window of the downtown office of the Pacific Telephone Company.

Through these exchange exhibits, San Diegoans and visitors to their city have become acquainted with the lovely art work Japanese children do in their schools. This work expresses a freedom and spontaneity that has evolved with the educational goals which reflect the country's closer alliance with the Western world. The art expression of Japanese children is as dynamic in its evolution as was the change that took place in Vienna in the first quarter of this century. (See Chap. 2.) This new direction in Japan is nationwide and is strikingly illustrated in each copy of *Zuga-Kosaku*,[12] which, translated, means "picture book." There is a series of twelve Zuga-Kosaku booklets, two for each grade, published in Tokyo. These booklets have literally hundreds of color illustrations of the

*Board of Education,
Municipality of
Yokohama, Japan*

346

work of Japanese children, together with some black-and-white drawings and photographs of children at work in the classroom. Professional and public school libraries, as well as college libraries, would profit by securing a set of these booklets.

The reproductions of children's art work in these booklets reflect the natural and highly artistic temperament of Japanese children: their imagination, their versatility, their ready acceptance of contemporary design, their skillful handling of a variety of materials, and their individuality. Japanese children have an inborn sense of aesthetic values and design qualities, which is seen time and again in examples of their public school art work.

Interaction through children's art exhibits with any city in a foreign country is a stimulating experience, which can lead to broader cultural understandings.

## REFERENCE MATERIAL

1. *Exploring the Hand Arts.* New York: Girl Scouts of the United States of America, 1955.

2. *Girl Scout Handbook.* New York: Girl Scouts of the United States of America, 1953.

3. *The Book of the Camp Fire Girls.* New York: Camp Fire Girls, Inc. "Creative Arts Crafts," pp. 168–85.

4. *The Camp Fire Girl.* Published monthly by Camp Fire Girls, Inc.

5. *The Blue Bird Book.* New York: Camp Fire Girls, Inc.

6. *10 Steps. A Guide Book for All related to the Organization of Cub Packs.* New York: Boy Scouts of America.

7. *American Junior Red Cross Journal.* Published monthly by the American National Red Cross, Washington, D.C.

8. Clarke, James Mitchell. *Public School Camping.* Stanford, Calif.: Stanford University Press, 1951.

9. Powell, Lydia. *The Art Museum Comes to the School.* New York: Harper & Brothers, 1944.

10. Chase, Alice Elizabeth. *Famous Paintings: An Introduction to Art for Young People.* New York: The Platt & Munk Company, Inc., 1951.

11. Craven, Thomas. *The Rainbow Book of Art.* New York: Harcourt, Brace & World, Inc., 1956.

12. *Zuga-Kosaku.* Distributed by Nippon Shoseki Kabushiki Kaisha, Bunkyo-ku, No. 108 Hisakata Machi, Tokyo, Japan, circa 1960.

## READER PARTICIPATION

Discuss the environmental influences in the district where you live. What types of cultural enrichment do they offer to children?

Make it a point to become acquainted with the opportunities for out-of-school art experience provided by the Girl Scouts, the YMCA, and all other agencies in your community.

Have a conference with the director of the local Junior Red Cross and evaluate the projects suggested in terms of the extent to which they fulfill both children's and service needs.

Investigate what camping experiences for children are available in your area and how the arts and crafts program at camp may be further developed through school experiences.

# 14

# *Strengthening the Enjoyment of Art*

Helping children to realize their potentialities for aesthetic growth is a challenge to a teacher. Appreciation and enjoyment of art can be made a daily experience in the classroom when the circumstances are favorable and the teacher is sensitive to art values. Through wise guidance, the place of art in life becomes increasingly significant to children as they mature.

## THE TEACHER'S PART

Appreciation and enjoyment are interchangeable and contribute to the art experiences of children. Appreciation may be thought of as an ever-maturing understanding of art and the principles of its structure, and enjoyment as the personal pleasure that a work of art gives. Because of the infinite variety of art forms, an approach which holds aesthetic significance can be found for every child if a teacher will but try. From very small beginnings in any learning, a teacher knows that children may be guided into richer experiences through skillful teaching and appropriate motivation. While every creative activity has its correlative aesthetic experience, this is not enough to satisfy a teacher who believes that possibilities for aesthetic appreciations inherent in children can be developed into realities. To do this effectively, the teacher will refine her own thinking

349

through study, reading, observation, conversation, and active participation[1] in an art of personal interest to her. For a home study course, consideration may be given to a series of portfolios on painting, lavishly illustrated with color reproductions, that is compiled and sponsored by the Metropolitan Museum of Art in New York City and distributed by the Book-of-the-Month Club, Inc.[2] Films are available which are mature in their presentation. One such film narrates a conversation between an artist and a young woman on the meaning of modern art. Its title is *What Is Modern Art?*[3] Two points of view are presented and the viewer is left to make his own judgment. A beautiful film that a teacher could share with her class is *Grandma Moses.*[4] The background music, Copland's *Appalachian Spring,* is as typically American as the painting. A third film, which is a presentation of rhythms and designs, is called *Art and Motion.*[5] Shown to mature children, this film could be a constructive as well as an enjoyable art experience.

Art structure in creative work is the result of good organization in the handling of the particular materials and techniques chosen by the artist or craftsman. No matter what art form is the medium of expression, painting or weaving, pottery or sculpture, the result is wholly satisfying when the work meets the two goals of organization: form that is functional, and unity that has variety. These are mature concepts, and even though good organization is demonstrated by children in their own work, it is more likely to take place through an instinctive use of the plastic elements of form, line, color, texture, and space rather than from a conscious and preconceived plan. Nor will a child always realize how well he has done his own work. If abstract concepts of organization and the elements of composition are to become meaningful to the child, they should be presented and interpreted through the common and familiar things of life which he knows and understands. To proceed from the known to the unknown is ever good practice in teaching.

Progress by children toward the subtleties of aesthetic awareness will be slow; but from a simple beginning that is primarily enjoyment, latent aesthetic responses within a child will be stimulated. Then, too, it must always be remembered that some of a child's progress rests upon what he has been accustomed to in his home environment and the attitudes of his parents toward art. Attitudes may be broadened and overcome when a new cluster of experiences is offered. This the teacher tries to do in her art teaching.

## FINDING OUT ABOUT FUNCTION AND VARIETY

There are many ways of demonstrating the goals of organization with common things which are fine in design. One choice illustrative of function in form with which children are familiar is a ball-point pen. A ball-point pen is admirably designed to fulfill its function. It can be held easily in the hand, and it contains a replacement unit for writing. The shape is gently rounded and the length is tapered, allowing for a comfortable grip. Then pen is balanced so that it can perform its function and the writing fluid will flow onto the paper. The case of the pen is smooth in texture and pleasant to the touch. While these qualities are recognized, a comparison with a penholder with its steel penpoint and its bottle of ink would emphasize their meaning for children.

Nature provides countless examples of unity with variety. A frond of a sword fern is one of the sharpest examples a teacher could hope to find. Each frond is a design complete within itself. The way every leaf grows upon the stem demonstrates variety as each changes in size successively, starting with small leaves which become larger and swell the contour of the frond, and then diminish gradually until the leaves are infinitesimal in size in the final delicate coil of the stem. Furthermore, color gradation varies subtly from the darker value of the older leaves to the lighter shade in the fresh growth. Texture, too, shows similar changes between the coarseness of old growth and the delicacy of tender new parts.

Such commonplace examples as are typified by a pen and a fern aid children in understanding better what are meant by form which has function and unity which has variety. When numerous examples of a similar kind are provided, the meaning of organization will become increasingly clear as children mature.

## THE TEACHER'S APPROACH

A teacher who is sensitive to children's aesthetic needs and who has a fine personal background will reap rewards in her teaching of art. While good art teaching is many times the outcome of a moment of strong intuitive feeling, the importance of a planned program is not to be minimized. One good approach used by many a teacher is to share with her class some phase of art which to her has deep meaning. It is certain

351

that if a teacher feels secure herself in a particular type of art, she is bound to awaken aesthetic responses in children, so sensitive is the art spirit in them.

Aesthetic experiences in a class never need to be stereo-typed or repetitious. There is such a vast wealth of art expression for a teacher to draw upon that she can keep her own interest as fresh as that of the children. And as her interests broaden, she will wish to vary her approach to art appreciation. Moreover, the very act of living in a changing world will prevent her point of view from becoming static.

### IDENTIFICATION WITH THE CHILD

A teacher who can identify herself with the children through the memory of her own childhood experiences has a means of evaluating artistic development. She may remember her early and awful appreciations and consequently wish that when she was a child someone had been interested and willing to help her to understand art values. From analyzing her personal experiences, a teacher will grow more convinced that any and every opportunity that will foster growth in aesthetic enjoy-ment should be explored and the best developed.

### INCREASING OPPORTUNITIES FOR ENJOYMENT

Skillful teacher planning can multiply the opportunities for aesthetic enjoyment which are possible for children in a year's work. Pupil participation is a psychological asset and gives clues to children's interests and needs which the teacher is seeking. The element of surprise stimulates children's interest, and there is every reason to utilize this natural charac-teristic when initiating an art appreciation experience. When a teacher wishes to share something of her own with her group, why not bring it to school wrapped in colored paper, packed in an attractive box, or hidden in a pretty basket? How much more dramatic the presentation will become and how pleasantly the children's expectations will be fulfilled when the surprise is revealed. To open a package, to enjoy what it contains together, to arrange the material in an appropriate place for later quiet enjoyment, these techniques help to captivate visual attention and stimulate pupil response. A bit of showmanship has never failed to help along an art lesson.

352 Many times satisfying beauty first comes to children

*San Diego Fine Arts Gallery*

through a picture, especially if the subject is a child. Picasso is a sensitive painter of children. *The Little Shepherd*[6] and *The Artist's Son*[7] are representative of an early period in his work. Renoir had a lifelong interest in children and painted them with tenderness. His *Portrait of a Young Lady*[8] is really of a child, as a class will recognize upon seeing the picture. Before making a selection, a teacher can look at small color reproductions in a commercial catalogue of art prints.

      Art prints may be featured each month or oftener in the classroom. Well mounted and attractively displayed, a series of pictures gives opportunity for children to see many kinds of painting techniques and subject interpretations. In upper grades, a theme may be developed for the year as children's interests become apparent to the teacher, or the choices may be made by the children as a result of seeing reproductions of the work of artists whose painting children have grown to like in books and portfolios placed on the library table. When prints have been selected in this manner, it has been noticed that children have an appreciation for contemporary art which is often surprising to their teacher. One sixth-    353

grade class consistently chose the work of contemporary painters throughout the year, with the single exception of the Christmas season. The teacher
had not anticipated this because he taught in a school which was located
near a housing project where it might be expected to find children culturally
predisposed toward a different kind of art. The school system had a large
collection of art prints for circulation and the teacher brought several
examples to class each month and let the children choose the one they
wanted to keep. It was also a fortunate circumstance that early in the year
there was a fine loan exhibition of modern art at the fine arts gallery in the
city and the class was taken to see it one Saturday morning.

It is an exceptional experience for children when they are
privileged to have a teacher who has a deep appreciation of nature. Love
of nature and sensitivity to art values are usually synonymous and the
combination of such personal qualities makes possible an outstanding
experience for children. There are many ways to demonstrate art structure
through nature,[9] and one effective way is to have flowers and plants in the
classroom. To arrange flowers[10] with children participating or watching is
both a graphic and a practical experience in the composition of line, color,
balance, and proportion.

The craziest thing happened. Our teacher went to the country on Sunday and
brought back a bunch of old, dried-up weeds. It certainly didn't look like anything much when she opened her car and took them out, but I helped her drag
them in. But you should see what she did with them. She found a flat bowl, it
was more like a tray, and it was brown, too, like some of the colors in the weeds.
And then, one by one, she stuck those old weeds into a holder. Some were bunchy;
they were buckwheat. Some were heavy and tall and scaly; they were dock. Some
were sharp and spikey; they were teasel. There were some that were spidery,
reddish in color, but the teacher didn't know what they were. Neither did I.
When those old weeds were put on top of the bookshelves, she pinned up a piece
of colored paper in the back and put a little straw mat (we have some just like it
at home) underneath the bowl, and then she found the cutest little squirrel you
ever saw. It was carved out of dark wood. She put it up there along with those
weeds and the bowl and the paper and the straw mat, and it all looked fine. Who
would ever think you could make old weeds look so nice?

The spiritual values of life find expression through the
artist's creative effort to share with the world the things of the spirit.
Children with frequent opportunities to experience visually great creative
work will strengthen their own understandings as they mature and find
meanings that lie beneath the vocabulary of art—color, line, form, and

texture. A simple and touching story of man's fidelity to something greater than himself that is readily understood by children is the color film *Morning Star*.[11] An allegorical treatment of the Twenty-third Psalm is the closing sequence in this documentary film of a shepherd taking his flock to new grazing lands.

In a life barren of art experience, children could become rigid and indifferent in their aesthetic responses through lack of opportunity, and their innate love of beauty could seemingly vanish from their personalities. A full and rich art program is a child's right so that he may be prepared to enjoy the art of our age and the art of ages past.

## REFERENCE MATERIAL

1. Churchill, Winston. *Amid These Storms*. New York: Charles Scribner's Sons, 1932. "Painting as a Pastime," pp. 305–320.

2. *Art Seminars in the Home*. Distributed by Book-of-the-Month Club, Inc., 1960.

3. *What Is Modern Art?* 16mm. film, 18 min., sound, color; produced by The Princeton Film Center, Inc.

4. *Grandma Moses*. 16mm. film, 22 min., sound, color; distributed by Bailey Films, Inc.

5. *Art and Motion*. 16mm. film, 17 min., sound, color; produced by Encyclopaedia Britannica Films, Inc.

6–8. *Fine Art Reproductions: Old and Modern Masters, 1956 Supplement*. New York Graphic Society.

9. Feininger, Andreas. *Anatomy of Nature*. New York: Crown Publishers, Inc., 1956.

10. Carrick, Margaret. *Creative Flower Arranging*. New York: M. Barrows & Company, Inc., 1955.

11. *Morning Star*. 16mm. film, 36 min., sound, color; produced by Encyclopaedia Britannica Films, Inc.

12. Lowry, Bates. *The Visual Experience*. Englewood Cliffs, N.J.: Prentice-Hall, Inc.; New York: Harry N. Abrams, Inc., 1961.

13. Shahn, Ben. *The Shape of Content*. Cambridge, Mass.: Harvard University Press, 1957.

## READER PARTICIPATION

Pay a second visit to the art museum of your choice.

Make a collection of a wide variety of all types of material that represent good design. Seek an evaluation of your choices by someone whose art judgment you respect.

Select those books from the chapter bibliographies which you think would be most helpful in a school professional library to assist teachers in developing children's possibilities for growth in aesthetic enjoyment. Visit book stores and libraries to augment the list.

Keep on the alert to find films high in aesthetic qualities, yet suitable to the different maturation levels within a class.

# *Appendix*

The following are the addresses of distributors listed in the chapter references.

American Petroleum Institute, 1271 Avenue of the Americas, New York 20, N.Y.

Artex Prints, Inc., Westport, Conn.

Bailey Films, Inc., 6509 De Longpre Ave., Hollywood 28, Calif.

Book-of-the-Month Club, Inc., 345 Hudson St., New York 14, N.Y.

Bowmar Records Co., 4921 Santa Monica Blvd., Los Angeles 29, Calif.

Boy Scouts of America, 2 Park Ave., New York 16, N.Y.

Bureau of Publications, Teachers College, Columbia University, 525 W. 120th St., New York 27, N.Y.

Camp Fire Girls, Inc., 16 E. 48th St., New York 17, N.Y.

Coast Visual Education, 5620 Hollywood Blvd., Hollywood 28, Calif.

Coronet Instructional Films, 65 E. South Water St., Chicago 1, Ill.

Encyclopaedia Britannica Films, Inc., 1150 Wilmette Ave., Wilmette, Ill.

Eye Gate House, Inc., 146 Archer Ave., Jamaica 35, L.I., N.Y.

Filmscope, Inc., Box 397, Sierra Madre, Calif.

The Ford Foundation and The Fund For The Advancement of Education, 477 Madison Ave., New York 22, N.Y.

Ford Motor Company, Motion Picture Dept., American Rd., Dearborn, Mich.

Girl Scouts of the United States of America, Film Library, 830 Third Ave., New York 22, N.Y.

Herrmann, Erich S., Inc., 225 Fifth Ave., New York 10, N.Y.

Indiana University, Bloomington, Ind.

International Film Bureau, Inc., 57 E. Jackson Blvd., Chicago 4, Ill.

McGraw-Hill Book Company, Inc., 330 W. 42d St., New York 36, N.Y.

New York Graphic Society, 95 E. Putnam Ave., Greenwich, Conn.

Princeton Film Center, Inc., Box 431, Princeton, N.J.

Prothman, Dr. Konrad, 2378 Soper Ave., Baldwin, L.I., N.Y.

Raymond and Raymond, Inc., 54 E. 53d St., New York 22, N.Y.

Syracuse University, Syracuse, N.Y.

Tabletopper Productions, 111 E. 6th St., Box 706, Carson City, Nev.

# Index

359